Cocaine Cassie

COCAINE CASSIE

SETTING THE RECORD STRAIGHT

Cassie Sainsbury

First published in 2024 by New Holland Publishers
Sydney

Level 1, 178 Fox Valley Road, Wahroonga, NSW 2076,
Australia

newhollandpublishers.com

A record of this book is held at the National Library of
Australia.

ISBN 9781760796693

Managing Director: Fiona Schultz
Project Editor: Xavier Waterkeyn
Designer: Andrew Davies
Production Director: Arlene Gippert
Printed in Australia

Keep up with New Holland Publishers:

f NewHollandPublishers
@newhollandpublishers

Contents

Introduction
What Would You Have Done?

In the twilight of naivety, at the age of 22, my life took an unexpected turn. The web of deceit was spun delicately, trapping me in the sinister dance of the wrong crowd. The person I cared deeply about, the confidant of my secrets, turned out to be the architect of my downfall. The invitation overseas seemed like an escape; an adventure painted in the hues of misplaced trust. Little did I know, it was a one-way ticket to a nightmare orchestrated by the very person I believed would protect me. Abandoned, isolated in a foreign land, I felt the first chill of betrayal.

Then came the unspeakable horror. Drugged and violated by someone I never saw coming – a sinister twist to the nightmare that had become my reality. Escape became a desperate plea, but the shackles of circumstance bound me. The absence of funds, the looming threat of police involvement with these people, and the whispered intimidation left me in a web so entangled that even the thought of freedom seemed elusive. The magnitude of the predicament I found myself in slowly dawned upon me, a reality more daunting than I could have imagined. This life, with its twisted tales of deceit, was not the one I had envisioned for myself. The weight of my suffering in Colombia surpassed the collective burden of my entire existence.

In the intricate tapestry of deception, I realized I was in too deep. The threads of betrayal had woven a complex narrative, each knot tying me further into the darkness. The prospect of walking away from this labyrinth of lies carried the ominous risk of jeopardizing lives I held dear, perhaps even my own. The depths of the entanglement seemed insurmountable, like a sinister force conspiring to keep me ensnared. To extricate myself meant navigating a treacherous path, where every step could have consequences echoing through the lives intertwined with mine. The choice to walk away, while seemingly liberating, bore the heavy burden of potential casualties in its wake.

In the shadowy realm of uncertainty, my own existence became a pawn in the game of survival. The complexities of the situation whispered a chilling truth – I was not just battling against external forces; I was wrestling with the shadows within, grappling with the fear that untethering myself from this web might unleash a storm of unforeseen consequences. As I stood at the crossroads, contemplating the risks of disentangling from the web of deception, the weight of responsibility pressed upon me. The lives I cared about, the fragments of my own existence – each delicate thread held the potential to unravel, leaving a trail of chaos in its wake. The suitcase, a silent accomplice in this sinister plot, held more than just clothes. A large bag, heavy with the weight of secrets and potential ruin, was placed under my unwanted guardianship. My family's safety was threatened if I dared not to go through with what they wanted.

The question echoed relentlessly: What would you do when trust crumbled, and every avenue seemed shadowed by betrayal?

In the darkest corners of despair, the list of allies dwindled. The police, once a beacon of hope, now loomed as potential adversaries. The very person who should have shielded me had become the puppet master of my misfortune. The web of deception tightened, leaving me gasping for a breath of autonomy. Yet, within the shadows, a glimmer of resilience flickered. The search for an ally became a quest for survival. Who could be trusted in a world stained by duplicity? Who held the key to unlock the chains that bound me to this nightmare?

As the chapters of this harrowing tale unfolded, the true test of strength lay not just in enduring the horrors but in the relentless pursuit of a lifeline – a hand to pull me from the abyss. In a story where trust had crumbled, leaving the reader to ponder their own choices, the narrative begged the question – When betrayal shadows every step, who becomes the beacon of salvation?

Prelude

I was 17 and on my own, renting a house, I toiled as an apprentice chef in pubs and worked in take-away shops, simultaneously while completing my final year of high school. I would do whatever it took to get my life on the right track, I learnt that I could not really depend on anyone. The fear of failure, a spectre that haunted my dreams. After completing year 12, I needed a career now that cooking no longer had any apprenticeship opportunities. This propelled me toward a passion for fitness and nutrition. Devoting myself to this new-found purpose, I worked tirelessly to succeed. I opened a personal training business and still continued to work at a takeaway shop to make sure that I would always have enough sustainable income. I refused to leave the shop until I had a big enough client base, which soon came. I had over 20 clients and it was going great, I was achieving incredible results with my clients, but this wasn't enough. The culmination of my efforts materialized in a dream – owning a gym. Undeterred by the scepticism of locals, I plunged into the venture, investing all my savings in the equipment, and hoping against hope that it would succeed. It was hard. I had no disposable income. Everything that I would earn from my clients would go straight to the rent and then household expenses. You would think I deserved this had I not looked into whether there would be interest in a gym or not, but the thing is I did look into it, and I was assured that I would be supported. Yet, as time progressed, the harsh reality set in. I felt failure was setting in. Membership sales dwindled, and between business and home expenses, I found myself drowning. Amidst the judgment and the absence of familial support, the weight of failure pressed upon me. What could I do?

At 19 years old, I found myself caught in a painful tug of war between hope and despair. No matter how hard I tried to hide everything I was going through, I couldn't deal with it anymore. Showing weakness was the worst thing I could do, so many people expected me to fail, and I couldn't bear thinking they were right. Attempting to conceal my struggles behind a facade of normalcy, I entered a relationship that only strained my emotional well-being further. Faced with financial difficulties and the overwhelming pressure of societal expectations, I succumbed to the belief that I deserved the worst life had to offer. In a moment of desperation, I ingested a cocktail of painkillers and sleeping pills, seeking an end to the internal torment. I didn't want to exist anymore. I couldn't be myself. I didn't have a good life. I hated my relationship. I hated that I was a failure. Everything I touched would turn to shit. It was a very weird feeling when the pills kicked in. It was peaceful actually – drifting off to sleep. Awakening in a hospital bed, I grappled with conflicting emotions – unhappiness at being saved and an unshakeable conviction that life held no value.

During my hospital stay, the reality of loneliness enveloped me. No visitors, no family – a stark reminder of my isolation. I wouldn't have been missed. I wasn't allowed to be released from hospital until my bloods were normalised and unfortunately, for some reason the nurses opted to drawing blood from my groin veins. It was ridiculously painful. It was the day after Father's Day that I was finally released. Returning home, I confronted a betrayal of the deepest kind. My ex had moved out, leaving an empty house. Literally he had left me with an empty house. Everything and anything that he had bought had been removed while I was in hospital. Now, I understood that those were his things; however, to do all of this to an unstable person while they are in hospital, that was next level shitty. And not only that. This was a symbol of perceived failure.

I was almost convinced that I was paying the price for not conforming to societal norms, I questioned why I couldn't be 'normal.' The silence of the empty house echoed with self-doubt, a haunting chorus of failure that everything that had gone wrong in my life was because I had caved into my temptation of my attraction to women, it was a sin. I really believed I needed to be normal in order to have a steady life.

Refusing to surrender to the weight of despair, I resolved to navigate the storm of pain and rediscover solid ground. The ending of this relationship, it was almost like I was being forced to acknowledge the feelings I had towards a girl. That same girl who I craved to be, she was so brave being openly out and proud.

As the doors of my gym closed, I felt so horrible, bankrupt without legally being bankrupt, there were a head full of memberships that I wasn't legally required to pay back due to the fact that the business had closed due to bankruptcy, and that it had been listed in the clauses of signing up, it didn't mean that I didn't feel responsible to pay people back, and I planned to do that once I got back on my feet. I sold all of the equipment that I could to gather money together, I engaged in conversations with the understanding owner, settling the outstanding dues with a mutual understanding that dispelled any potential animosity. Although, some people decided to spread rumours saying that I had left owing thousands of dollars, no one knew anything. I needed to get away, I needed to leave this small town.

Amid the rumours concocted by those who claimed to know the truth, I embarked on a journey to Adelaide, seeking not just a change of scenery but a chance at personal reinvention.

However, this move, intended as a turning point, only ushered in a more profound sense of isolation. I thought it would be more fulfilling. At 21, stranded in an unknown city, unknown, because I didn't know Adelaide, I had never really seen anything in Adelaide. For a brief moment I dated a girl. She was gorgeous, complex, olive skin, with long chocolate brown hair. I thought I had overcome my biggest fear, I thought I could have been on my way out of the closet. We lasted no longer than a month, she wanted to be public with the relationship and I wasn't ready for that, unfortunately, it wasn't something that she wanted to live. She left me, told me "Good luck!" She told me I had too much emotional connection about coming out, I was too scared of being rejected, more than what I had grown up with. Her comments wore heavy on me. I grappled with a relationship that served as a disguise, concealing my true identity. My boyfriend, Scott, a mere façade of attraction and affection, failed to ignite any genuine connection. The struggle to come to terms with my sexuality amplified the chaos of my life. I yearned for normalcy, a functional existence free from the shackles of pretence. Yet, in the clutches of a self-absorbed partner, I found a temporary reprieve, a tenuous stability born from our deliberately distant relationship. Scott wasn't really my type, dark hair, he was a gym junkie, it was the only thing we had in common was the gym. We would train together, but other than that, we didn't really click, and I think it was because I didn't want too. On the surface he was kind and non-judgmental but in private he was different. He would often go out clubbing with his friends or to festivals, but I didn't really step foot into those scenes often, I wasn't a party animal but more of a home body so we really only connected with the gym.

In the midst of this tumult, a familiar figure emerged – Wendy. Our paths had crossed during our shared time at the fitness institute, someone who at the time was a course mate, we would share small talk and often eat lunch together, but we never actually had a real strong friendship. So running into her now seemed like fate. She was beautiful, shoulder length dirty blonde hair, slim masculine build. She had the perfect face profile. Her jawline was impressive. She had a pretty smile, one that I would probably never forget as it was my defeater, and her presence provided a sense of comfort and camaraderie. Despite intermittent separations due to my relocations, not having a close friendship. I regarded her as a friend, a reassuring beacon of shared experiences. In the sanctuary of our conversations, I confided my deepest secret – my struggle with my sexual identity. She told me that she too struggled with the very same situation, that hopefully together we could overcome it. She made life suddenly worth living. She made me believe that we were going to take this path together. That she was that girl for me, that one that finally gave me the courage to come out. We started to spend a lot of time together, Scott was in his own world. I think because I was so involved in what this meant for me that I had no desire to discover what he was doing in his free time.

Wendy, one day in a surprising revelation, disclosed her role in managing men's clubs. Misinterpreting it initially as fitness establishments, given her background as a personal trainer, I soon discovered the reality – a world of gentlemen's clubs, entirely unfamiliar to me. She seemed quite upset and I watched as her eyes watered up talking about it. In her vulnerability, she admitted facing numerous challenges, from financial theft to the abrupt disappearance of hired personnel. She told me she felt like she was failing, and those were words that I myself had felt ever since I was 14 years old. Wendy offered me a job as a receptionist, urging me to keep a watchful eye on the operations. She said that she needed me, I was the only person she trusted. Feeling the weight of my unemployment and financial woes, Scott not working and contributing much, it meant it was up to me to keep a roof over my head, and although those were the more important reasons, the only thing that stuck in my mind was the fact that she needed me, what if I could save her, help her be happy, then we could be happy together. I watched her cry in front of me, I longed to ease her pain like I wished someone had done for me. Wendy extended an unconventional lifeline – she offered me a job as a receptionist, urging me to keep a watchful eye on the operations.

In the shadows of secrecy, I agreed to Wendy's plan, motivated by desperation, looming bills, and a genuine desire to help. She stressed the importance of maintaining our connection under wraps, emphasizing the need for discretion among the other employees. She didn't want anyone to know that I was there under her request, that they were being spied on. Despite the strangeness of the request, I consented, driven by a desire to be the person who could alleviate her problems. It felt good being needed. As the plot thickened, Wendy urgently summoned me to Sydney. The prospect of a solo flight to another unknown city heightened my anxiety, but Wendy arranged for my stay in a hotel upon arrival. I'd never been to Sydney alone before. I had never travelled anywhere alone before, and it was definitely nerve-racking. The job she described seemed promising – an hourly rate, flexibility, and the chance to distance myself from the unwanted aspects of my life. I eagerly embraced the role, seeing myself as the rescuer in her time of need. What could have gone wrong?

Yet, the reality of the job unfolded differently. Upon arrival at the club, the receptionist, unaware of my impending presence, suggested I assume a role beyond that of a receptionist. Uncomfortable and confused, I sought clarification from Wendy. This wasn't what I had been told, nor offered. Her response, filled with jests about my beauty and attractiveness, left me perplexed. "Just be yourself. Please do this so no one picks up on why your there. I'll deal with the receptionist. Be your sexy self." The lingering question, "Did she like me?" swirled in my mind, adding an unexpected layer of complexity to our relationship. I mean, I knew that I liked her, but we hadn't ever really ventured down that conversation whether she liked me. Unwilling to disappoint her, I reluctantly complied, exchanging my tracksuit for what could only be described as period undies and an old bra – a humorous yet bewildering twist. I thought to myself, "How sexy! Granny panties and an old bra, surely no one would find this attractive."

In this naivety, I found myself unknowingly entangled in a world I had never fathomed, all while harbouring a secret admiration for Wendy that had quietly blossomed into something more. She was everything that my 13-year-old self-envisioned in a girlfriend, beautiful, smart, business minded, caring. She was guarded and scared to open up, trust issues and I wanted to be there for her.

I wanted her to be more than my friend.

The initial encounters in the world of the gentlemen's club were far from what I had anticipated. I was asked to do an introduction to a client, sitting in a smack booth covered by a curtain, I walked up, rocking my old undies and bra. The other women were all dressed up in fancy lingerie and heels, I was no match, thankfully! Struggling with the uncomfortable proposition of being chosen, why would I have been chosen next to all those women? What the actual fuck? I stood my ground, refusing to compromise my authenticity. Sex work wasn't in alignment with who I was, and the receptionist's insistence only fuelled my internal turmoil. The first encounter with a client left me nauseated, a wave of discomfort washing over me as he undressed. A million thoughts running through my head, how did these women do this, how could they stand this? I stood there, not moving an inch, disgusted at what I was seeing, as if I didn't need enough fuel to not like men. Though he eventually sensed my lack of interest, he sat down on the bed, completely exposed, and spoke to me, "You don't belong here. I'm sorry I picked you. I'll come back for another lady", and he left without incident. The experience left an indelible mark on my psyche.

Days turned into a blur of tears and confusion as I navigated this unfamiliar territory. The receptionist's hostility and mistreatment added to my distress. Yet, amidst the chaos, a glimmer of connection emerged in the form of Lynda. She was a bigger lady, jet black hair, cat like makeup and her bubbly nature and empathy became a lifeline, offering solace in a tumultuous environment. Lynda extended a hand, promising a better job outside this disorienting world. She told me that this was her hobby, it wasn't a job. She liked being someone completely different here. It was surprising, intriguing to think that there were women that actually enjoyed this. Despite the hardships, the moments spent with Wendy provided a unique comfort. When she was around, we clung to each other, and her comments, about how I was her saviour that I was beautiful, kind and she even said that she liked me, though keeping me on edge, brought a sense of familiarity. In those instances, I felt a semblance of being myself, a stark contrast to the facade I wore during the working hours. Was this me finding the strength to open the closet door?

Yet, beneath the surface of camaraderie, doubts lingered. Naturally I didn't understand anything about this kind of work, but something sat wrong, that gut instinct that you get. Discrepancies in the financial records hinted at potential wrongdoing, but my loyalty to Wendy clouded my judgment, surely, she wouldn't be doing anything wrong. I mean she wouldn't bring me into some messed up business right? I brushed off the concerns, unwilling to believe she could be involved in such activities. The persistent requests for my presence escalated, Wendy would tell me that when I wasn't there, big amounts of money would go missing. She continued that she needed me despite my discomfort. The need for income because Scott still was not working or able to help out with the costs of the home. I had hoped he would be able to cover his half but that was unlikely at the time. However, a traumatic encounter with a construction worker shattered any illusions of control that I thought I had of this situation, I mean up until now. This worker, he was big, I mean like overweight big. He was unshaven, rude, and it seemed he had a bit of a 'domination' type attitude. Like usual, when I was asked to do the introduction, it was done with disgust, and he actually asked me if I wanted to be picked and I flat out said no. His disregard for consent, forcing me to, and the subsequent dismissal by the receptionist left me shaken. She told me that I had no choice but to complete the booking, that she was sick of having me around and not actually creating any profit for the business. I walked into the room, I was sure to be in control, I would tell him that maybe a massage or something, but he was crazy to think I would let anything else happen considering I had told him 'no'. But I didn't know what I had just walked into. As I closed the door, the man was right behind me, he slammed me into the door and was trying to force my clothes off, with one hand, while the other pinned my arms behind my back. The soundproof rooms echoed, ignoring my cries for help. He almost managed to force himself inside of me when I found the force to kick my leg back, kicking him in the testicles. He dropped my hands and fell back. This was my escaping point, I pulled open the door and ran. I hid in the dressing room and the incident forced me to confront the harsh reality of the environment I was entangled in. I couldn't do this.

Outside, nursing my wounds, Lynda became a beacon of support, she was always that friendly face beside Wendy, she was very calming. The decision was clear – it was time to sever ties with this toxic world. I had wanted to help Wendy, and I had wanted to make sure that I still had a roof over my head, but I had nearly just been raped for what? Lynda provided a lifeline in the form of a job opportunity via a friend, she promised me that it wouldn't be anything like this, that she had been offered it, but she wasn't interested in an office job and with a new-found determination, I was ready to leave it all behind and went back to Adelaide, to reset and consider what I would do. But, one thing was sure, I knew my relationship with Scott was not right.

Wendy's attempts to reconnect tugged at my emotions, she begged me to go back, that she would ensure that things would change, that she would fire the other receptionist and she just continuously stated that she needed me there. She couldn't do this without my support. Even her visit to Adelaide stirred conflicting feelings. Yet, despite the affection, I stood firm in my decision, I wouldn't return back to that place. With Centrelink offering only minimal support, I struggled to make ends meet, still stuck in the same situation with Scott. I needed to do something. I reached out to Lynda's friend. It was for a chance at a normal job.

Upon having a conversation with Peter, he asked if it was possible to present myself for a job interview, in his office in Mascot. I decided to accept, and I headed over to Sydney to do the interview. He picked me up from the airport in his shiny Mercedes Benz and then drove us to his office. I took a good look at this man. He was a bigger man but short in stature, well dressed and he didn't look Australian. He had olive skin and spoke slightly with an accent, but I couldn't pick it up. He was very respectful and polite. The office was probably five minutes from the airport, and it was a cruise line/travel agency office. Peter continued to tell me that he was looking for a new assistant and office administer as his other worker had moved to their office in New Zealand. He explained that the job was very simple, general sales and office duties and occasionally working with teams of sales reps. I liked the idea of have a steady and simple job. In the back of my mind, I thought of Wendy and that if I lived in Sydney I could be closer to her. I will admit that she was part of the reason for wanting to accept. Peter offered me a 75k salary package and help to relocate. It sounded like a dream come true, finally a breakthrough after all the bad things that had happened.

Peter, my new boss, ushered in me a sense of stability and decency. Working as an assistant in the world of poker cruises felt like a genuine job, a stark departure from the disarray and chaos I had left behind. It was very refreshing. The allure of a fresh start beckoned, prompting a decision to completely relocate from Adelaide to Sydney. This move, coupled with the promise of authenticity in a real job, offered a glimmer of hope and a chance to reclaim the person I had lost in the tumultuous journey so far.

However, the illusion of normalcy shattered when Peter's true intentions emerged. I was only a couple of weeks away from relocating to Sydney. I hadn't told Wendy yet. I wanted to surprise her. However, the comfort of a genuine job was replaced by the uncomfortable proposition of trading my dignity for employment. Peter hinted about extra benefits that I was required to commit too. Extra benefits that I knew nothing of. He wanted me to be his mistress, as he was happily married, he expected me to travel with him and have sex with him on demand. Refusing to compromise myself once again, I declined Peter's advances, only to find myself unemployed once more. But this time, I was possibly in a worse situation as any money that I had put aside had been spent on deposits which were non-refundable for movers and well, a house. I had nothing to live off, and no help. The disappointment was palpable, and I faced the harsh reality that even seemingly respectable environments could harbour unsavoury elements.

Amidst the setback, Wendy extended a lifeline, we hadn't really spoken much, I felt like she had distanced herself a bit, something I thought I had provoked when I didn't commit to continuing to help her, she offered me work that involved assisting with invoices, billing clients and various tasks between the clubs. I didn't realise that she was involved in other clubs. Despite our tangled history and lingering doubts about her involvement in dubious activities, I found myself accepting the opportunity. The need for income and the familiarity of working with Wendy overpowered my reservations yet again, but this time I promised myself that if there were any signs of sex work again, I was out. Ideally all I wanted was to move forward and get ahead, I wanted to be happy. That lingered in the recesses of my mind.

The work proved less demeaning than my previous encounters, and I found solace in the routine of handling administrative tasks, I dealt with a lot of money, I was often required to do bank drops, pick up money from other clubs and bring it back to her, but I was never required to do anything I didn't want too. Our interactions, laced with comments that kept me on edge yet again, stirred a mix of emotions. I often wondered if she actually liked me or if it was to have me around. But considering I wasn't used to receiving female attention, I took it all in. The allure of her company conflicted with the uncertainty that clouded our association. As I settled into this peculiar arrangement, I couldn't shake the feeling that I was dancing on the edge of something bigger of a precipice. The fear of falling back into the chaotic world I had escaped from haunted my every step. I remember, one day I was on the train with one of the other workers from the club, I was headed into the city, and she was supposed to get off before in one of the suburbs, that day in particular was the client drop off day, which meant we were handed envelopes with what I believed to be invoices or paperwork, we were always told that we should never look in the envelopes. We didn't sit together, I was 'lower class', yet I watched her open up one of the envelopes that was addressed to her client drops, I watched this lady, pull out one the envelopes and open it. For some reason, I suddenly felt unsafe, I looked around as if I felt like someone was watching, then returned to looking at my phone. I decided to pretend that I hadn't seen anything. I got off the train in central Sydney and began to head down to some businesses, a couple of travel agencies, dentists and lawyer firms. I never stopped to chat, it was always a quick drop off, no conversations and back to the club. I never felt like I was doing anything wrong, I guess because I had never seen a different side of the business that actually indicated to something illegal yet.

Something was different this time, the women were different, they always seemed drunk or drugged, yet I never saw any signs of drugs, if I had seen them, I would have been out of that place quicker than I walked in there. Drugs were not my thing. I had seen them destroy some of my closest friends. I refused to be around them. The financial irregularities I had observed earlier resurfaced, again casting a shadow of doubt on the legitimacy of my new-found employment. How were they moving this much money? How was it possible in one day, that the club was turning over 15k after paying the ladies their cut? And I mean the cuts weren't great, it was a 60/40 set up.

Yet, despite the lingering concerns, I pressed on, desperate to cling to a semblance of stability and not only that, but I also actually wanted to know what was going on. The decision to relocate had been driven by a yearning for authenticity and a chance to rediscover myself. The journey, however, continued to be fraught with challenges and unanswered questions, I tried to ask Wendy about a business partner, how and why they moved so much money when the club wasn't exactly that busy. Yet she would always say that we could chat about it in private, but that never happened. In this uncertain dance between the past and the present, I tread cautiously, hoping that the elusive promise of normalcy would eventually become true. I didn't want to return to Adelaide, I didn't want to be Cassie that everyone thought they knew, I wanted out. I wanted a fresh start and I wanted to be free. And for some reason whenever I was around Wendy she made it seem like it was all possible. I was miserable. At the end of the day, I wanted to finally stop being what everyone expected me to be, and be my free, happy gay self, allowing me to break free from the tumultuous cycle that had defined my recent history.

A Trip to Remember
November 2016

It's interesting to think, I had very few times spoken to a Nick while working with Peter, I never had a name to the face, but his accent was British. His phone calls would always come through on WhatsApp as an overseas number. Peter told me that he was a business partner, I never thought twice about this. Until later, when Wendy introduced me to a Nick, saying he was her business partner, now if he hadn't spoken, I wouldn't have put it together but when he did, I heard that same British accent that I had once spoken to over the phone. He was tall, tanned, closely shaven head, lots of tattoos on his arms; snakes, dragons, and foreign words. But he was very well dressed, businessman like actually. Wendy told me that he was in town as he was about to head overseas with some girls as they often go with him for business and get to do sightseeing and travel. I thought it was rather intriguing, I did ponder for a minute and wonder what the work entailed but I didn't want to go down that rabbit hole and get stuck in a situation that I didn't want to be in again. I was surprised, this same man was in both the tourism and sex club industry?

Wendy mentioned to me later that she would be going with Nick for work and that she wanted me to tag along, that we would finally get some 'alone time' without everyone being in our business, she said she wanted to travel and get away with me so we could finally be honest with ourselves. I did not see this coming, not from her, not so direct, I think I had finally convinced myself that there was nothing between us and now she goes and says all of this? Brazil, a land of hot, cultural, Latin chaos. She told me how she wanted to spend each moment with me, it was music to my ears. She told me that Nick was going to have a chat with me and fill me in on when we were supposed to travel, she told me that she would take care of everything else. "You saved my ass here. Now let me treat you. I will treat you the way you deserve to be treated."

After agreeing to Nick's proposal, the process became a chaotic ordeal. Wendy expressed dissatisfaction with the initially planned travel dates and later conveyed her unavailability for the trip. It was all stop and start continuously. I began to believe that it wasn't going to happen, which was somewhat disappointing.

The departure dates would be provided – 10th December – 28th December – 19th January – only to be changed repeatedly at the last minute. The intended destination was Brazil, specifically São Paulo, and Wendy and I enthusiastically began crafting extensive travel plans, outlining what we intended to explore during our stay. I was now officially excited. I didn't know how much homosexuality was accepted over there, but I was excited to explore where this trip would take our friendship.

It was now February. I hadn't heard any updates. I was anticipating confirmation of our booked flights. I awaited the news eagerly. However, in an unexpected turn, Nick informed me that he had assigned Lynda. Same Lynda from the Club. He would send ladies from the club to the Brazil trip instead. His rationale was based on Lynda's familiarity with the client and the country, and he expressed concerns about Wendy and me navigating the unfamiliar terrain. I will admit, the fact that we had planned a whole trip based around Brazil had been shut down, I really thought that this trip was never going to happen. Nick then disclosed his alternate plan to send us to either Hong Kong or England. Given my long-standing desire to visit England, I expressed my preference for the latter. Wendy continued to tell me about the plans to go to England, "I can't wait to take you to England so you can see where you're partly from, I'm so excited to do this for you. I want to be the one to spoil you on this trip. I want to show you how much you mean to me. Just imagine everything we can do over there!" She told me that she dreamt of being with me. I would finally get to see where part of my family had been born. Nick assured me to be patient, assuring me that he would coordinate the details and liaise with Wendy. My dream destination. Were my dreams finally becoming a reality?

Fast forward to the end of March 2017, nearly two months later, I received a phone call notifying me that everything was arranged for the first week of April and that I should prepare accordingly, which meant it was time to pack. It was finally happening. An email containing the flight itinerary and confirmation of a reserved and paid-for reservation was promised. On the 27th of March I received the flight details, revealing a journey to London scheduled for my departure from Australia on the 2nd of April. It was days away. I was so close to leaving. I could taste the freedom. Excitedly, I immediately called Wendy to share the news, discovering that she too had received the itinerary, which I should have expected really, considering we were going together. Despite her initial expectation of backpacking in South America, she acknowledged the allure of exploring London's many attractions. "We get to see so many other exciting things" she told me, "Big Ben, the Queen's Palace and that famous bridge. Heck, we can even visit Sainsbury's supermarket and you can take a photo out the front." She genuinely seemed excited about the trip and being with me.

2 April 2017

As I stepped into Adelaide airport, the air thick with anticipation but exciting at the same time, I was about to have my first international flight with the girl that I was crazy about, but I found myself running late. Hastily navigating the check-in process, I declared my destination as London while bringing up the email I had received. The lady doing my check in seemed a little confused and asked, "Are you sure that's your final destination?" What? A startling revelation awaited me – the flight paid for concluded in Bogotá, Colombia. Bewilderment etched my face. Where the fuck was Bo-go-ta? I wondered if it was a stopover somewhere that Wendy or Nick had forgotten to mention. I convinced myself that had been the case, but I proceeded with check-in, my mind racing, intending to question Nick upon departure. I needed to confirm that they had done the booking correctly, last thing I wanted to do was end up somewhere alone and somewhere dangerous!

Attempting to reach Nick was challenging; his phone sent me to voicemail. A message left, I wanted answers. I rang Wendy, I presumed she would know what was going on considering it was her business partner! "Oh Cassie, don't worry! Everything is okay, Babe! Are you scared because it's your first time travelling?", Wendy asked me. She made me feel pathetic for being worried about this. However, Wendy reassured me, explaining her delayed check-in and dismissing any concern about my solo journey. Of course I was leaving Adelaide, and she was leaving Sydney. An hour later, Nick responded, "Cass, everything's OK. Problem with flight plan but everything on track, enjoy your time with Wendy."

He was claiming ignorance but still assuring me of a rearranged flight to London. However, an unexpected layover in Colombia was now part of the plan. Nick sold it as an opportunity, "Hit the streets, try some amazing Colombian food! You'll love it over there!", urging me to explore with Wendy and he emphasized the safety of English-speaking locals. I received a text message. He swiftly forwarded a Bogotá hotel address, assuring me that he had secured reservations and would send money for expenses via Western Union once in, and that in the meantime, Wendy had everything we needed for the trip.

Departing after an exhaustive 8-hour wait in China, Wendy's absence concerned me. Where the hell was she? Wasn't she supposed to be here before me? Amidst the uncharted territory of international travel, an unsettling feeling crept over me in the Chinese airport, a sensation of being watched or followed, a feeling that I had once felt before, back in Sydney. I dismissed it as nerves. Surely, I was safe, but that gut feeling was back, the one I had once ignored, tempted to acknowledge. I didn't. I gave Wendy and Nick the benefit of the doubt.

I was already starting to get anxious, considering as I wasn't supposed to be travelling alone anymore. To top it off I was denied boarding onto the plane because, apparently, I had no return booking from Colombia. Anxiety gripped me, something that I had completely missed, in the excitement of travelling I realised that I hadn't actually ever received a return flight. How had I been so stupid to not see that! I messaged Nick, asking for the returning flight number to Australia because I wasn't allowed to board without it. I was nervous, this seemed a little too disorganised now. I wasn't being told something here. I was beginning to suspect something was going on. Nick's reassurance brought temporary relief. After all, he was my lifeline and with this, I waited for confirmation of my departure from Colombia. In the chaotic swirl, Wendy's nonappearance heightened my concerns. In the meantime, I still waited for Wendy to magically appear and to make this whole process a little bit less scary, I wondered if something had happened to her in her travels. I was worried about her, after all, I was on this trip for her. She was the one who was supposed to be working on this trip with new clients, not me. I was useless without her.

An email arrived minutes before check-in's closure, revealing a departure from Bogotá on April 7th. I was quite confused, I called Nick and confronted him, "Why am I leaving Colombia on the 7th when I thought it was just a stop over? Where is Wendy, why am I alone? Why do I feel like something else is going on here that I'm not being told about? I was demanding an explanation. His response, citing urgency and a change of plans, "I'm so sorry Cass, there has been a mix up in the plans, I'm fixing it! I need you to meet with a client in Bogotá before flying to London. You'll be fine. Just do as your asked." This compelled my presence in Colombia. Protesting, I expressed my discomfort with the country and the desire to return home. "I don't want to be in Colombia, that place isn't safe! Why would you do this to me last minute, did you plan this the whole time?! I refuse to do this, I refuse to go alone, I am not boarding this plane in Los Angeles." Nick countered, " It's too late Cassie. You're in this whether you like it or not. I have invested a lot of money to send you both over there, you will do as you are told, or you will suffer the consequences. Remember, you overshared your life with Wendy & I know everything I need to know to get what I want from you." He was invoking financial repercussions and client issues.

I was speechless, what had just happened. What was I supposed to do? Trapped, I boarded the flight, somehow, I felt that this was about to get 10 times worse. I didn't know what was waiting for me upon landing but something that was sure to me was that this wasn't the trip that I had planned with Wendy, and it most definitely wasn't going to be my dream trip. An ominous feeling settling in.

3 April 2017 - Day One in Colombia

Arrival in Bogotá unveiled a foreign landscape, the shock amplified by Wendy's absence, still no sign of her? Why? While walking up to customs, panic was setting in, I was stuck here, on the other side of the world. Alone. Customs passed in silence, my limited Spanish failing me. From what I had heard so far, no one spoke any English. Great, add that to the list of problems. I struggled to read the directions to get out of the airport, everything in Spanish. I made it downstairs, and I stopped to change currency for a taxi.

The desolation intensified. I had hidden hope that when I made it to the exit she would be there, Wendy would be waiting there to make this all better, no one awaited me. I was completely alone and phoneless, I chose a taxi, hoping answers lay at the hotel. Maybe, just maybe Wendy had gotten in early and was there. I hoped that this was the case. I sat in silence in the taxi, I just looked out the window, Bogotá didn't look good. It looked dirty. Lots of people on the streets with stalls. Did I mention dirty? After about 30 minutes, the taxi arrived at the hotel, "97 mil peso" the driver said to me. I blanked. What the hell was that? He said " Money, Money" I took out what I had exchanged earlier, and the taxi driver grabbed two 50,000 notes, leaving me with another two of 50,000. It seemed like a lot of money. Did I just let him steal from me? The driver then got out of the car and helped me with my luggage. Without a word, he returned to the car and left. What just happened?

Hotel Inter Bogotá.

Walking in, it kind of resembled a cheap motel, and much to my disappointment, held no trace of Wendy's reservation. Language barriers intensified the ordeal. My pleas for information met with baffled stares. But one thing became clear, there was no reservation for me. Forced into an uneasy acceptance, I paid for a night, clinging to the hope of Wendy's imminent arrival. The room cost 93,000 pesos, all the money I had left. Wendy was the one who was supposed to be paying for everything and not only that the room was supposed to be paid for. This wasn't good. Room 601, equipped with a surveillance camera right in front of my door, became my uneasy sanctuary. It somewhat made me feel better knowing there were cameras. It seemed the only security I felt.

Connecting to Wi-Fi, silence echoed.

No messages awaited. Why had no one asked if I was okay?

No assurances.

Why hadn't Wendy checked in?

An irate message I sent to Nick revealed my predicament, the sense of abandonment and deception seeping through my words.

"What the hell is going on? Why does it seem like I've been set up to come here? Why isn't Wendy not answering me? Where is she? Why the hell am I here alone? I didn't sign up to come to the other side of the world alone and abandoned. What the fuck is going on! I want to go Home!"

I sank into the bed, awaiting a response, the weight of vulnerability settling in the foreign room. What had I done? Had Wendy really set me up for something more? Had I been so stupid?

Surely not.

I'm sure everything would be all settled the next day.

Darkness gave way to a phone buzzing, Nick's messages revealing Wendy's arrival. "Calm Down Cassie. Wendy is in Bogotá. I will deal with you tomorrow." I must admit, the whole "I will deal with you tomorrow" was a little weird. What did that even mean? But I focused on the fact that Wendy had arrived. I would be seeing her soon. Everything was going to be okay!

But the reunion never occurred. Wendy remained elusive, the two blue ticks on the phone mocking my pleas. She was ignoring me. Had I done something wrong? Had I upset her? Alone and apprehensive, tears marked my slumber. The reality of my entanglement with Nick's sinister web beginning to surface. I wanted to understand what was going on, yet I couldn't seem too. I blamed myself for Wendy ignoring me, had I upset her by asking Nick too many questions? Was she offended? Had I fucked this up like I seem to do with everything?

I needed to know what was going on.

4 April 2017 – Day Two in Colombia

Daylight brought minimal solace. My isolation was compounded by unanswered questions. Nobody was answering me. Being alone in this hotel, no one spoke English, I didn't know how to even order food, let alone pay for it. Reception called through to me. I didn't understand anything that I was being told, until a different voice was speaking to me, very simple English she spoke. "Cassandra, ahh, Western Union for you. You go. You boss send ah, money. Goodbye". Before I could ask the lady anything she had hung up on me. Forced to navigate Western Union alone, I googled the closest one near me, yet when I left the hotel I had no internet. I had to guess roughly where it was located. Walking the streets of Bogotá alone, it was scary, yet I couldn't shake that feeling of being watched. Everyone was looking at me. I obviously stood out in the crowded streets, no one else around me was so blonde and so pale. I wondered if that was the weird feeling of being watched because everyone was looking at me. But something really made me doubt that. I just couldn't shake the feeling of, I wasn't safe. It took me about 10 minutes to find the Western Union, it was hidden amongst a bunch of smaller shops. Walking into the Western Union, the man behind the counter looked me up and down and began speaking at me so quickly and I must have had the blankest look on my face because he stopped talking and laughed, "Pasaport."

Passport.

OK.

I handed over my passport without flinching. Why did I just hand my passport over to a stranger that I can't understand! What is wrong with me! I retrieved funds 1,500,000 Peso, the equivalent to $700, I received the receipt and walked back the same way I had come. Walking into the hotel, booked the room I was in, until the 7th of April, because I doubted that I would be leaving sooner. The hotel staff, seemingly privy to my circumstances, hinted at their knowledge. The hotel staff, seemed, a little too understanding for my liking, but I brushed it off for them feeling sorry for me. That was it, right? The loneliness echoed, exacerbated by Wendy's silence and a persistent, unsettling awareness of being watched. Sleep. That's all I wanted to do. Maybe if I slept long enough, I would wake up from what was turning into a nightmare.

5 April 2017 – Day Three in Colombia

The isolation in the heart of Bogotá's unfamiliar streets mirrored the void left by Wendy's resounding silence. Despite the desperate messages I sent, she continued to ignore me, the two blue ticks on WhatsApp acting as cold confirmation. Each unanswered plea intensified the feeling of abandonment, my only lifeline left dangling in the abyss of uncertainty. I was left with my own thoughts, overthinking every aspect of my life since meeting Wendy, I hadn't imagined everything had I? I really needed answers. I craved them.

Summoned by an unexpected phone call from reception, the person speaking spoke Spanish to me and all I could spit out was no Spanish, and then someone else was talking "Cassandra, you come down to meet me now, I wait for you in the reception", a male spoke to me, his voice held a heavy accent, not excellent English but by far the best I had heard.

Who was this man?

The demand for my presence downstairs set an ominous tone. Anxiety gripped me as I reluctantly informed Nick of the situation, sent him a message, "Who the hell has come to meet me in the hotel?" His response, a volatile cocktail of anger and caution, did little to ease my escalating fears. "Who the fuck have you spoken too? Who have you told that you're here? You better not have fucking spoken to anyone Cassie". I replied, "I haven't spoken to anyone! I've been waiting for Wendy!"

He replied quickly "Go downstairs and meet the person, you better fucking report back to me who the fuck you've seen." He was aggressive, I hadn't seen this side to him yet, it wasn't nice. It actually scared me even more, why would he think I would have spoken to someone, and what was the big deal if I had? I mean, I was there on a holiday supposedly, right?

Descending into the lobby, I confronted a man. He wasn't what I had imagined him to look like. He was short, dark skinned, he was well dressed, wore a golfer's hat which covered his bald head. I looked at his face, he had a huge scar along his face. His eyes, lifeless. He carried himself in a manner that would make anyone else feel as if you were below him. He presented himself to me as Carlos – a mysterious presence whose grip on a tightly held bag exuded an unsettling menace. Why did he hold his bag like that? But something else bothered me.

I saw Wendy.

At first I thought I was seeing things, but I was almost certain it was her standing in the doorway, talking on the phone. Thank God! Wendy was finally here. A feeling of ease ran through me. Everything was going to be okay now. However, what I definitely didn't expect was for Wendy to completely ignore me. I smiled at her, and she looked me up and down as if I was some pathetic bystander checking her out. What was going on? I must have upset her, but how? Carlos, I'd nearly forgotten that he stood there. He must have seen me looking at Wendy. He said, "My girlfriend," smiling and gesturing to Wendy. I snapped back to reality, a million thoughts running through my head but none of them making enough sense to string a sentence together. What did he mean girlfriend? Why hadn't she told me? Why had she lied?

What the *fuck* was happening?

The revelation that he was Wendy's boyfriend sent shockwaves through my already fractured understanding of reality.

My attempts to comprehend the magnitude of this revelation were cut short as Carlos orchestrated an unsettling outing to McDonald's under the guise of acquiring sustenance 'needing to eat'. I didn't need to eat, I needed to understand what the hell was going on. I was on the other side of the world, stuck with no understanding of how this had happened!

Carlos and Wendy both sat across from me at McDonald's, he had ordered me chicken which I didn't really want to eat, I had no appetite. Being tricked and lied too for months would do that to you. Carlos proceeded to tell me how he used to be a part of the Brazilian politics and was very well known, that he had connections everywhere. "Cassandra, you know why you are here. You need to keep your head down and not question anything you are told to do and say. We invest lots of money in you workers and we know how to make you pay if you don't do as expected. Remember you are now in my country. I have complete control of you here, no one can help you". I tried to speak and say that I actually didn't know what I was here for, but the words didn't come out.

In the fluorescent-lit fast-food haven, Carlos' warnings reverberated with ominous intensity. Veiled threats lingered in the air, leaving me shaken to the core. Why was I here? What had Wendy done? Why had she done this to me? The only thing that had now become clear to me was that I knew nothing and that I had been so stupid, so naive, how did I let this happen, how did this happen? What could I do? Thoughts were racing through my head. I needed a plan.

I waited quietly for Carlos to finish eating, once he finished he stood up and said in broken English "You go back to the hotel now and you speak to no one but me or Wendy. You do as you are told! You don't want me to have to make you." I just nodded in fear, I didn't know what else to do, so I got up and walked back to my hotel. This just went from bad to worse.

Wendy's betrayal, combined with Carlos' cryptic demeanour, deepened the shadows of the sinister labyrinth I found myself entangled in.

8 April 2017 – Day Six in Colombia

Days blurred into a monotonous routine of solitude. Wendy's silence persisted.

Nick remained unreachable. My sense of entrapment deepened, was I ever leaving Colombia? Or was I going to be here forever? Why did it feel like something way bigger was being planned for me and I had willingly walked into this? I still remembered Carlos' comments of, "You must blend in, be a tourist, you cannot make people suspect you." Although, I didn't really understand what I was going to be suspected of. Carlos was well known. He was respected by authority which meant, I didn't know who I could talk to too. Could I ask for help? But from who? Carlos' ominous reminders to venture out as a tourist rang hollow, a stark reminder of my vulnerability in this foreign web of deceit. I had never felt so trapped and stuck in my whole life, how was I supposed to deal with this, what was I supposed to do?

As I explored options for escape, I realised that Wendy had planned this really well. I was broke. She was the one who had said that I needed no money for this trip, that everything was paid for, and I stupidly believed that I wouldn't need anything. So even if I did find a way to go home, I didn't have any money. I found a travel agency close to the hotel and I ventured down to look at flights, although I couldn't really communicate with them. I hinted 'Australia'. I was shown a price that had lots of zeros and the reality of an expensive flight sunk in. I walked back to the hotel feeling flat because I thought I had found an option to get myself out of this mess I had gotten myself into and then an unexpected threat came through from Nick, "I don't know what you're playing at here, looking for flights to Australia, you think people don't speak about a girl looking for a flight out of Colombia? You dumb shit. Maybe we haven't made ourselves clear enough! You do as you're told, or you will pay the price Cassie. Do as you are *fucking told*. Are you that stupid you can't understand it? Stop talking to people. Stop fucking with us. You are *fucked Cassie*. You do this job or it will be the last thing you do. We are watching you; your every *fucking* move is being watched."

And just like that, his voice was gone. His threats about my being under surveillance paralysed me. I looked around, wondering if I could spot someone, but I saw nothing. Helpless and abandoned, each passing moment intensified the horrors of my living nightmare. Part of me knew that I wasn't getting out of this easily.

9 April 2017 – Day Seven in Colombia

The glimmer of hope radiated through the email's flight itinerary, promising an escape from the nightmare that had become my reality. I thought this day would never come. I was almost certain it wouldn't. I thought I had been brought over to Colombia to never leave again because that's what it felt like! Relief washed over me as I absorbed the news of my imminent departure from Bogotá. Nick's call, however, shattered the illusion of liberation. Carlos, the ominous puppet master, would be reaching out, and compliance with his demands was my only ticket out of the tangled web I found myself in.

"Carlos will be talking to you later today. You wait for him. You go nowhere until he sees you." What could he possibly want now? All I wanted to do was return back to Australia, part of me began to think this had begun long before I had met Wendy. I felt like I had been set up by someone else, someone who knew how vulnerable I was with my sexuality and that I would be an easy target due to my own insecurities.

Motivated by the prospect of returning home, I ventured out to purchase souvenirs and trinkets, desperately trying to grasp onto a semblance of normality, something that was actually easy to do when I knew I was on my way out of this nightmare.

A phone call from Carlos: "Where are you? Why did you leave the Hotel? Wendy is there looking for you!" I tried to tell him that I was out shopping but I was cut off again. Wendy, supposedly searching for me, had now became a watchful eye on my every move. "Meet me at the McDonalds," he said, "I will come for you. I think it's time you learn your lesson for not following the rules." I wasn't sure what that meant, learn my lesson? What had I done wrong now?

At Carlos' behest, I waited near the infamous McDonald's, wondering if Wendy would join in. I watched as a taxi pulled up and Carlos got out, he called my name, and I walked over to the taxi. The surreal encounter began with an eerie compliment. Carlos went to grab my hand and said "Wow, don't you look beautiful today!" I knew that I had bed hair, track pants on and most definitely not looking anything close to beautiful. Things quickly escalated into a demand that I spend the night with him and Wendy at his apartment. "It seems Cassie, you can't be trusted" he began saying as I was pushed into the taxi, "Nick told me that you have been troubling him a bit which is very sad to hear. I thought we had an understanding. Hmm, how disappointing." I had no words, I looked at my hands in my lap, I didn't know why I was in Colombia yet. Why did he think that I knew? The rest of the trip, we sat in silence, I didn't want to converse with anyone. The taxi stopped in front of an apartment building. We walked in and took the elevator up, level 8 – room 812. His apartment.

Upon entering, Wendy was stretched out on the sofa. She was watching something on the tv and didn't seem bothered to see me. She smiled, but she wasn't smiling at me it was at him and then she said something to him in Spanish. What the fuck? When did she learn Spanish?! Seeing her in her element here, she was comfortable, she was being herself. I watched her stand up and greet Carlos with a big hug and kiss. Disgust, that's all I felt was, disgust. She had lied to me for months, she used me, she had been manipulating me. How had I not known? Why had I been so desperate to believe in her? She was in on this. This was the real Wendy and suddenly she became very ugly to me now.

The apartment was well furnished, paintings on the walls but no personal photos anywhere. It actually made me wonder if it was rented. I sat down on the sofa and observed. I dared not speak. I couldn't reveal how terrified I was to be there. Carlos sat his bag on the table, that same bag I had seen since day one, and began to pull objects out of it, revealing a handgun and three phones, made it clear that any resistance was useless. The danger beginning to be less hidden and more obvious.

As the evening unfolded Carlos' demeanour grew increasingly menacing. They made me feel like I was missing an inside joke, but I knew I was the joke here. Wendy's laughter echoed through the room. Wendy fooled me so easily, yet I felt angry with myself, I had *let* her fool me, I should have known that no one would have made me feel that special. I had been so absorbed in my thoughts that I must have stopped observing them. The night took a horrifying turn as Carlos' aggression escalated, culminating in a violent assault that left me paralysed.

I would remember only parts of my violation.

They ate pizza and I picked at mine, I wasn't hungry, since arriving in Colombia I hadn't eaten a meal, I couldn't stomach anything. We ate the food and then they continued to watch another movie. I barely spoke to him. I didn't speak to them. I sat in silence. I didn't even know what to talk about anyway. What was I supposed to do? Have a conversation about *Colombia*?

Yeah right.

I turned and asked Wendy for some water because I had no intentions of drinking alcohol. She sighed. I did notice that she made a brief moment of eye contact with Carlos, but I put it down to their weird relationship.

She went and brought me a glass of water and I drank half of it straight away. I realised I was actually thirsty; I hadn't drunk anything since the early hours of the morning, I held the glass in my hand, not willing to let it leave my sight. Only a few minutes had passed when I tried to pick up the glass again when I realised that I didn't feel good. Suddenly I started to feel sluggish, slow. I felt like I was drunk, the room seemed to be spinning and that wasn't possible because I had only been drinking water.

Suddenly I had lost all the strength in my body.

My tongue felt sticky and heavy. I couldn't speak.

My mouth was dry.

My eyes felt heavy.

I felt dizzy.

It was horrible trying to move but not being able too, I had no strength in all of my body. I suddenly saw Wendy's face in front of mine, and she had a nasty smile and said, "It's done" and I lost sight of her. I was fighting against what was happening to my body.

I couldn't follow her or watch where she was going because I couldn't move.

Then I felt it.

I was being pushed down, my head hitting the armrest of the sofa. I heard a loud crack, yet I felt no pain and then, there it was, something that I think I had been fearing arriving. I felt a huge weight on top of me and what was worse than anything was that I knew everything that was happening, but I couldn't do anything. I tried to speak, and the words wouldn't come out, and it felt like my tongue had filled up all of my mouth. I thought I was going to suffocate. This was it, being raped and suffocated. I closed my eyes and wished that this would all end, wished that it was just a bad nightmare, that none of this had happened, that I hadn't been set up from someone I thought cared about me, someone whom I cared for.

I felt him pulling down my pants. I felt him force himself inside me, roughly, something that should have hurt and yet I couldn't feel anything. He grabbed a fist full of my bum to pull my legs apart.

No pain.

Nothing.

It was literally like I was paralysed.

I remember feeling the tears falling down my face as he did what he wanted with me whilst I lay helpless. I wasn't sure when this sensation would finish, and I would be able to fight back.

My eyes began to get droopy and after what felt like only minutes of being asleep, I woke up. I was on the floor, not where I had remembered I had last been.

I had blacked out last night because I couldn't remember having feeling again until now. I had a horrible headache. My body felt weak and when I tried to move it hurt so much. I looked down at my body. I had bruises on the inside parts of my legs. I was naked, nothing covering me.

Once I managed to stand up from the couch.

Only when I got up did I see blood on the couch where I suddenly had flash backs and I looked down at my legs, I had dried blood on my legs.

I quickly dressed myself and went to the bathroom, leaning against the walls for support. I cleaned the blood and when I tried to pee it was so painful, it felt as if someone was sticking a knife in my vagina and the toilet had blood in it. I had no idea what else this man had done to me, but I was terrified. This man had no limit and he had done what he wanted. Was this the *lesson* I was supposed to learn? What the hell was wrong with these people? When I left the toilet Wendy was waiting at the door, she just smiled. I couldn't look at her anymore, she disgusted me. She was evil, pure evil. When I walked back into the living room area, I couldn't hold back the tears. I felt them rolling down my face. How was it possible that she had planned all of this?

I grabbed my things and said I wanted to go.

Carlos smiled and said something in Spanish to Wendy. Carlos turned to me and said, "I will take you back to your hotel, you are not to leave, not for food, not for anything, you speak with no one. If I find out you are talking to anymore travel agencies you know what will happen. This was nothing."

I just looked at the ground. So *this* had been *what*? My warning to do as I'm told or what? I never wanted to go through something like this ever again. This was something that I couldn't bear to live through again. I followed him out of the apartment and down to the taxi, we sat in silence and when we arrived at the hotel, he said nothing. But I could see his beady eyes said it all.

I entered the hotel and didn't look at anyone, I went straight for my room. Behind that closed door, I broke down, the tears kept coming, I sat in the shower fully clothed, holding my legs to my chest and just cried. What was going to become of me? Was this it? Why me? Why had she picked me for this? I wanted to be okay, I wanted to find some strength to be okay, but all I felt was pain and more pain, physical and emotional. I felt disgusting, I didn't know what to do with what I had just been through. I felt sick.

Awakening the next day I was greeted by the aftermath of the night's brutality. Physical and emotional scars marred my body. I remembered Wendy, the orchestrator of my suffering, who had met my gaze with a chilling smile. Carlos' threats lingered in the air as he left me at the hotel, a constant reminder that my every move was under scrutiny.

I obeyed him, and I didn't leave my room, speak to anyone or even eat, not that I could stomach anything anyway. I was in so much pain, but I had no idea how to get pain relief. This was painful. I had to live with it. I had to use it as fuel to get through the next few days. I needed to get angry, I needed to stop being this pathetic, vulnerable thing, because this is why all this was happening to me. It was all my fault, I had somehow provoked this, I deserved this for being so naive and stupid.

I sent a message to Nick, a declaration of defiance and a vow to expose their heinous acts, served as a feeble attempt at reclaiming control. In response, Nick's cold and menacing words echoed through the screen, shattering any illusions of escape. Trapped in a nightmare, I realized the true magnitude of the darkness I had unwittingly entered, and the harsh reality of my life in its clutches.

12 April 2017 – Day Ten in Colombia

The vibration of my phone disturbed the silent pre-dawn hours, an email delivering my flight details. Departure for London was set at 10:00 pm, with an unexpected final destination – Hong Kong. Hong Kong? What was this? My stomach sunk. This wasn't over yet.

Almost reflexively, I considered reaching out to Wendy, my one-time confidante.

But I couldn't. I wondered how many other people had Wendy done this too and how many more people were there to come? I knew I couldn't have been the first.

An unwelcome phone call at 8:00 am. I answered, it was his voice "You go to the pub at the corner of your street. You be there before 1:00pm, no later. Remember, do not speak to anyone. We are watching." I put the phone down, thinking to myself, I guess today I knew how this was going to end and that I would finally understand their plan.

Another call directed me to await further instructions. The caller remained anonymous.

Nearly two days had elapsed since my assault. Memories of the ordeal stirred a turbulent mix of anger and revulsion, the throbbing pain from the bruises serving as a relentless reminder. I couldn't sleep much, I only managed to get an hour or two of sleep each time before I would start having nightmares. I would wake up in a cold sweat and with the constant urge to vomit, and then I would shower and scrub my skin until I felt somewhat clean. Succumbing to fatigue, I allowed myself to drift back into a restless slumber, awakening at noon to confront the imminent unknown. I sat and waited. I wondered what would happen to me today. I must have drifted back to sleep because I suddenly was dreaming about something I was possibly already fearing. From a third eye perspective I watched myself being arrested and not leaving the country. I watched myself beg the police offers for help and would be shocked to see Carlos' face, laughing at me. I scared myself awake.

I decided to pack my suitcase, I was going to be okay, I tried to convince myself, surely Wendy wasn't capable of bringing someone to the other side of the world to have them thrown in prison, right? I think I was just trying to convince myself of this, I believed she was capable of it, especially after everything that had happened. Packing my clothes and shoes up, unexpectedly, a sharp knock reverberated through the room. I wasn't expecting anyone. I slowly cracked open the door and Wendy was standing there.

"Why are you still here? You are supposed to be waiting for Carlos! Oh Cassie, do as you're told please, I can't bear to see you go through something like the other night again." I looked at her confused. Was she being sincere? I really didn't know anymore. Before 1:00 pm, we were en-route to the pub, the atmosphere was filled with tension. I sat in silence, analysing what Wendy had said before, I really felt stupid, I knew she was the reason all this was happening to me yet the fragile, vulnerable part of me wanted to believe that she really did care about what Carlos had done to me.

Carlos' entrance commanded deference from the staff. It seemed that they only picked places where he was well known. Interesting.

He ordered a perfunctory meal and beer, then ordered me outside. Carlos entrusted me with an envelope, "You care for this with your life. You do not open it. You do not look. You do not leave it anywhere. You must leave it in your carry-on luggage. It cannot leave your eyesight. This is what you are here for. This is life or death. You get it?" While standing there, I saw Wendy leave and walk towards the hotel. Where was she going? Then as I turned to follow, Carlos grabbed my upper arm and pulled me towards the pub entrance, his touch sickened me, and I vomited in the middle of the doorway.

Wendy was gone for what I guessed was 20 to 30 minutes. I wondered what she was doing, then suddenly she was sitting in the seat next to me, she had a bag full of some groceries, it was odd, I wondered why she had chosen to go and do that now.

Upon our return to my hotel room with Wendy she showed no interest in me it seemed. Then Carlos stormed towards me and grabbed a handful of my hair and with an exchange of Spanish between the two of them I heard a zipper being pulled down, was this my suitcase I wondered. I tried to wriggle around to see, but he pulled my hair harder. I heard the zipper again and then Carlos, not releasing my hair, directed me towards the door. Accentuated the tenuous nature of my predicament. As Wendy and Carlos exited, a sense of powerlessness enveloped me. They lead me back to the pub.

Carlos and Wendy sat there talking in Spanish, then she turned to me and said, "Its nearly time. I've put up with your pathetic bullshit for months. Just for this moment, you do as you're told. What Carlos did to you the other night, it's nothing compared to what *I* can do."

By 6:00 pm, Wendy dictated the next move – collecting my belongings from the hotel. We had been at the pub this whole time, and the only thing that was running through my mind was if they had put something in my suitcase, I didn't understand. I mean, Carlos had given me the envelope that I needed to take, right? Standing in my hotel room, I should have been excited to go home, yet I felt a panic attack coming along. A glance at my hand luggage revealed the lock had been tampered with. I grabbed the last couple of things that I had forgotten to put into my suitcase and yet to my surprise, I couldn't open it, my lock combination had been changed, I thought I was going crazy, that maybe being so nervous was causing me to forget the combination, but I was definitely sure. It was my birthday and now, it wouldn't work. I turned and looked at Wendy, I wanted to ask for help, yet she was smiling to see how scared I was looking. Before I could even begin to argue, Carlos had walked through the door "What the fuck is going on here? You're supposed to be in the taxi and on the way to the airport! Don't fuck with me, Cassie." I watched as he placed his little man bag on the small table, and pulled out his gun and sat it down next to me.

A cryptic phone call transpired this time in Spanish, yet again and Carlos' mood shifted, and he no longer negotiated but presenting a final ultimatum backed by a final threat. "Why don't you look at your phone. You know these people?" The images on my phone he had seen, they were of my sister and her children, and of course Scott – all targets in a cruel game I never consented to play. I was confused as to why Scott had been put into the threats as Wendy knew how I really felt about him due to my sexuality. I focused on my sister. She had nothing to do with this.

This wasn't fair, I didn't want my family to get hurt because of me.

What more did these people want to put me through! "Tell me Cassie, you or them? Make a decision," Carlos said.

I stood there for a moment, looked at my luggage, wanted to run, leave this behind, scream for help, and run to the first person who would listen to me, yet I didn't know if I could. I was completely alone in this in this situation, and this is how they had always planned it. I turned and grabbed the suitcase and the carry-on bag. I walked out the door, knowing that this was it, I had no choice but to finish what I got myself into. I left Wendy and Carlos in the room.

Descending to settle the bill, I walked out to the taxi that was waiting for me, yet to my surprise, I wasn't alone in the back seat. Wendy was there.

As we approached the airport terminal, the weight of Wendy's surveillance settled upon me, extinguishing any vestiges of hope for escape. "Your every move is being watched, it seems you didn't value your life enough to do as asked so now we put your families lives in the game, if you don't do this, you will live the rest of your life knowing *you* killed them." The way she smiled while saying this was sickening. But her point was clear, there was no turning back.

I walked into the airport, I felt like I would have a panic attack at any moment, I could feel the tears wanting to fall out of my eyes, and all I could think about was how could I have been so stupid, how had I fallen for all her bullshit? I should have seen the manipulation. I should have seen the lies. The unfolding events like a script penned in a movie.

Immigration offered a fleeting respite, where body scans and routine procedures unfolded without incident. The envelope's contents remained an enigma, a deceptive calm before the storm, I thought that the envelope wouldn't have made it through the scanners, I thought that it was the worst part of this. Was I really on my home stretch? I looked in the duty-free shops, wanting to disconnect and forget these last 10 days. Yet, I couldn't, anxiety filled me, I couldn't breathe properly. Part of me knew this wasn't over, they wouldn't have made things this easy at the end. Buying souvenirs, a futile attempt at normalcy, filled the void while waiting for my flight. A mere ten minutes into the wait, an unexpected summons to the desk unravelled the semblance of order. "Cassandra Sainsbury" and something in Spanish. I looked up at the desk, and there they were, three police officers standing there.

The Arrest
12 April 2017 – 10:50pm

In the hushed corridors of the Colombian airport, a sense of foreboding draped over me like a suffocating shroud.

As I stepped into the interrogation room, the harsh fluorescent lights exposed the vulnerability of my suitcase on a cold metal table. This was the next stage of my nightmare.

A chill ran down my spine. It was a warning that my life was about to be irreversibly altered.

Wendy, once the confidante of my deepest fears, had become my downfall. How could she do this to me, why did she do this?

Two police officers waited at a desk.

I felt nauseous. I vomited.

The officers' expressions were marked by an eerie understanding. If only they knew how many lies had been told to me to get in this exact place. But would anyone actually understand?

The room echoed with the metallic scrape of zippers and the ominous snap of gloves. Each item extracted from my suitcase was a piece of my soul torn away.

When the hands of the officers reached the nondescript fabric bag, I knew the universe had conspired against me. This was it: I too would finally know what the contents of the bag held.

Inside the bag held six wrapped cubes.

The cubes were unwrapped, revealing headphones – an absurd twist, in a nightmare I couldn't comprehend, headphones weren't that bad right?

Then ... these small black rolls were pulled out from the insides of each box, the police cutting into each roll and testing it. Cocaine ... in box after box. COCAINE.

Fuck.

It was the unveiling of a betrayal, each layer peeled back the depth of Wendy's deceit. And the same question that had echoed through my head the whole week, why? Why me?

A person I had adored had become the architect of my destruction.

Handcuffed, I faced the cold reality of the anti-narcotics station amidst the rapid-fire Spanish police around me. How could anyone understand this language! Tears came to my eyes. It was a lose-lose situation of ultimate betrayal from Wendy.

The police sergeant wielded his power with an unsettling oddity.

Google Translate bridged a linguistic gap but couldn't bridge the abyss of my vulnerability.

"Do you want a lawyer?" the Sergeant asked and demanded that I unlock my phone. As I did this, I watched as he stored it away in his personal drawers. He asked questions without a lawyer being present and proceeded to ignore my questions of my request for a lawyer, in fact his behaviour struck me as odd, when questioned if there was anyone else involved and I told him that everything he needed to know was in my phone, the one that he had stored away and he just nodded, something told me that phone was long gone and I had this horrible gut feeling that I was eye to eye with one of the insiders of Wendy's crew.

Hours crawled by.

The sergeant exercised his power with as you would expect and the cavalier trampling of my belongings.

An eerie comment about safety in prison sent shivers down my spine. "You won't be safe there, especially if you don't keep your mouth shut." Had I just been threatened? I was made to sign several papers without comprehension as someone said something about 'credit cards', money, property and when questioning, again I asked for a translator to help or assist me and again I was told that I wasn't going to be granted *anything* to help my situation.

At 4:45 am, lawyer-less and lost, I faced a transfer to 'URI.' Police drove me through the city.

I was 22 and now contemplating prison. Prison in a third world country. Prison in Colombia.

The police van ran through winding back streets – the city was beautiful and complex, something that I hadn't even seen up until now. They took me to an unexpected destination – a doctor's clinic. What was that about?

The lady officer's phone explained that this clinic would conduct a check to ensure I hadn't been mistreated or assaulted by the police.

This urgency to validate the legality of my arrest seemed a little belated.

We waited an hour. There were curious glances from those who passed by.

The police officer diligently filled out paperwork, and soon we entered a room where a nurse waited.

Seated at a desk with a checkbox sheet, the nurse began probing into the treatment I had received from the police.

There were questions about physical mistreatment. I answered truthfully. That I hadn't been mistreated or hit by the police since my arrest.

I acknowledged the disregard for my rights.

She asked me to disrobe down to my underwear. She saw the bruises on my legs, in-between my legs and it was a painful testament to what had happened before. Something that I wanted so badly to forget.

I clarified that the bruises predated the encounter with the police.

The nurse and the officer scrutinized the bruises on my upper arms.

The nurse's frustration was evident as the officer repeatedly denied any physical abuse.

Were you attacked by someone? Were you hurt? A question hung in the air, and with a heavy heart, I nodded in acknowledgment of the violation I had experienced.

The nurse, sighing with empathy, asked me about any lingering pain.

I told her about the continuing pain and the unsettling amount of blood in my urine.

The medical assessment concluded with routine measurements and documentation. Fingerprints were captured in a digital system, and photographs were taken. This was something that never in my life I expected to be doing. The nurse engaged in a final discussion with the police officer, her gestures towards my legs met with a shrugged response.

The language barrier left me in the dark.

The nurse's evident anger hinted at a discrepancy, an unsettling undercurrent that added to the enigma surrounding my predicament. Something told me she had tried to talk to the officer about my bruises and there was no interest.

The clock inched toward 8:00 pm, which was to be the time of my accusation hearing.

Escorted by the lady officer and the newly appointed translator, we made our way to the courthouse. I was told that I needed to meet with my prosecutor before the case because she wanted to talk to me in private. She was short but quite beautiful and extremely stern, which is what one might expect in a prosecutor. She pointed to the chair for me to sit and then the police officers left the room. She had Google Translate ready on her computer and she typed. "I'm sorry you're going through this, and I'm sorry for what's to come. I see situations like yours all the time, however, I have to do my job. I can help you if you help me."

As I read this, I still didn't know if this was a trap, if she was in on this, Carlos and Wendy had really scared me into thinking that everyone here couldn't be trusted. I reached for the keyboard and began to type.

"I don't know who I can trust"

I didn't know what else to say, it was the truth. I didn't want to die because I didn't keep my mouth shut. The prosecutor nodded, seeming to understand the situation and typed.

"I understand, but this means you will go into the system, it will be tough, try to be strong, I believe you are innocent in this, but I can't help you, I have to follow the law."

I felt that there was no need to type back, I nodded in understanding. She had a job to do, and I broke the law.

Security-laden corridors screamed confinement and the gravity of the situation became real of what was happening.

The courtroom was stark. The atmosphere was heavy with formality.

They led me to a designated seat, flanked by the translator and my newly assigned lawyer, the one who had shown a sudden interest in my case just hours before.

Seated at a desk laden with paperwork, my lawyer engaged in hurried conversations with the other legal professionals present. A sense of urgency filled the room as they navigated the complexities of my case, something that I didn't even understand, but it left decisions about my immediate future hanging in the balance.

The minutes ticked away. The judge entered the room, exuding solemnity.

Spanish became an impenetrable barrier, leaving me to decipher the gravity of each moment through the subtle cues and expressions of those around me.

The prosecutor presented the charges.

My lawyer, in a hurried defence, articulated arguments that I could only hope were in my favour.

The translator's voice became my lifeline, because I couldn't grip even one word of Spanish, it was so hard to understand, it all just sounded like word vomit.

Witnesses were called, each testimonial a puzzle piece contributing to the mosaic of my case. The gallery had a mix of curious spectators and those with a vested interest in my predicament. They observed with a mix of detachment and scrutiny. The weight of their gaze intensified the isolation I felt.

A sense of helplessness engulfed me.

The prosecutor's arguments seemed relentless. My prosecutor claimed that I was the mastermind behind this, that I had thought, planned and set myself up. Something I just didn't understand as to how she had come to this conclusion when I had told the police officer earlier that I didn't do this!

The defence didn't do anything, he just sat and listened to the charges and what the prosecutor was saying. I didn't know if he was doing his job or not because I had never been in anything to compare this too.

Suddenly the stark realisation that my fate hung in the balance of these legal deliberations and Spanish conversations.

The gavel fell. Its sound marked the beginning of a new chapter – one that was to unfold within the cold confines of a remand prison cell. Not an actual prison, a holding cell while space was made for me in a prison because of over capacity of people in there.

The reality of incarceration set in. Each step away from the courtroom felt like a step deeper into the abyss.

The lady officer – a constant, if not sympathetic, presence throughout this ordeal – guided me through the logistics of my imprisonment. Explaining that from here I would be taken to a police holding cell until Monday and they would reassess whether the prison would have space for me.

The clinking of metal doors and the echoes of distant voices marked my descent deeper into the abyss. What would become of me?

Detention Centre or Hell?
13 April 2017

We arrived at the police station, a place that had only existed in my nightmares until now. The nightmare had become my reality, and there was no escaping it. As the police officers escorted me into the station, I couldn't help but feel an unusual sense of vulnerability, I think I had actually been feeling this since leaving Australia but every single thing that was happening was making me more and more vulnerable. Did they really think I posed a threat? The glances from those inside the station, a mix of curiosity and speculation, made it clear that I was an anomaly in this setting. Something that I didn't think was a particularly good thing.

Inside the station, I found myself seated in the same place they had placed me earlier that day. Two police officers remained with me while the other two approached a door that would lead me to an as-yet unknown fate. Little did I know what awaited me beyond that door would become the darkest 48 hours of my life, a period that, despite its horrors, couldn't surpass the ordeal I had endured. Upon entering, I faced a room where the police meticulously recorded my details before subjecting me to a full-body search. And when I say a full body search, I mean clothes off in front of everyone, spread your legs and squat and then if that wasn't enough, having all these eyes on me from men who had probably not seen a naked woman in God knows how long. The male police officer proceeded to stick his fingers up my vagina, which was extremely painful, and the police officer laughed. This felt like it went on way too long and then I was allowed to get dressed again. The harsh reality of the detention centre revealed itself – a space filled with about 2050 men, not confined to cells but free to move around. Their stares and comments, incomprehensible to me due to the language but their body language said enough, they were suggesting sex, this added to the discomfort.

The cells were not what I expected or even what you would see in movies. One large cell housed around 30 men, and where I was headed comprised a shared area with three cells – two smaller ones and a larger one. Each area with 15 to 20 men. The hygiene conditions were deplorable – a single shower and two toilets without doors, offering no privacy. The pungent mix of cigarette smoke and an unmistakable smell of weed lingered in the air, making breathing even more difficult and, exacerbated by my asthma.

Placed in a small, dirty cell with minimal amenities, literally all it had was a concrete bench. I felt a profound sense of despair. The absence of bedding left me to rest on a cold concrete bench, next to an unsettling presence – a small pile of shit. I could only assume it was human shit.

What the fuck.

The police officer's nonchalant attitude as she locked the cell amplified the nightmare of the situation.

The men from the adjacent cells gathered in front of mine, their intense gazes fixed on me. Their remarks, incomprehensible but undoubtedly vulgar comments added to my mental strain. How was one supposed to deal with this? How was it actually legal to be placed into a men's holding facility. I hadn't been given any bedding, and sleep seemed like a distant luxury.

As the hours crawled by, my chest tightened, a familiar sign of an impending asthma attack. Panic set in when I realized the police had confiscated my asthma puffer. A young man, not so fluent in English, came to my aid. Amidst the chaos, he handed me a bottle of water and shared his discontent with the police, who were demanding money in order to help me. This man's assistance was a brief respite in the hostile environment.

The night unfolded with uncomfortable stares and unsettling comments, which I had yet to understand from the men around me. Sleep eluded me. Each passing moment felt like an eternity. I wasn't exactly sure when morning came, I woke up exhausted, feeling as though I had aged decades in a single night. I was pretty sure that I had only managed to close my eyes not even minutes beforehand.

Amid the pervasive, unrelenting tension, I summoned the courage to venture towards the toilets. The desperate need to relieve myself outweighed my disgust of the deplorable conditions. The toilets, stained and covered in shit stains, no seat, just the bowl, seemingly untouched by cleanliness, offered no solace. I entered one of the cubicles, strategically choosing the one furthest from the entrance. I needed to take advantage of the fact that it was mealtime and that everyone was lining up outside for the food and I could use the toilet facilities safely. The lack of proper seats forced me to improvise with toilet paper to create a makeshift barrier. As I squatted down, I struggled to overcome the discomfort, I was still hurting so much, the stench, and the unnerving awareness that privacy was a luxury denied to me. In the midst of my solitary ordeal, a man entered the toilet block. He stood in front of me, I barely had time to pull my track pants up, he looked at me in a very weird way, almost hunger like. His presence was ominous, and he walked past without acknowledging me. I tried to push past him; I knew I was in a tricky situation. He pushed me back. I lost balance as the back of my knees hit the toilet bowl. I tried to stand up, but he was standing over me, he grabbed a handful of my hair and pulled me to my feet, he licked my face. For some reason I had no voice to scream. He was trying to pull down my pants, I closed my eyes, I didn't know how to fight anymore, I thought to myself this can't be happening again. I heard voices, someone was coming, I felt the sudden urge to try and escape this man again. Then I saw his face. I assumed, perhaps naively, that I had escaped his notice. But as I finished and rose to leave, our paths intersected.

This man, the same one I had seen engaging with the police in hushed conversations before, approached me. He was unpredictable, and the language barrier intensified the impending sense of dread. He uttered incomprehensible words in Spanish, his tone growing more assertive. Instinctively, I pushed his hand away as it encroached upon my face. Panic set in as I tried to move past him, I couldn't go through something like this again. The isolation of the toilet block intensified the vulnerability of the situation. The echoing silence was shattered by the realisation that no one was within earshot, and I was at the mercy of a stranger's unpredictable hostility. In the direst moments, a stroke of unexpected fortune intervened. The English-speaking man, who had proven to be a brief ally in this place appeared on the scene. He questioned the unfolding situation, concern etched on his face. I mustered a shaken response, telling him that I was not okay.

In a protective gesture, he intervened. He pulled the man away from me separating me from the mysterious man. The tense confrontation subsided, but the residue of fear lingered. The man who spoke English guided me back to the area where I had spent my first, agonising hours. I couldn't shake the feeling of violation, a sense that my vulnerability had been ruthlessly exploited. I knew that if he hadn't found me, I knew what would have happened. As I reflected on the incident, I grappled with the harsh reality of my surroundings. The detachment of the police, they didn't care about the inmates, in fact they would ask for money from them, and the predatory nature of some of the inmates painted a bleak picture of the system I was trapped in. I wondered if prison would be easier, better being with women. Surely something had to be better than this. The detention centre, devoid of compassion and basic humanity, became a crucible where survival meant navigating a treacherous path of uncertainty, I assumed violence would present itself, and of course, despair.

The lack of communication and understanding made the situation even more challenging, something that I couldn't wrap my head around. The police's indifference to my well-being and the unsanitary conditions heightened my anxiety, I honestly thought that prison or whatever this stage of my process was, had better conditions. The arrival of a public defender, seemingly uninterested in my case, only added to my growing sense of hopelessness. I mean, if I didn't have a lawyer that cared about me, that meant it was over before it even started.

My surroundings became a haunting labyrinth of uncertainty. The looming accusation hearing and the prospect of facing years in prison cast a shadow over my already tumultuous journey. The next chapter of my life seemed destined to unfold within the cold, unforgiving walls of the detention centre, a place where humanity and compassion were scarce commodities. Although I knew that the hearing could be dragged out, or it could be over and done with, all I wanted to do was prove that this wasn't my doing, that I wasn't a drug smuggler, I WAS NOT a bad person. Fuck, how could this be happening?

It was early, I couldn't see any sunlight coming through the only window in the holding cell. One of the officers entered, collecting the remnants of my belongings, shooting me a glance that silently instructed me to trail behind. As I lingered in the corridor, flanked by two more officers, the cold metal of handcuffs closed around my wrists, I actually wondered what was going on, had the days gone and I didn't realise it was Monday? And the sinking realization hit me – the day I had feared had arrived.

It was time to make the journey to EL BUEN PASTOR CARCEL. The end of my days.

17 April 2017 – 5:30am

The journey to El Buen Pastor was a nightmare that seemed to have no end. I wondered if it was going to be worse than the few days I had just spent in the male's holding facility, or what I had gone through with Carlos and Wendy. These were thoughts that never left me alone. I often thought of how I wished I could just disappear or how I had wished they had just killed me for not going along with them. The police officers treated me with contempt, handling me roughly, the handcuffs were so tight that they were cutting into my wrists, and they would pull me around by them, making them much more painful. They tossed what was left of my belongings on the floor as if they were garbage, kicking them around in the mud to do a 'search' for prohibited items, something that had been done so many times now, I wondered what they thought they were going to find. The van ride was a tumultuous ordeal, their erratic driving seeking out potholes with seemingly malicious intent, with my hands cuffed, I had no way to hold myself up once knocked down. The anticipation gnawed at me, wondering when we would finally arrive.

Abruptly, the van halted, and anxiety clenched my chest.

The male officer gestured for me to disembark, guiding me to a side door. Confusion lingered as I found myself in a different compartment.

Desperately, I scanned the surroundings, hoping to catch a glimpse of the prison. My expectations, moulded by scenes in movie scenes, left me unprepared for the reality that awaited.

The van slowed to a stop before a colossal blue door. I watched nervously. I thought I was going to vomit from the fear I felt. Being in front of this big blue door, it marked the complete end of my freedom. It really did scare the shit out of me. A female officer guard stepped out, she wore a blue military-type uniform, she had quite a stern look, she spoke with the officers and then, disappeared into a booth beside the entrance. A small door opened, and the police officer now entered. Questions swirled. I wanted to catch a glimpse at what waited for me, but I was more focused on the fact that there was a queue of people with bags, containing what appeared to be essentials for prison life which was toilet paper, clothes, and hygiene products. Prison essentials? It was odd to see this, were they willingly admitting themselves, or was that something they can prepare for here? It was very confusing.

I waited for the officer to return, retrieving my bag to inspect its contents once more, I was left with a smelly cardigan, a book and two pairs of track pants. Everything else had been taken by the police. I watched as the prison guard looked in the bag and tipped the contents out onto the muddy floor.

The selection process continued, leaving me with almost no clothing. The officer pulled me out of the van with the handcuffs. The reality of entering El Buen Pastor hit hard. My emotional turmoil seemed lost on the officer, who, upon noticing my tears, only responded with a harsher grip on my arm. I don't know what I was supposed to feel, say or do but I felt numb, after the last few days my life just seemed so unbearable and I knew it was only about to get worse.

Walking through the blue door, my eyes fixed on a massive antiquated old building with clothing strewn about the sides of the walls of the building. There were more guards waiting for me, and as we approached a smaller door swung open. The officer pushed me through the small door causing me to fall face first in the mud. I couldn't get up on my own and I looked down at my wrists as they were now bleeding from all the pressure from the cuffs. I felt some tears leaving my eyes, and only a quick reaction from a guard prevented me from stumbling and falling apart further with my emotions. I sat there for a moment, wanting to feel sorry for myself, but I knew I couldn't, and that at the end of the day I had stupidly got myself into this mess whether I had meant to or not. A guard walked over and helped me stand up. I had managed to graze my arms and my face. It was painful but it was nothing compared to the pain and heartache of my situation I was feeling inside. Unspoken exchanges occurred as my passport changed hands and without a backward glance the officer departed through the blue door.

Now under the guard's custody, I was led toward an intimidating figure who scrutinized me with disdain. Locking eyes with the less-than-friendly guard, I sensed a chilly reception. I don't know why I expected any differently, I was a prisoner after all, but I could have done with one reassuring face but that was too much to ask for.

The two guards conversed briefly while I fixated on the peculiar sight of clothes adorning the buildings. The significance of this escaped me. I wondered if that's where I was going to live, if that was going to be my home for the next 30 years. The thought of leaving here when I would be 50 terrified me.

A freezing holding cell awaited, I was alone in here, and, absurdly, I was kept in handcuffs. I actually wondered if this was where I would be kept. Guards passed by, casting strange glances my way. I felt like I was an exhibit in the zoo, everyone stopping and looking at me. I just sat in silence, looking at the floor. I didn't know how to process everything that had happened. Eventually, the door swung open, and a less threatening guard led me out. Handcuffs were removed, revealing my bleeding and bruised wrists, I saw that she went to say something then stopped, that drew a sympathetic shake of the head from the guard. She lightly touched my wrists and reached for a tissue and placed it over them to stop the bleeding, she smiled at me slightly, something that I hadn't expected.

In a small office adjacent to the cell, the guards attempted to talk to me. Frustration. Spanish sounded like word vomit, as much as I wanted to understand I couldn't, so Google Translate became the intermediary, the guard wrote on the computer:

"I'm Andrea. I need to do your entry process for the prison. I will ask you questions, and you can help me answer them please."

I nodded, I didn't want to be difficult, I just wanted this to be over.

"Full name, age, address, tattoos, birth marks or defects."

I nodded again, I wrote down my full name, age and address. I then showed her my only tattoo which was located on my rib cage.

"What does this say?"

I wrote down, "It says 'I only swear I'm up to no good.'"

Realising now that the tattoo was ironic given where I was and why. Harry Potter was my favourite movie but, in the moment, I felt stupid for having that tattoo. The guard nodded, she didn't ask me any more questions, instead she handed me a plank that had numbers on it. The number read: 129074570 it then had the date 17 April 2017. I felt more tears coming, I didn't want to cry, I couldn't show weakness, I needed to get through this. The importance of these digits eluded me, I watched as the guard Andrea wrote something on a piece of paper and handed it to me, they were the same numbers I held on the plank. I pocketed the paper. A sense of foreboding lingered – had the time come to officially enter El Buen Pastor?

Confused by the absence of English speakers in official capacities, I begrudgingly provided information. Andrea, seemingly more empathetic, informed me of the necessity for a shower.

She led me back to the cell and on her phone she had Google Translate, she wrote "You're smelly. You must shower. Do you have clean clothes?" Irony hit, *of course I stank*. I hadn't showered in days, she grabbed my pathetic bag of items and looked inside of it and shook her head, she said in broken English, "Ah police do this? Or guard?" I didn't know if it was a trick. I shook my head and she sighed. She said something in Spanish and disappeared. In the corner there was a shower and toilet, it was all in the open, I guess this was what life was going to be like now, I had to get used to it. I was shy and this wasn't exactly something that was going to be easy, the guard walked back in and handed me a small pile of what looked like clothes – leggings, a bra, and a singlet. She said, "For you", and then pointed to the shower and walked off.

Resigned to my situation, I began to take off my smelly clothing. I stood naked in the corner of the holding cell, watching as male guards would walk past, stop and look before moving on.

I navigated the frigid water, it was ice cold, something that I had never had in my life, a cold shower. I looked down at my body, revealing a body battered and bruised. I wondered if that's what the guards were looking at. I had bruises on my arms, up and down my legs, in between my legs, on my wrists. The bruises were a dark purple, blue. Standing in the water, it was burning my feet it was so cold, and I stuck one leg in at a time before managing to get more of my body under the water. The cold on my bruises hurt more than I expected. I would have been in the water a whole two minutes before not being able to do it anymore. Drying off with a tank top that was in the pile the guard had given me. It didn't fit me. I wasn't exactly a size 8 and apparently that's what she thought I was! I could barely get a leg into the pair of leggings she gave me. I hadn't laughed in days, and I found myself laughing at the irony of everything, I thought to myself I was losing it. I had finally lost the plot.

I redressed myself in my smelly clothes, I knew the guard wouldn't be happy but it's all I had that fit.

The holding cell began to fill up with women.

Contrary to expectations, I waited alongside other women. Their curious glances and attempts at communication hinted but I couldn't understand one word, these people spoke so quickly.

As lunch arrived, I gave my portion to a fellow inmate who seemed in greater need. One look at it and I knew I wouldn't be able to eat, it was boiled meat and rice. If I had been hungry I would have tried to eat it, but I just couldn't. The other lady who took it from me seemed to be enjoying it. This made me wonder if life was harder for them on the outside then inside a prison.

Later navigating the unfamiliar landscape, I was herded through a series of inspections. A guard entered. The only word that resonated with me was 'dos,' – 'two' – and a sinking feeling gripped me – I knew it was time for the next stage. The unspoken understanding spread among the women, and we were ushered out to encounter a group of five young men in crisp uniforms. Each of them was assigned to one of us, leading us into a room on the left-hand side.

Inside, the room housed five small cubicles. The guard accompanying us proceeded into each cubicle, initiating a thorough inspection of our belongings. My gaze fixated on the male guard who handled my possessions. There wasn't really much to go through, but he examined them thoroughly. It made me think about the other girls who had hidden things, well everything they could. Without uttering a word, he unceremoniously emptied the contents of my bag onto the cubicle floor, a ritual that seemed redundant given my earlier inspections. I observed, bemused by the routine that treated everyone as if they were hiding something.

When the guard seemed satisfied with his intrusive search, he spoke to me in Spanish, assuming I understood. My bewildered expression must have conveyed my confusion. He grasped my upper arm roughly as if I had been disobeying and directed me into the cubicle. The realization dawned – it was the dreaded body search.

A mixture of apprehension and disbelief set in. Did I really have to strip for this man?

The legality seemed questionable, but in this unfamiliar world, legality was a concept I struggled to grasp.

I stood there, hesitating, as the guard gestured to me to remove my clothes. Realizing the waiting eyes and the silent expectation, I reluctantly complied. The guard stood by, watching intently as I undressed, something that I would have to get used to eventually, I guess. In here there would be no privacy, I had removed everything but my bra and I decided to retain my underwear, but he signalled for their removal. I stopped there for a moment. Why were men searching us and not women guards? How was this legal? The body search commenced, I stood there, nothing hidden, the guard approached me, he brushed his arms over my upper body but stopped as he passed my breast, I closed my eyes, wanting this to go by quickly. I felt as he grabbed my breast. It was more of a grope rather than a swift search. I remained calmly with my eyes closed. I couldn't bear any of this. I felt as if his hands left my breast and moved down. He kicked apart my feet, spreading my legs.

Part of me knew what was coming yet I didn't want to believe it would until I felt it, the guard had pushed his hand between my legs and was trying to push what seemed like his fingers into my vagina. My eyelids flew open, and I tried to push him back but as I did so, he pushed his fingers inside me, no hesitation. Tears rolled down my face, I was in shock. I tried to scream but the scream got stuck in my throat. The guard pulled his fingers out. He brought them up to his nose to smell them.

I should have kept my eyes closed.

The guard then put his hand on my shoulder and turned me around and continued. He brushed over my upper body and then I felt his whole body up against me, I couldn't believe this. I felt him. He was hard from this.

He then pushed my shoulders down for me to squat down and I presumed it was to see if something would fall out, although he already knew there was nothing in there. And then he was down next to me. Yet again he was trying to push something inside of me. I pushed back and I sensed he was about to fight me when there was a bang on the cubicle door and suddenly, he was standing right against the door, as far from me as he could. I turned to face him; disgust written all over my face.

This was my reality. It was my nightmare come to life. I needed to learn to deal with this as it happened otherwise, I was going to go insane here.

As the ordeal concluded, he walked out, leaving me to hastily re-dress. Once again, I gathered my belongings strewn carelessly on the floor.

I emerged from the cubicle to see the gazes of the other women. I wondered if they had just gone through the same ordeal I had, or if the guard had merely taken advantage of the fact that I didn't speak the language. Opting to avoid their judgment, I focused my attention on the floor.

The subsequent steps of passing through a metal detector and enduring yet another body search unfolded with mechanical precision, however, this was nothing like the other I had just gone through. We were then lined up beside a metal door. Something was behind that door that I wasn't ready for. I grappled with my expectations, shaped by cinematic portrayals of prisons with orange uniforms, courtyards, and cramped cells. I didn't know what waited for me, what prison was going to be like in Colombia, I really didn't know, I hadn't ever been in a situation like this before. All I had seen was what prisons looked like in the movies, and something told me this wasn't going to be anything similar. This was no movie.

The guards opened a small window and issued commands in Spanish. The process unfolded mechanically as, one-by-one, we were propelled through the metal door. Each of us had the same scared look. As the last in line, I hesitated, reluctant to confront the reality on the other side. Closing my eyes as I felt myself being pushed to the other side, I entered, I heard the door slam shut behind me, I had no choice, bracing for the unknown horrors that awaited within El Buen Pastor.

The moment I opened my eyes on the other side, the realisation hit me – I had officially entered the prison, I mean, of course I had been in holding cells and locked up, but *this* was prison, an actual prison. Confusion and disbelief washed over me as I scanned my surroundings. Closed doors surrounded me, and two figures in worn cream and orange uniforms caught my eye. Were they workers or fellow prisoners? They seemed friendly. A woman in a similar uniform spoke to a guard, mentioning "patio uno." I had no clue what that meant, but the others seemed to understand and followed her. Unsure of where we were headed, I hesitated but decided to join the group, I wasn't too keen on being left behind. As we turned a corner, the scent of fresh bread filled the air. Where the hell was that coming from? Fresh bread?

Passing through a small gate, I was met with the real essence of prison life. To my left, guards at a desk berated a crying woman at the gate. A cacophony of voices echoed as around a hundred women pressed against each other, shouting and screaming. I watched as they pushed past each other, pulling each other out of their way. Was that going to be me? On the opposite side, another gate revealed a more serene scene – women sitting peacefully on steps, engaged in conversation. The purpose of these gates remained a mystery. Were those the yards? What did these different areas mean?

Moving forward, I encountered another desk with guards flanking gates on either side. However, the distinct smell of weed permeated the air, something that I had just spent days smelling when I was in the men's holding cell. Were these the infamous jail cells? The group continued, and my curiosity heightened. Beyond another gate lay a basketball court and, to my astonishment, a park with children playing. Children in prison? The abnormality of the situation left me bewildered. Why were there children here? Surely they hadn't been imprisoned. This prison was huge, it seemed never ending, it made me wonder how many women were in the prison.

On the other side of a passageway, a wooden stage, concrete benches, and even a church came into view. This wasn't the prison depicted in movies. My expectations shattered as I struggled to comprehend the reality unfolding before me.

What the fuck was this place?

Passing through yet another gate, the endpoint became visible. A desk with only two guards awaited, one of whom had a kind demeanour. The girl leading us conversed with the guards, guiding the others to the very end. Little did I realize that this marked the entrance to what I would soon recognize as hell, although after everything, you would like to think I would have recognised it.

The guards now walking behind us herded us into a small room. It wasn't concrete, it was a tin cell. Locked inside, I wondered if this was to be my cell. As I glanced around. I noticed roughly ten unfamiliar faces with mattresses and belongings. Was this their permanent living space? Though I hadn't moved from my spot, I remained alert, trying to discern friendly faces amid the unfamiliar crowd.

My attempt to survey the cell was interrupted when a group of women seemingly residents, approached. One of them, noticing my confusion, attempted to communicate in broken English: "You bien?"

I looked at her? What was 'bien'? I shook my head, unsure what I was saying no to. The lady tried to converse again, "You speak family?" This time I understood. I shook my head "I don't know how to I said in English. How do I ring them? I have no money. I haven't got anything." I blurted this out realising that the little English they had didn't keep up with what I had just said. Frustration mounted as I struggled to comprehend their words and to have them understand mine. Eventually, they abandoned their efforts, leaving me alone.

Amidst the gazes, a black-haired woman with huge facial scars whom I assumed to be their leader, caught my attention. I was caught off guard by her. She wasn't tall, yet she was dominant. She was stocky but not fat, and she had crutches, her leg held together with metal bars, and I wondered what had happened to her. I looked at her, she had slits in her cheeks, and I couldn't help but stare as she stuck her tongue out the slits. Why would someone do that to their face? But intimidation set in as she approached. What did she want from me, especially considering my lack of Spanish? She whispered incomprehensible words, then said something I understood, "Chilli, me, Chilli" and as she signalled to her group, two women approached. What kind of a name was 'Chilli'? Was she considered spicy or what? What did they want? Why did no one understand that I COULD NOT UNDERSTAND THEM!!! It was beginning to get really frustrating for me. Something told me that I was their target, I knew I needed to find somewhere safe and away from them, out of sight. I avoided eye contact, as they now stood in front of me, speaking and looking at me up and down, but Chilli's group's laughter hinted at an ominous future. Although I hadn't been threatened by her, and even if she had, I didn't understand it, but I could feel it, the way they watched me and detailed my every move, I knew I was in trouble. I just didn't know when they would come for me. I walked away from them. I didn't think I could take much more for today.

Soon, the guards opened the door, and everyone streamed into the patio area. The two older ladies who had tried to talk to me earlier attempted to give me a tour, indicating the locations of phones, washing areas, and toilets. The shocking revelation of the prison's living conditions unfolded – a bathroom with two leaking toilets and showers without doors, all shared among the women. There was no privacy whatsoever, I walked into one of the toilets and it was full of shit, I don't know how long it had been there, but it smelt disgusting and I instantly felt vomit coming up to the surface. I swallowed, not wanting to show weakness.

The stark reality overwhelmed me. This was nothing like the movies. Not even ten percent of what you see in movies.

The ladies persisted in trying to communicate, resorting to hand gestures to convey the idea of calling 'family' I looked at them trying to understand what my family had to do with anything, and the confusing look made the other lady signal to the phones and related 'family'? Realising my lack of understanding, they guided me to a phone. "I have no money, I can't call anyone, I have no money." I continued to repeat this over and over again. After a complicated process of trying to explain this, I gave up and watched as they scratched some sort of bank card, and call a heap of numbers. Then the woman turned to me and said, "Your number family." This whole broken English thing wasn't easy to understand especially when you were used to people speaking good English, but beggars can't be choosers and I decided to grasp what they were saying, and I handed over my sister's number. The phone said something in Spanish and then I heard my sister's voice. "I don't have time." I yelled into the phone. "I'm in prison. I'm here. I hate it. I'm scared. I'm terrified. Tell the embassy, I need a law..." and just like that the call cut off. The brief conversation left me yearning for a connection with my family. I hadn't even managed to have a conversation. I was truly alone and on the other side of the world.

Returning to the patio, I observed the seemingly joyous atmosphere. It baffled me – how could anyone be happy about entering prison, or happy about being here? It was odd seeing this, these women found happiness in their day-to-day activities. Sitting on the ledge, I observed the surroundings, feeling detached from the apparent cheerfulness.

I was consumed by my thoughts when the guard's shouts signalled a change in routine. All the women, each with a weird tray from the holding cell, formed chaotic lines. It resembled a zoo, with women pushing and yelling at each other. Reluctantly, I joined the line at the back, unsure of what awaited me but scared to be left behind or without. It was dinner time, I wondered if it would be better than what lunch had looked like, though I was doubtful. Prison food wasn't meant to be luxurious.

As the line progressed, I tried to catch a glimpse of the mysterious food. Some women were already sitting on the ledge devouring their meals, treating it as a delicacy. Maybe dinner was actually nice? At the front of the line, I observed crates on the floor and women serving food with their bare hands, no gloves. Apprehension grew as I hesitated, how was that okay to be served food off the floor and with their bare hands? God knows where they had put their hands! But a sympathetic guard intervened, and I received a filled tray.

The woman serving it, however, made a mockery of my reluctance, possibly seeing a disgust in my eyes as I had watched her serve others, spilling soup on my clothes. She practically threw the soup into the tray, pouring it all over my clothes. I sighed, if high school hadn't had enough bullies, here was high school 2.0. The lady gave me a small handful of rice and an onion and tomato salad. As I walked back to the ledge I saw a worm in my salad, and I instantly gagged.

Back inside, I sat alone, unwilling to eat the questionable meal. One of the women who had helped me call home approached me, gesturing for me to eat. Unable to communicate, I allowed her to take the tray. Her rapid consumption surprised me, and to my amazement she was so happy while eating and she spat out "Thank you! Thank you! I hungry! Muy hungry!" What did 'muy' mean, I wondered? I watched as she walked away with my tray, but to my surprise she washed the tray for me and brought it back, she said "thank you" a few more times before leaving me alone with my thoughts once more.

The day wore on, and I remained in my corner, contemplating the surreal events. Eventually the guards announced the end of the break, everyone returned to the cell. I followed as I hadn't understood anything. Exhausted, I tried to sleep, hoping to escape the nightmare reality I was in. It was the only thing that would make time go by quicker.

I settled into the routine of prison life marked by the rhythmic clanging of metal doors and the oppressive atmosphere that hung in the air. What felt like ten minutes had probably been hours. We lined up like cattle. The new guards performed their count, a ritualistic exercise in the monotony of incarceration. They scribbled in their notebooks, indifferent to the people reduced to mere numbers. We were nothing here. Nobody.

After the formalities, a brief respite beckoned. A five-minute toilet break allowed us to relieve ourselves, hastily filling bottles with water before the cell doors clanged shut once again. I didn't have a bottle of water, that was a luxury here. The bathroom became a shared space, devoid of doors – an unspoken agreement of privacy in the midst of captivity. No one looked at the other while they would do whatever they needed.

The act of peeing, an intimate act forced into public view, was a strange adjustment. Yet, it was preferable to the alternative – the leering eyes of perverts. Each person, in turn, filled a bucket of water to flush away the evidence, a routine that became second nature, mechanical in its repetition.

As I filled my bucket, I noticed her again, – the source of my unease – Chilli. I remembered our brief encounter from earlier in the day and I hadn't managed to shake off the uneasy feeling she had left me with, but I couldn't help but wonder 'why me?' I took another good look at her. She wasn't ugly. She would have been pretty if it wasn't for the scars and scary presence. Her eyes were jet black and she had an olive skin complex and long black hair.

Aggressively, she suddenly pushed me. I couldn't comprehend the reason for her animosity, but I didn't intend to find out. I wasn't here to cause problems, stepping back, I avoided a fight that I wasn't inclined to start nor finish and I wasn't a fighter, I wouldn't have known what to do, take a hit I guess, if it came down to it. All I knew was that I had to keep my distance.

Retreating to the cell, I sought refuge in the corner, all alone, my head resting against the cold tin, the unforgiving wall. I wondered if I would even sleep, not with Chilli and her crew lingering. A throbbing headache pulsed through me, it had been a very stressful day, exacerbated by the fear that lingered from my encounter with Chilli. I closed my eyes as the doors shut, hoping to find solace in sleep, an escape from the living nightmare. But my dreams were no escape from reality, I would see Carlos and Wendy. I would relive the last few days.

However, the respite I sought eluded me. Broken sleep plagued me, interrupted every few minutes by startled awakenings. Even as time passed, with others seemingly asleep, a different kind of unrest persisted.

In the dimly lit corner, Chilli and her group engaged in quiet conversations. I wish I could understand the language so I could be ready. Two of them ventured towards the belongings of newcomers, sifting through bags with an air of authority. Is this what they do? I mean, as it was we would arrive with next to nothing and then that was raided by other inmates? Helpless, I observed as they showcased their findings to Chilli, seeking her approval or disapproval. It was such an odd thing to watch, I knew I shouldn't have, but it was so captivating to witness how it worked in here.

My belongings, confined to the same garbage bag they had floated around in for days, were not exempt. Amidst the murmur of Spanish, the term 'gringa' caught my attention. I wasn't sure what it meant but for some reason, I felt that it was about me. I was silently watching, careful not to draw attention to myself when a sudden cough drew their focus to me, prompting footsteps in my direction. Who the hell had coughed? I didn't have time to look around. Panicking, I feigned sleep, keeping my eyes shut, hoping to escape their attention, yet their curiosity prevailed. I lay there, closing my eyes as tight as I could but then I felt it, feet pressed against my ankle, pain shot through me, my eyes now wide open and the atmosphere thickened with tension. And again, I watched as one of Chilli's crew stormed their foot down on top of my ankle, I tried to look around for help, yet everyone seemed to still be sleeping, or so it seemed. Suddenly, I found myself pinned down, the intrusion unbearable. I didn't see which one her followers was doing this, but she was forcibly searching my body, as if I were hiding something. Unfamiliar hands violated my privacy, searching for something that wasn't there. As tears streamed down my face, their violation intensified. I turned to pull away, I tried to push her off me but then my arms were being pinned down by another girl and the only thing that was left for me to do was to scream, but as I went to do this, I felt something being shoved into my mouth. I couldn't see it, but I could smell it, it was disgusting, maybe a dirty sock.

I was helpless, and the next thing the girl who had been searching my body was pulling my pants down, fingers probing. Part of me knew what was about to happen but I didn't expect it, she smiled at me, and then roughly stuck her fingers in me, feeling around for something, yet there was nothing. The pain was excruciating, and I sobbed silently uncontrollably. One of them tasted their intrusion. I couldn't believe this kept happening to me over and over again. I watched the girl bring her fingers to her face, she smelt them, and then sucked on them and smiled at me again. What the hell was happening ? What was wrong with these people?

I watched the girl stand up and look over her shoulder and I tried to follow where she was looking but the other girl holding me down wouldn't release me. Chilli's approval signalled a false end to the attack. Then they let me go, I grabbed what was in my mouth when I thought it was over, but the assault continued – a barrage of kicks from faceless tormentors. I tried to pull up my pants, but the girls stood kicking me whilst I lay on the ground, I had no escape.

I curled into a ball. I endured what was happening. Surely they would get tired of all this? I wondered what I had done to deserve this brutality. As they finally retreated, their laughter echoed through the cell. I prayed for the nightmare to end, retreating into myself as sleep became an elusive refuge from the harsh reality of prison life.

The Next Day

The initial 24 hours in prison felt like an endless descent into an unfamiliar and harrowing world. Two ladies, their eyes fixated on me, observed as I hesitantly nibbled on the bread roll, their 'pan'. The conversations around me blurred into an indecipherable stream of rapid Spanish amplifying my sense of isolation.

The monotonous routine of incarceration persisted. Lost in my thoughts, I was jolted back to reality by the repeated calling of my name – "Cassandra." The lunchtime line formed, and the ladies, seemingly with their own agenda, pulled me along. I could barely walk, from the bruised ribs to my swollen ankle, I tried to make it seem like it was nothing, but I could barely hold myself up. My injured state didn't escape their notice, and the word 'Chilli' surfaced in their conversation. It became evident that the events of the previous night were not concealed; my vulnerability was laid bare for all to see. I didn't dare tell anyone what had happened last night, I couldn't. I was almost sure I would cop another beating if I did.

In the food line, the same woman from the prior day met my gaze with a disdainful look. The uniformed lady's presence seemed to alter her disposition, offering me a forced smile. A minuscule portion of boiled meat, rice, lettuce, onion, and a piece of boiled banana did little to stimulate my appetite. A worm wriggled in the banana.

Yesterday the salad, today the banana. I couldn't believe people actually sat down to eat this. I would rather go hungry then risk getting sick eating this.

Returning to our seats, the ladies who had helped me yesterday attempted to coax me into eating, but the mere sight of the tainted food brought tears to my eyes. I just couldn't do it. They shared their portions when my reluctance became apparent, even taking the unexpected step of washing my tray. The smallest gestures of kindness stood out in the harsh reality of prison life.

An abrupt announcement by the guards disrupted the day, prompting a return to the confines of the cell.

Alone again, the door sealed shut, I dared not look around, and not look for Chilli. Somehow, I needed to find the strength to push through this. I didn't know where I was going to find it.

As fatigue settled in, I contemplated the uncertain future within these walls. Sleep seemed elusive, but eventually, the door creaked open, and the routine shifted. Everyone left the cell, leaving me alone. The ladies returned, attempting conversation, but comprehension eluded me, and a sense of emptiness pervaded my being. Only 24 hours in, and the weight of fear and doubt pressed heavily upon me.

Hours passed in a daze, observing the inmates who seemed oddly at ease in their confined surroundings, and I wondered how? I really didn't understand this, how could one be happy with these people, these conditions? The guards' intrusion signalled another round of lining up for food trays. Disinterested, I remained seated while the two ladies departed to collect their meals. The guards, inquisitive, engaged them in conversation, but my concern was solely for reprieve in the form of sleep.

The return to the cell brought back haunting memories of the previous night's torment. The routine mirrored the previous evening – two toilet breaks and the 'contada' – the counting. I retreated to my corner, uncertain if sleep would embrace me. Terrified and overwhelmed, I found solace in tears until exhaustion claimed me, dreading the unknown. Minutes that awaited in this unforgiving environment.

Movement?
20 April 2017

"Cassandra Sai... Cassandra." The call echoed through the prison corridors, the guards struggling with the pronunciation of my last name. I would have laughed at how they tried to pronounce it if it hadn't been for my current situation. The two ladies who had been helping me earlier now guided me down the walkway. I was still crippled from the horrible beating. I was sure most of the women knew what had happened but not one person spoke of it. The guards, recognizing my English background, didn't bother to try and talk to me, they pointed toward a tall, skinny girl on the other side of the bars.

"Hey, I'm Lily," she introduced herself.

I was shocked it was decent English. She was extremely tall, with long black hair, a gentle smile and very skinny. I smiled in recognition, to be honest as nice as it was to hear English, I wasn't in the mood to speak.

"I need to take you to the 'Capitan.' They need to speak to you."

The 'Capitan'? Why? What was going on? Was I being let out? Was this all over? Lily gently took my arm to aid my limping walk.

As we strolled, Lily engaged in small talk, inquiring about my origin, well-being, and the treatment I had received so far.

"So where are you from? How have you been? Have the others treated you well?" My responses remained concise. I answered the questions but gave not enough information. "Australia. I'm okay. I'm surviving, and well, I've been treated as well as you can expect for a prison." There was no way I was snitching on the beating I had received. What if she was friends with Chilli? Curiosity nudged me to question our destination and purpose. Lily explained that we were to see the Capitan and the 'Mayor' to determine my situation in prison. I felt a spark of disappointment, although I knew it was impossible to be released from prison, part of me had really hoped for it. However, confusion lingered – was there something worse awaiting me? What did that mean, to determine my situation? The office, situated near my initial entrance into the prison, felt familiar yet distant. Only three days had passed since I walked through that door, yet it felt like I had been here for entirety already. Lily exchanged words in Spanish with someone at the doorway, granting us access. We seated ourselves before a tall, skinny lady and a short, chunky one – I assumed they were the Capitan and the Mayor.

Mayor Nancy, though initially intimidating, had empathetic eyes. A rare sight in this judgemental unforgiving environment. Lily translated while Mayor Nancy asked questions.

"What is your name?"

"Cassandra."

"Age?"

"Twenty-two."

"Occupation?"

"Personal Trainer."

"Why are you here? What did you do?"

"Drug Trafficking."

"Do you consume drugs?"

"No. Never."

I was sure no one would ever believe that I hadn't ever consumed any illegal substance but it was true. I was terrified of drugs. I'd never even smoked a cigarette. Once I provided the answers, Mayor Nancy communicated further with Lily. I wasn't sure what was being said but then Lily continued, posing questions about my knowledge of Spanish, family in the area, and legal representation. The Mayor, seemed dissatisfied, directed a pointed question about my injured ankle and medical attention.

"The Mayor wants to know what happened to you. Did this happen in the patio? Have you seen the prison doctor?"

"I ... ah ... I fell over. I haven't gone to the doctor. I'm OK."

Mayor Nancy was sceptical did she believe me? Surely they knew that I couldn't really tell them what had happened. The Mayor exchanged words with Lily.

"The mayor says you have no reason to be scared to speak here. This is a safe place. We are here to ensure nothing bad happens to you."

I smiled in acknowledgment, but the truth was, there was no safe space anywhere, something told me that the walls had ears and it would all get back to Chilli if I told anyone.

The Mayor, writing on a card with my mugshot, seemed to have made a decision. Lily informed me, "You are being transferred to 'Patio Five' – a place she assures you will be better there. In the afternoon, your name would be called, and you need to collect a mattress and personal supplies before returning."

Walking back in silence, I sought clarity. Lily shared that "The Mayor intends to place you in Spanish classes. You need to learn to communicate, Cassandra. There are women in here who will use you."

The news of relocation stirred conflicting emotions. What awaited me in 'Patio Five'? Concerns about the fate of the two ladies who had aided me nagged at me. Although we couldn't communicate, they had made me feel less alone, now I was going to be all alone again.

Upon returning to Patio One, where the ladies awaited, I tried to communicate my impending move with five raised fingers. They must have understood. Their smiles and laughter suggested they were pleased for me. Had they influenced this decision? As they assisted me to my usual spot, guards opened an unnoticed door on the other side of the yard. Intrigued, in a moment of wry amusement, I pondered, had that always been there?

As I stood there, the guard's shout jolted me out of my contemplation, and the group began moving towards the previously unnoticed door. What did she say? I felt so stupid, not understanding anything. I had no choice but to follow everyone else. Stepping through the doorway, I was met with an unexpected sight – a vast expanse of grass, surrounded by fences and watched over by towering guard posts. I mean, it wasn't some hidden Eden garden, but it was refreshing to see something other than tin cells and concrete walls. I hadn't known such an area existed within the confines of the prison. People were scattered around, engaging in conversations, or simply sitting and enjoying the rare outdoor space. They all seemed at peace. The ladies guided me towards a lady who they introduced as Johana, conversing with her, but my mind was preoccupied with the impending move. When? And what would it be like encountering new faces? Would I go through another beating like the one I had just had here? Was I going to be, okay?

Lost in my thoughts, I barely registered the guards standing on the grass, shouting what sounded like "contada." Confusion set in as everyone scattered, forming a line. Yep, it was time for a count. The midday headcount seemed unusual; my limited understanding of prison routines left me questioning the unexpected timing. Maybe something had happened. Once the count was done, I scanned my surroundings, and that's when I noticed several lesbian couples, unapologetically displaying affection. Hugs, kisses, and shared moments unfolded openly, their happiness palpable. Watching them, I couldn't help but admire their comfort in being true to themselves, disregarding judgment or societal norms.

Reflecting on their authenticity, I questioned my own struggles. Why couldn't I embrace my identity with the same confidence? The answer seemed complex, rooted in years of fear and societal expectations. I had spent years in relationships that felt stifling, all because of the fear of judgment. Pushing these thoughts aside, I couldn't confront this internal battle in the midst of prison life. The disdain I already faced made me hesitant to reveal another layer of myself. Would they hate me even more if they knew I was gay? I yearned to blend in, to fade into the background and be forgotten in this unforgiving environment. Yet, I wanted what they had, after all that's how I had ended up here.

I sat and observed the daily routines unfolding around me – the rhythmic hum of conversations, the meticulous washing of clothes, and the crafting of small items. This was prison life and they all seemed to be enjoying it, or maybe I was imagining it, but they definitely didn't look like they were *suffering*. My gaze fixated on some women, again, unashamedly displaying affection for their girlfriend. They appeared so happy, and as one couple made eye contact and smiled at me, I swiftly turned away, awkward, my cheeks flushed with embarrassment. Could they sense my curiosity?

Did they somehow know? I mean, I had heard of the 'gaydar', but was it really a thing?

I seemed to spend most of my time lost in my thoughts and yet, sometimes I wasn't even thinking anything. I noticed a distant call of my name, but my senses were dulled by the constant chatter about me. It took a moment for the realization to hit: someone was genuinely calling my name. Emerging from my daze, I spotted Lily by the gate, accompanied by a guard.

A wave of relief washed over me – it was time to leave Patio One. Lily instructed me to gather my belongings, but I confessed to having none. Which was true, after Chilli's crew attacked me the first night, I had been left with nothing. Her sad nod conveyed understanding; she likely knew the story. We set off to retrieve my mattress and the monthly personal supplies that were infrequently distributed. Lily told me that the prison was supposed to supply us monthly with toilet paper and pads, but we would only receive them once every 8–10 months. I kept my silence; commenting on the irregularity of supplies seemed unwise. This was bad where would I get toilet paper from?

Following Lily to a different office, she explained its purpose, noting it as a place to find a social worker for discussions about the embassy, family, or intimate visits. The term lingered in my mind – 'intimate visits'. What did that entail? Did people engage in sexual visits here? An elderly lady joined us, and Lily conversed with her in Spanish. My name and 'Australia' caught my attention, as they continued their conversation. Struggling to stand due to my throbbing ankle, I opted to sit in a chair across from the office. The women from Patio One, standing in line, intrigued me. Were they also being relocated?

Observing, I noticed the old lady handing Lily a bag containing pads, a roll of toilet paper, and other personal products. Lily relayed that this was a monthly supply, which raised eyebrows considering its scarcity. Lily directed me to another office to collect bedding. Assisted by Lily, I limped to the office, where we encountered university students in white coats, studying the practical stage of social work. Astonished by the presence of volunteers in such an environment, I couldn't help but wonder about their motivation. Lily spoke to a student, who handed her a paper for me to sign. The student disappeared briefly, returning with a plastic bag containing a thin, grey blanket, and another student followed with a paper-thin mattress. Lily emphasized its uniqueness and the need for careful preservation.

Now equipped with my belongings, we approached Patio Five, reputed as the safest. I guess I would soon find out, although, I wasn't convinced I would go through anything worse than what I had before arriving here. Lily's reassurance provided a hint of relief, but escaping Chilli too easily left an ominous feeling. Would she send someone after me? I looked around, trying to see if anyone was eyeing me off. Lily noticed my concern, offering a comforting smile and words of reassurance. "Let's go, I'll help you get settled in. You'll be okay."

Patio Five – Getting Settled
20 to 22 April 2017

Lily and I crossed the gate, and once inside, she engaged in a lengthy conversation with the guards, I wished I could understand, although occasionally mentioning my name and the word 'Australia', I knew I was the topic of the conversation.

Lily informed me that I was assigned to cell 32 in Tramo 2A. I was not sure what 'tramo' was, but I just followed. Lily assured me that she would guide me, helping me settle in and introducing me to my new cellmate. A wave of gratitude swept over me. Having someone close who could assist in navigating this foreign environment was a comforting thought. Especially in my language, you have no idea how nice it was to understand something!

The guards swung open the gate, and a lady took my mattress out of my hands and disappeared upstairs. I had a momentary panic; did I just get robbed? "Hey!" Was the only thing that I managed to spit out in the shock of it. I heard someone laughing next to me, it was Lily, it irritated me that she would find me being robbed as funny! Lily chuckled, "Oh Cassandra, what did they do to you in the other patio? These ladies, they were merely helping with your transfer, here we try to help each other."

Relieved, I climbed the stairs to the second floor, acutely aware of the attention I drew from others. Lily whispered, "You'll get used to the people, we don't like people we are not accustomed to as new cellmates, or newcomers really, and well, you're not from here, which makes it a little worse."

Upon reaching what was to be my cell, I encountered my new cellmate, Carina – a woman in her 30s with black hair adorned with purple streaks. Her friendly demeanour offered a sense of calmness, contrasting with the anxious atmosphere of the prison. Her face was covered in freckles, she had a friendly smile and quite a delicate voice. She wasn't anything similar to the people I had just spent my last few days with. Lily mediated our introduction. I presumed she was telling her that I had no belongings and spoke no Spanish. Carina's eyes held genuine concern, and after Lily left, she assisted me in placing the mattress on the top concrete bunk.

Despite the language barrier, Carina's warmth transcended words. She handed me one of her blankets and introduced herself in Spanish and I looked at her, confused, so she tried again "Ah, me, ah name es Carina."

I smiled at the attempt to communicate with me, I replied "I'm Cassandra and thank you," I said, while indicating to the blankets. I reciprocated, feeling grateful for her kindness. Attempting to communicate, she gestured towards herself and mentioned something in Spanish, creating an awkward pause. Carina then retreated to her belongings, leaving me standing in the corridor. Ahhh! 'Tramo' meant passageway or corridor – interesting word. Outside, I stood at the wired barrier and observed. Below there was a basketball court and various activities, a stark contrast to the confines of the cell. In front of Patio Five there was another big building, and I could see that it was another Patio, of course it had been the weed-smelling patio I had walked past days ago.

Feeling the weight of the stares, I stood alone minding my own business. This was something I had learnt very quickly. Don't look at anyone and do not engage unless they do first. I was consumed in thoughts until Carina tapped my shoulder, inviting me back into the cell for privacy. She handed me a pile of items, sparking confusion as I hesitated about accepting due to lack of funds, I had no money, I had nothing. I shook my head and spoke "I have no money, I can't take this, I can't accept it, sorry." Carina's expression of confusion was the same as the one I had carried around since arriving in Colombia. She laughed and said "Que, What?" No money" I tried again, slower. "Ahhhhhh nooo" – then she proceeded to speak Spanish and again stopped and said "No money, ah no problemo, ah you" she then pointed to the items. Carina's reassuring smile conveyed her genuine intent, and she signalled towards her nose, subtly indicating my need for a shower. Yeah okay, I know, I stink. I mean it had now been what, over a week in the same clothes. What did these people expect? Gratefully, I accepted the clean clothes and personal products she provided.

Guided by Carina, we navigated to the communal bathroom – a space with two toilets, three showers with makeshift curtains. This was different. The other patio had left everything exposed. I was already beginning to see the difference in the patios. Without hesitation and not wanting to make Carina uncomfortable with my smell, I had no choice but to shower. The freezing cold, three-minute shower left me, well, forcibly refreshed, although I couldn't feel anything in my body, at least I didn't smell bad anymore. I put on an oversized maroon jumper and grey tracksuit pants Carina had generously given me. Words couldn't express how thankful I was for the clothes and soap. I couldn't help but marvel at the unexpected presence of a microwave.

Returning to the cell, my sense of direction wavered, I walked until the end of the passageway and realised I had forgotten which cell was mine, this was very stressful. What if I entered the wrong one? I was about to give up and just stand there until Carina's call redirected me. Climbing into the bunk, as I settled into the cell with Carina, she demonstrated kindness beyond my expectations. However, a momentary misunderstanding left me momentarily flustered, revealing my vulnerability in this unfamiliar environment.

As Carina and I engaged in an awkward attempt at communication, she suddenly pointed to my dirty clothes and then to a bucket. What did that mean? Was it the dirty bucket pile? Perplexed, I questioned her intent, fearing that she might be taking my belongings, but I thought 'Surely not!' After all, she had just given me clothes, I placed them into the bucket and suddenly some redheaded lady walks in without notice, picks up the bucket and leaves. She just stole my clothes! The possibility of theft flashed through my mind, igniting a momentary panic. Carina, sensing my confusion, burst into laughter, the sound echoing within the confined space. She assured me through gestures that my clothes were safe and that she intended to assist me with something related to the bucket.

Relieved, I followed her lead, putting the clothes in the bucket as she continued to chuckle at the misunderstanding. It was a moment of vulnerability for me, a realization that in this new environment, where language was a barrier, misinterpretations could lead to unwarranted fears. Carina's laughter, infectious and warm, served as a reassuring balm, reminding me that amidst the challenges, there were moments of light-heartedness and understanding. She said "um ... clean ah ... ropa" what the hell was 'ropa'? I couldn't put it together until I followed the lady who had stolen my clothes and saw filling the bucket with water, what was she doing? The girl looked at me, she probably noticed that I was very confused and said "Me, ah, clean" then she pointed to my clothes, what the heck, was this a thing? Did people do this? She smiled as I probably continued to look more confused and said "Ah, Carina, for you." I just nodded, although I was over the moon to see that these women were trying to communicate with me, it was very hard to comprehend what they wanted to say with their broken English, nevertheless, I gathered that Carina was behind this lady cleaning my clothes. The incident highlighted the importance of patience and the need to navigate the complexities of prison life with a sense of humour, even in the face of seemingly mundane activities like laundry. I laughed at myself, twice in two hours I thought I was having my things stolen.

Man! Chilli really had left me traumatised.

Carina's laughter, infectious and genuine, eased my nerves. The misunderstanding showcased my vulnerability, but Carina's kindness prevailed. The cell, though small, became a haven, adorned with personal touches by Carina. She had pictures of her kids all over the walls, and everywhere she could put them. It was sad to see, I felt for her, I couldn't imagine being a mother and leaving them outside on their own. I didn't have any photos, and part of me didn't want to, however, the loneliness persisted, overshadowing any attempt to make it more bearable home. I pondered the significance of decorating cell walls and questioned if I would ever embrace such a practice. The cell, despite Carina's efforts, remained a silent testament to the loneliness of these prison walls. I was curious about Carina, I wanted to know why she was in here, but I didn't really know how to ask, not yet.

The morning routine in Patio Five was an early wake-up call, and I quickly realized that the expectation was to be ready, showered, and dressed before the morning headcount.

The ice-cold showers in the prison were a brutal reminder of the harsh realities of the gaol. The bathroom, with its two open toilets and three showers shielded only by hanging sheets, offered minimal privacy, but it was better than nothing. The icy water further intensified the discomfort of an already horrible situation. Would I ever get used to this water?

The frigid water hit my skin like a thousand needles, creating a burning sensation that lingered long after stepping out. God, I missed hot showers.

The lack of privacy with no doors to shield the showers added another layer of discomfort. The vulnerability of being exposed to others in such an intimate act as bathing intensified the emotional toll. The sheer visibility made an already challenging experience even more humiliating, as the absence of personal space stripped away any sense of dignity in here and there were women who loved it, I slowly was beginning to analyse people. I needed to do it to survive.

In this environment, the basic act of personal hygiene became a physically and emotionally demanding task, where even the most personal and basic routines were stripped of comfort and rendered as stark reminders of the loss of autonomy and privacy.

It made you think about all the luxuries you would take for granted on the outside.

However, my attempt at a discreet morning routine didn't go unnoticed. There was an unfriendly woman watching me from the line that was there. She was short with brown hair with brassy blonde highlights in her hair, she didn't have a kind look and with her painted-on eyebrows she looked like one of Cinderella's evil stepsisters. She seemed to take pleasure in my discomfort. She exchanged smirks and comments with her companions, I wish I could understand what she was saying, just so I could be one step in front of her.

Then out of nowhere, a sudden cascade of freezing water drenched me. Shocked, I turned to the direction the water had come from, and the horrible lady stood there with the bucket in her hand, what a bitch!

I clutched the soaked clothes to my body, wondering what I had done to deserve this. I didn't retaliate though, part of me knew it wasn't worth it and then another part of me knew that I was showing people yet again, that they could do what they wanted, and I wouldn't react. I carried the bucket back to the cell; I walked away feeling like a wet rat with no other clothes to change into. Great, what was I going to do now?.

Carina, perched in the doorway with her coffee and cigarette, looked at me with a mix of shock and amusement. She shook her head, smiled, and shouted to Christina, the lady from the neighbouring cell, to take the bucket from me. I watched as they engaged in conversation, they looked at me and laughed, I didn't feel that this was actually funny, especially not when I was freezing my tits off and with nothing to change into, but then, I don't know if it was a nervous laugh, or a 'life is so fucked' kind of laugh, but I found myself laughing yet again. I sensed that humour might become our common language, a way to communicate without words.

Entering the cell, I placed my personal products back in their spot and left my towel on the bed to dry. Carina, who had apparently been behind me the whole time, reached past me and grabbed my towel. This unexpected action startled me, and I turned around to see her hanging it on the inside of the cell door. Everything had its place in the cell, I was learning this as each day went on.

Carina muttered something about a "key," leaving me bewildered. Had she found something in my wet clothes? Again she said, "A Key", pointing to the back of the door. I nodded, but what did 'A Key' mean? She kept talking, and I stood there, I was really trying to understand words, try and piece together sentences but I had nothing to base them on, I was screwed, I understood nothing! When she said "café," I was confused, but she pointed to her cup. It took a moment, but I realized she was offering me coffee. The idea of a café in prison seemed absurd, right? Maybe cafe meant something else here, did it mean coffee? I wasn't complaining, but I accepted, hoping it might provide a boost of energy.

As I sipped the strong black coffee, Carina surprised me again by producing a bag of bread rolls. The smell of fresh bread wafted through the air, making my stomach rumble. I gratefully took a roll, munching away, appreciating every bite. It was a simple pleasure; one I hadn't experienced in days. Yet, I wondered, where had the bread come from?

The combination of the coffee and bread momentarily distracted me from the strange encounter in the shower. The coffee, though not my preferred style, I don't think I had ever drunk black coffee and definitely not without sugar, became more palatable with each bite of the delicious bread roll. As I leaned against the bars, watching the morning activities unfold, inmates running to the showers, hanging out washing, I felt a hint of gratitude for these small privileges in an otherwise challenging environment. Just as I finished my coffee and bread roll, the word 'contada' echoed through the Patio. The morning headcount was commencing, and I was relieved to have finished eating. I realised that I was actually learning words and remembering them, which I hoped meant that learning the language wasn't going to be too hard. The guards didn't shut the gate after the count, leaving me wondering if it meant freedom of movement during the day. Regardless, I had no intention of staying cooped up in my cell. I needed to steer clear of the mean woman and avoid any more awkward conversations.

I had always been a loner growing up, so being alone wasn't the problem. The hardest part was actually feeling alone. I was surrounded with thousands of women yet I felt so alone that it physically hurt.

Later, as I entered the cell, there was a friendly face waiting in one of the chairs. She told me her name was Denise, and to my surprise, she spoke fluent English. She greeted me warmly, offering assistance whenever needed and expressing her willingness to practice English through conversations. Denise shared that she was half African and half Dutch, hailing from Holland, then she proceeded to overshare. She had been here in Colombia on a vacation and had been caught smuggling over fifteen kilos of cocaine and had been sentenced to five years and ten months. She had already served two years of her sentence. That was a crazy amount, I thought my nearly six kilos had been bad, but fifteen? And she only got five years and ten months, it made me hopeful that if I were to be sentenced it would have to be less than her sentence as she had nearly three times the amount.

Carina spoke to Denise in Spanish, and their conversation seemed serious. Once they had finally finished talking, Denise turned to me and said, "She asked me to warn you to stay away from a woman named 'Mariana'. She has stolen money from people in both Patio Five and Patio Four. I wasn't sure which lady it was, and Denise stepped out and showed me the lady, I hadn't really seen much of her, she was a huge lady with long hair. Just from looking at her I got a bad vibe. I was done ignoring gut feelings. Denise, seemingly kind, cautioned me about 'Mariana', but I couldn't shake off a sense of discomfort.

Carina hadn't come in to sit down yet and she continued talking to Denise in Spanish. Even though I couldn't understand their conversation, Denise, proficient in Spanish, was able to engage with Carina effortlessly. I was jealous, that's what I needed, I needed to learn this damn confusing language. Jealousy crept in as I watched them communicate so seamlessly. Denise turned to me and explained that Carina had asked her to translate to facilitate communication between us. "Carina doesn't want you to feel uncomfortable and she wants to help you where she can. She will teach you how to wash your clothes and she wants to give you phone credit. Family is important, it keeps you sane."

I laughed and said, "She obviously has a normal family. Mine drives me insane. They give me no peace of mind!"

But it was true, right now, they were my only connection to the outside world. "Cassandra, do you not eat? Carina tells me you don't eat. What is wrong with you, girl?" Denise spoke with her heavy African accent, I shook my head, "I can't eat this food, I know it's all there is to eat, but I can't do it. I've had worms, hairs and for all I know maybe toenails in my food. I can't stomach it!"

"You'll get used to it." Denise said sadly, "You're better off eating that, than getting sick from not eating and dying. In here we come to die, we have no medicine, no health. A Russian lady dropped dead the other day because the doctor here told her she had nothing, and five days later, she was dead." This shocked me and I was left speechless, surprised at the lack of medical treatment and it touched me that she cared. Denise continued translating as Carina spoke, outlining a plan to make my prison life a bit more manageable. According to Denise's translations, Carina intended to take care of my dirty clothes, ensuring they were washed. Denise even offered to cover the expenses until I could stand on my own feet financially. Carina continued to express the importance of eating and encouraged me to help myself to coffee and bread rolls whenever available.

Denise informed me about 'expendio.' "'Expendio' is for the rich here," she said. "They sometimes sell bread, plantain and sometimes even chocolate. Other times they may sell tinned foods but that's it. However it's better than the food we get. I don't get 'expendio.' My family do not give me money, so I just eat what we get." I figured that would be my case too. Who was going to give me money to survive here?

"Carina was trying to make me feel as comfortable as she could to help me ... what ... find my feet here I guess you could say," Denise continued, "and that she would bring me a few things each time they sold items." She also explained the routine, including morning water heating by Christina, an opportunity to watch TV (which Carina planned to move for better visibility), and a heads-up about Mariana's rudeness. Feeling overwhelmed by the unexpected kindness, I took in the information and tried to express my gratitude. Carina handed me calling cards with 15,000 pesos to call my family. Although, I wasn't sure they were going to be encouraging or give me motivation to be okay, I didn't feel like I could lean on my family, I mean, what had it been, two or three years since I'd actually had a proper conversation with my mother? Denise continued translating Carina's words, assuring me that my phone code was mine alone and advising me against sharing it. As Carina left, I couldn't help but feel touched by her generosity. Denise, too, seemed surprised and remarked that I was lucky to have someone like Carina looking out for me. She reminded me where her cell was and left me to process the whirlwind of emotions. In that moment, amidst the uncertainty of prison life, I felt a glimmer of hope. Maybe, just maybe, Patio Five wasn't as bad as the other Patio, and perhaps, with Carina's unexpected kindness, things were starting to look up – as much as they could anyway.

When lunch was served, I decided it was time to acclimate to prison life, the quicker I learnt to live and move in this underworld, the easier it would be, right? Carina joined me, guiding me past the other Patios into an open area across from the park and alongside the church.

Everything I had seen on my first day walking to Patio One. This Patio had a different food distribution process than Patio One, which was a relief, I wasn't keen on having someone's bare, dirty hands serving the food. As we approached the plain, white building in the middle, I noticed a massive line that eventually split into two. It was crowded, and I found myself squished against others. It was very uncomfortable, everyone was pushing into each other, all in a rush to get their delicious serving. The line led to six little windows where each person received different items: rice, meat, vegetables, soup, juice, and a mysterious sixth window that Carina ignored. I wonder what it had been, I tried to catch a peep, but I thought if Carina avoided it, there was a reason, so I copied.

Following Carina out, she stopped to speak to a guard on our way back. I paid little attention, I mean it wasn't like I would understand anyway, until I heard my name being called. The guard introduced herself as Jane, " Ahh, Me name es Jane" she said with a friendly smile.

Wow. Nervous and flustered, I quickly turned away, pretending not to be too interested. What the fuck was that, Cassie? You do *not* think that guard is cute? Carina tapped my shoulder, a knowing smile on her face. Had I been that obvious? I needed to compose myself. Look at the shit show you just got yourself into for liking a girl! Keep your head down and get out of this place!

Back in the cell, Mariana appeared, and I hastily put my food on the bed, retreating into my bunk. In silence, I picked at my meal – chewy meat, plastic-tasting rice, and a bland salad, of … well … onion. I skipped the soup after seeing it on Carina's tray. It was a funny colour. I don't think I had ever seen soups that were a dirty grey colour and smelt like poo. The prison cuisine was far from gourmet, but I reminded myself, this is what I deserved. It wasn't a five-star resort.

Amazed at how quickly others finished and enjoyed their meals, I threw my food into the bin, unable to stomach anything more than a couple of bites. I washed my tray in the shared bathroom, returned to the cell, and found the door shut. Was Carina already asleep? Could I just walk in? Of course I couldn't, it was shut for a reason! The decision to enter or wait outside felt like a crisis, and after much contemplation, I chose to go in. Carina was laying on her bed. I guess this was how she made her days go by. It wasn't something that I think I could handle. I needed to be proactive, do something. However, days of inadequate sleep had taken a toll on me, and exhaustion from over-thinking weighed heavy. I could do with a nap. I put my tray away and laid on the mattress, staring at the ceiling. Carina had the TV on. She was listening to Spanish, so I turned to face the wall.

Thoughts of Denise, serving nearly six years for carrying more drugs than I did, lingered in my mind. It sparked a sense of hope. Maybe my stay here wouldn't be as long as I feared. It wouldn't be anywhere near as long as the prosecutor had threatened me with. I resisted the idea of accepting any deal without a fight, contemplating the need for a lawyer. Perhaps Denise could recommend one? Maybe hers? Contacting the Embassy also crossed my mind, but I remembered that they weren't allowed to get involved with any legal type situations. The million ideas on what to do collided with the uncertainty of how to achieve them. My family most definitely didn't have the money for any of this, I could not rely on them. All I could think of was, getting through this, keeping it quiet and moving on with life, however things worked out, I just wanted to move past it eventually. Lying there, I couldn't manage to fall asleep. Every sound around me kept me alert. How did people actually sleep here?

The rest of the day followed the familiar routine – dinner, contada, and bedtime. Like every other day in this confined world, something that I would learn to adjust too. However this whole 'doing nothing thing' would eventually drive me insane.

The next day began early as Carina tried to wake me up. Despite her efforts and a language barrier, I couldn't understand what she was saying. It was a recurring frustration – people assuming I would magically comprehend Spanish overnight. Carina, realizing my confusion, left my tray on the bed. Breakfast time had arrived, and although barely awake, I descended from my bunk, limping downstairs. The paper-thin mattress that we were given wasn't enough to give ease from the cold concrete that lay beneath, unfortunately old injuries were starting to flare up.

As I walked out, a clock caught my eye, displaying an early 3:30 am. Who eats breakfast at 3:30am? Carina stood in line ahead, gesturing for me to join her, but not wanting to inconvenience anyone, I shook my head and waited my turn. It was my first breakfast in this place, and while not thrilled about it, I proceeded through each serving window, receiving bread, a green orange, a peculiar piece of cheese that was covered in white slime, and a white lumpy liquid, which I had no idea what that was!

Jane, the guard from the day before, stood by as I collected my breakfast. It puzzled me why I remembered her name. I had struggled to remember most people's names, yet hers, it was easy to remember. Feeling my face redden, I looked down, trying to ignore her gaze. Was this going to be an occurring thing? Shit, why did I always have to turn bright red when I was nervous? Back in the cell, Carina was already gone. Was she in the shower? Deciding to eat my breakfast, I sampled the strange white liquid first. It resembled porridge but had a different consistency and was less sweet. Although not unpleasant, it was sickly sweet, I couldn't quite stomach it.

After climbing back into bed, I left my tray on the shelf with the rest of my belongings. Sleep eluded me, and I lay there, listening to the mumbled conversations around me. Carina returned, flicking the light on and settling into her bunk. I wasn't sure what she was doing, and I ended up zoning out. The sound of her chatting with friends filled the air, but I paid little attention.

Today marked the first day I ventured outside our passage alone. It felt awkward, with people's curious stares, but I pretended not to notice. Leaning on the railing, I pondered my situation and the consequences of my actions. Lost in thought, a lady in her sixties, named Carol, interrupted. She spoke English, surprising me, and offered help, genuine concern in her eyes. I appreciated her kindness but kept my struggles to myself. She was tiny, she would have been no taller than 4ft 7" or 8". Quite cute really, she had brown hair with grey running through it, she was pale and fragile, yet something told me this women was tough.

Carol, enthusiastic about practicing English, signed up for non-existent lessons, lessons that I didn't realise I had offered. It was strange, a stranger approaching me so suddenly, but I welcomed the company.

It was nice to not be consumed by my over-thinking. As she chatted, about, well I'm not exactly sure, my mind, burdened by the weight of my situation, barely registered her words. Suddenly, my name echoed through the air. Anxious about another incomprehensible conversation, I hesitated. Carol offered to join me, and we descended the stairs, where a guard awaited.

Carol and the guard engaged in conversation, and I yearned for clarity. "We must go," she said to me, offering me no further clarity. Where was I going? We walked towards the area where we usually received food, but this time, we turned left towards a playground. My confusion deepened. Why was there a playground in a prison? Carol explained, "This area is for the children who are in prison with their mothers, they get play time, often too, some patios will be allowed to spend some time on the playground. It's nice when that happens. It's different". It was just part of the area, a bizarre detail that intrigued me. Oblivious to the surroundings and thinking about the fact that there were kids in prison, I hadn't noticed the classrooms filled with frustrated-looking women, confirming my suspicions about a prison school.

We came into an office where a tall, skinny man named Peter awaited, I felt uncomfortable. He was tall, had dirty yellow, horrible teeth, and thinning hair. His demeanour was unsettling, and I couldn't shake the feeling that he was overly touchy-feely. Carol translated Peter's words, "You are very beautiful," praising my beauty, making me uneasy, "very beautiful girl". It was very unsettling. The conversation shifted to a Mayor-mandated Spanish class. It was time to learn Spanish. I nodded, understanding little but relieved when the meeting seemed to end.

However, Peter insisted on showing me the library, he put his hand on my shoulder to guide the way, I tried to wriggle away from him, yet his grip tightened. We walked through corridors, up and down stairs, arriving at an area with a basketball court and a smelly toilet block. The pungent odour turned out to be marijuana. Carol translated Peter's question, "Do you do marijuana?" I shook my head, repelled by the idea, I even hated the idea of the idea. Peter's sleazy smile lingered as we entered a building filled with books, where a guard oversaw the so-called 'best prison library'.

Carol suggested looking for children's Spanish books to aid my learning. Meanwhile, I examined the limited English section, finding only a handful of books, mostly about God and meditation, neither of which were of interest to me. I mean, I wasn't about to start believing in God just because I was in prison. It felt fake. My eyes landed on *The Girl on the Train,* and I decided to give it a read. Maybe it would distract me. Carol returned with a stack of grammar books for kids and offered to help me learn Spanish during our free time.

Strangely, although I acknowledged the *necessity* of learning Spanish, funnily I resented being *compelled* to do so. Frustration with my situation lingered. I was beginning to feel, well, angry about my whole situation. As we checked out the books, Peter walked us back to the Patio, his unsettling presence a constant discomfort. Great! Now I was going to be near this man all the time.

After a while, the days blurred into one recurring nightmare, the same agony in an endless loop. Anger began to consume me, anger that I hadn't wanted to feel. The situations stood out more than the days, a constant reminder of my predicament. The Spanish classes, a supposed escape from the Patio, proved almost useless. Frustration mounted as the teacher, lacking English proficiency, couldn't explain or answer my queries. How was someone supposed to teach me a whole new language without being able to explain it to me so I could understand? I attended the class anyway, feeling more conspicuous among others. People made comments, and with an ineffective teacher, understanding them seemed distant. Fuelled by determination, I borrowed a dictionary from the library and tried memorizing words. I didn't need anyone to teach me this language, I would do it on my own. Because I was on my own in all of this. Yet, I hesitated to speak aloud, feeling foolish, I didn't want to be corrected, or laughed at, yet I knew one day I would finally speak out loud, but only when I was good enough.

The lawyer I had was supposed to be a lifeline, a source of reassurance. However, the broken English he spoke carried a bleak message – being in Colombia meant being in trouble. Which, well, was obvious. He suggested a plea deal, emphasizing that in Colombia, innocence rarely mattered in drug cases.

"No matter you innocent or guilty, here you do time. We cannot fight that. You must do time." Assurances of meetings with prosecutors and promises of everything being okay rang hollow. My lawyer claimed the prosecutor knew I was set up, that I hadn't orchestrated this, I hadn't planned to do this, yet they still aimed for a life sentence. Great. The absurdity struck me: "We know you were set up by an organisation, but you'll get twenty years in jail."

To add to the surrealism, I discovered that the entire country of Australia was now aware of my plight.

How, I couldn't fathom, but the news of my predicament had spread across borders.

Fuck.

Signs of Danger or The Right Move?
30 April 2017

We were waiting for food, something that had now become a regular routine. A stranger pushed her way into the line. She was very muscular, in fact, I would have mistaken her for a man if she hadn't been in this prison. Short, black hair and a sleeve tattoo, she smelt bad and was covered in scars. I watched not thinking anything of it, I was used to women pushing past and doing what they like, however, I didn't realise she was concealing a sharp object, and I suddenly felt her push against me and an extremely painful pinch in the back of each of my arms. A chilling sensation gripped me as I touched my skin, feeling the wetness, I looked down at my hands to see them full of my own blood. I looked around helplessly for the woman who had done this and then I saw Denise, my lifeline in this unfamiliar world, engaged in a tense conversation with the menacing girl in Spanish. The translation sent shockwaves through me – "You need to shut the fuck up about everything you bitch, you speak to no one, or we end you in here, it's easy" – a clear warning to keep silent, to avoid interaction at all costs. The woman was next to me and then I felt her hand on my hand and the force was very surprising as I felt my head moving backward and smashed into the wall, leaving my vision blurred, leaving me, teetering on the precipice of unconsciousness. I felt myself falling but I couldn't stop myself. I had been knocked out, I was trying to regain my senses, understand what had just happened, I remembered, the assailant vanished, leaving behind a scene of blood, confusion, and fear.

Was this going to be a regular thing? In the company of a guard and Denise, the urgency to report the incident clashed with the dread of potential repercussions. Fearful of the unknown I declined, emphasizing that involving the guards might only invite more trouble. I was advised that I had a concussion and to not sleep, that if I got worse as the night went on, that I would need to be taken to receive medical treatment. Great – Attack Number Two.

Denise became my constant companion, a tenuous link to the Spanish-speaking prison life. We spoke incessantly, seeking solace in the shared understanding. Yet, the attacker haunted my every step, was she talking about Chilli, or Wendy and Carlos? And who did she think I would be talking too? It's not like I can actively have a conversation with anyone in here other than Denise. I suddenly didn't feel safe anywhere. In response, Denise proposed that I move to her cell, 3A, where communication would be more effective, and she could look out for me. We drafted a letter to the Captain and Mayor, pleading for a transfer to celda 62-3A.

The weight of doom settled on my shoulders, an oppressive force that rendered each step heavier than the last.

Scared and small in the vastness of despair, I wandered through the dimly lit passages. The flickering lights casting long, foreboding shadows. I wondered when my next attack would be, it seemed it didn't matter that I had moved away from Chilli, there was always going to be a new threat and I stupidly kept walking into them.

I couldn't cry in front of anyone, I could show emotion, but it would put a bigger target on my back, I needed to be strong, even if it was for everyone else. I could swallow my emotions and deal with them later, right?

The day I moved to my new cell marked an unsettling shift in my prison experience. The unfamiliar faces scrutinizing me, great, I was the new girl again, coupled with the chatter surrounding my arrival, resurrected the initial discomfort of my incarceration.

But in the midst of adjusting to my new surroundings, the prison walls couldn't shield me from the outside world. Not anymore.

My sister had told me that she saw a Facebook post about one needing legal help overseas and it took a private matter and pushed it into the public eye.

The unwanted attention from the media descended upon me like a swarm of relentless mosquitoes, buzzing around, hungry for a taste of my story. Something that I hadn't accounted for, something that I never wanted. Something that I had said from the beginning that I didn't want.

Just two days into my new cell, a stranger called my name at our cell door. I stepped out to face a person I had never seen before. Panic gripped me as she smiled, I went to step back into my safety net, but she was seemingly harmless, conversing with Denise. The stranger's intention to offer me clothes appeared innocent, yet an uneasy feeling clung to the situation.

Denise reassured me, urging me to accept the girl's offer. "Girl, you have no clothes, you need all the help you can get." It was true, I was routinely wearing the same clothes on rotation, I did need help. A tug on my hand led me to the fourth floor, where the unease intensified, I hadn't been up this far, I didn't like going far from my passageway. In the unfamiliar cell, the girl thrust clothes into my hands, prompting me to try them on. It was quite funny watching them signalling for me to try them on. A discomfort settled in, an instinctive awareness that something was amiss in this seemingly 'charitable' act. No one was this nice to anyone here.

As I looked down, grappling with the discomfort, my name echoed in the cell. To my astonishment, a phone emerged, capturing a seemingly innocent moment. What the fuck was going on? Did they just take a photo of me? The girl who had forced her clothes on me said "Es mi birthday, ahh photo para family." I wasn't a genius, but I think she was trying to tell me she wanted a photo for her family. I sat between the two women, and I forced a smile, it masked my true feelings, and I succumbed to the peculiar request for a birthday photo. As soon as the pictures were taken, I found myself ejected from the cell, the odd encounter leaving me unsettled. Was I just used? Or was I just paid with clothes for a photo? I was so confused; these women were so weird.

Returning to my cell, I shared the bizarre incident with Denise, who, alarmed, emphasized the potential dangers. "Girl, are you stupid? Why you let them take a photo?" I was annoyed not only with myself, but also with her, did she not just give me the okay to go up there? The media's insatiable appetite for my story and the possibility of the photos reaching the person who had threatened me loomed ominously. I no longer believed that Chilli had threatened me not to talk. No, this threat had come from Wendy, she was letting me know that I wasn't safe anywhere. Torn between fear and the desire to dismiss the incident, I couldn't escape the haunting question: Why did they want a photo with me? The uncertainty gnawed at me, an unsettling reminder that even within prison walls, my vulnerability knew no bounds. Yet, I was to blame, yet again, I had stupidly believed the good in people.

The following day, my world crumbled further as I received an un-expected call from my mother. She confronted me about sending photos to the media. "Why did you do it? Why did you ask for photos to be sent out? Why would you do this? The media are going crazy over these photos, saying you look happy, that you being in danger is a joke, that you're fine."

Great, just what I fucking needed right now! Damn it, I knew something was wrong, but I hadn't expected this, how the fuck did those girls get these photos into the hands of the media?

With a heavy heart, I probed my mother for details of the photo. She described a scene where I sat beside a woman with her face blurred out. The betrayal cut deep, and frustration mingled with anger. The forced smile in the photo masked the turmoil within. I couldn't fathom why people would exploit my vulnerability for their gain. The desire for solitude, safety, and anonymity shattered in the face of ruthless opportunism.

"The media was outside the prison," my mother continued, "I'm guessing they offered money to the women to get photos of you inside prison, Cassie you need to lay low, we have a deal with a media outlet and you can't talk to anyone or have photos leaked."

I was taken aback but these girls here had tricked me and were obviously being offered money to get photos of me.

Distraught, I sought solace in Denise's presence. Struggling to convey the ordeal, I grappled with my emotions, attempting to articulate the magnitude of the situation. "Denise, they sold the photos to the media, the media has my photos, they're saying I'm fucking happy here, who the fuck would think that anyone in their right mind would be happy here?

As the minutes ticked by, in tense silence, Denise finally spoke. The gravity of the situation dawned on her, and she insisted on involving the guard,

"We must tell the guards." Her words, tinged with a hint of "I-told-you-so," stoked the embers of irritation within me. I grappled with the dilemma of reporting the incident and potentially being labelled a snitch, a pariah among the inmates. "Right now, you not worry about what people think in here, you worry about your life out there girl, you need protection, how many more attacks and photos? Huh, no more Cassie, you need help. If we don't stop these girls, others will do it too, I know they will."

Denise took me downstairs where I believe she asked to speak to the guard and from there, I presumed Denise had just told the guards what had happened with Tahlee, the girl who had 'gifted' me clothes, tricked me so she could get photos of me and sell them to the media, which was, illegal.

As minutes stretched into an eternity, watching and waiting, a different guard, distinctive in her prison police attire, approached us. She was short and stocky, but pretty, dammit. Why was that the first thing I was noticing? Denise informed me "This ah, lady she is the prison police, she is here to talk about what happened." I nodded; I still hadn't stopped looking at her. That she was a prison police officer and a more amiable presence than the regular guards. Her sympathetic gaze offered a rare contrast to the disdainful looks from others. It was, nice. While Denise conversed with the prison police officer (the 'PJ'), I remained oblivious. The inability to understand such basic things were extremely overwhelming and frustrating.

"I told her everything she needs to know to help you, Cassie. They are going to investigate what happened and how. But she say, it's no big deal and to embrace the fame, it will blow over."

Was she fucking kidding me? Did I look like I wanted attention? My thoughts were distracted when I saw the guards descending from the upstairs cells.

Fear crept in as Denise whispered to me that the phone wasn't found, that she couldn't see one, but the two women responsible would be summoned for questioning. A surge of panic overcame me, overshadowing the potential relief that the guards were taking action. The PJ, having completed her conversation with Denise, guided her towards the desk where other guards sat, and I trailed behind, adamant not to be left alone amidst the brewing storm.

In a hushed conversation, Denise disclosed the alarming truth – Tahlee, one of the women involved in the photo incident, had a sister who was a prison guard. The implication was ominous; my pursuit of justice might be hindered by the intricate web of relationships within the prison. The realization dawned on me that, in this environment, connections wielded more power than any pursuit of truth. But given everything I had gone through over the last few months, it was clear, this was the case everywhere.

Lost in my thoughts, Denise said, "You must fill in this paperwork, write down what happen to you, it doesn't need to be perfect, but make sure everything important is there." Obliged to document the incident officially, I began hastily narrating the events to the PJ, who produced a piece of paper for my account. The pen raced across the pages as I recounted the confrontation – the two women giving me the clothes, the betrayal, taking the photos, and the potential threat I faced within the prison of it happening again due to the media still waiting outside begging for more.

Completing the statement, I signed and left my fingerprint, sealing my plea for justice. Glancing up, I spotted Tahlee glaring at me from a short distance away.

Here we go.

My frustration peaked as I tried to focus on writing amidst the audible mutterings of accusations. Denise's response to Tahlee's claims hinted at a brewing storm – "Bitch! She's such a liar." The tension escalated when Tahlee was brought over for further interrogation, she was now standing no less than 2 meters in front of me, Denise translating on parts of what was being said. Tahlee was claiming that I had asked her to send the photos out to the media, that I had begged her.

How dare she? I wanted nothing to do with the media, everyone kept pushing me and my life into the media's view and it was the last thing I wanted!

Denise's silence during the chaotic exchange added to my sense of isolation, why wasn't she helping me understand everything here!

Suddenly, Denise's demeanour shifted, and without warning, I found myself being shoved against the wall. Stunned and not registering as to what was going on. I looked up to see Tahlee raising her arm, ready to strike. The intervention of guards prevented the physical assault, yet the emotional and psychological impact lingered, I was frozen, I couldn't move even if I wanted too.

What was wrong with me?

Jane, the PJ, and Denise formed a protective barrier. I was grateful for this. I wasn't sure how many more beatings I could handle. As emotions ran high, Jane exchanged words with Denise. What had she said?

Jane didn't break eye contact with me, nor did I, it was grounding me in all the trauma that was waiting to consume me. An abrupt return to the Patio brought no relief; instead, it marked the beginning of a perilous journey. Denise, resolute in her concern for my safety, urged me to contact the embassy, recognizing the heightened threat I now faced. The reality sank in – I had become an enemy within the prison walls, a target of hostility that extended beyond Tahlee to her network of associates. I didn't know whether Denise had wanted me to be labelled a snitch, but one thing was certain, *I* was now known as a snitch, and it was going to be fucking hell to move through these passageways. I walked straight back to the cell, no eye contact with anyone. Ignoring people wasn't a problem because I didn't understand them anyway.

In the privacy of the cell, Denise's anger and my own overwhelmed the room. Hours passed in stifling silence before Denise broke it with an unexpected shift in tone – a sudden, almost comical observation about a potential romantic interest from a guard. "Cassie, what did you do to the guard Jane? I sense some roooooooomance in the air ahhhh."

Laughter threatened to bubble up, a brief respite from the chaos, but the impending storm outside the cell demanded my attention.

"What did she say to you out there?" I asked.

"Never you mind Cassie, I'm sure she will tell you one day." Denise wasn't going to tell me, and I wondered why. Was she scared that I was gay?

Is This Goodbye?
23 May 2017

In the solitude of my cell, my thoughts spiralled into a relentless whirlpool, each dark eddy pulling me deeper into the abyss. In here, there was no distraction from everything that haunts you from within.

How would I deal with this? How could I? The palpable animosity from fellow inmates and the guards formed an impenetrable barrier, isolating me in a sea of hostility. The promise of decades behind bars, coupled with the stigma of my alleged crimes, cast a shadow that seemed impossible to escape. I was having a hard time confronting everything that I had gone through before being arrested, let alone everything else that was happening afterwards.

Prison would kill me.

I grappled with the concept of ending it all – contemplating the various methods as if browsing through a macabre catalogue of escape routes.

Overdosing: the promise of sweet oblivion.

Throwing myself from the fourth floor: a leap into the unknown.

Hanging myself: I did have options to do so, a swift departure from the pain.

The shame I felt wrapped around me like a suffocating shroud. I was beginning to convince myself that my very existence was a blight on my family, a stain that they would be better off without. I wasn't loveable, I mean if I were, why would someone organise for this to happen to me, right?

As I walked to the edge of the Patio, intending to steal one last look at the world beyond, I felt Denise's concerned gaze following my every step. Why wouldn't she just let me be? I hadn't understood more of a desire to leave this world then I had in these moments. I didn't want to confront the pain I kept burying. I didn't want to face more trauma and fear. I didn't want to be here anymore.

As I peered out at the street …

How cruel was this? To have a direct view to people out walking their dogs, playing with their kids. It was a sick and twisted punishment; I wasn't sure how this made people feel better.

Denise, sensing my internal struggle, remained silent, watching as I grappled with the weight of my emotions. I took a deep breath, preparing to take my last look at the world. Turning to Denise, I declared, "I'm done. Let's go." A serene smile masked the tumult within me. She had no idea what was going on with me, bless her. Being on the fourth floor, there was a huge gap where the stairs didn't finish, the gap went right down to the bottom floor. With each step towards the railing, I could feel a sense of relief washing over me. The pain, the shame, the scrutiny — all would be gone with one small step into the abyss.

I positioned myself to easily walk into the gap, where I planned to fall and not survive. I didn't want to survive over the rail, Denise was distracted by another inmate. I didn't want anyone getting in my way, it wasn't unusual for inmates to stand where I was, so I didn't draw attention until I took that step off the ledge staircase. A subtle force yanked me back. Confused, I scanned the faces of the three individuals holding onto me, strangers with no connection to my plight. Then, I saw Denise, her face drained of colour. "What the fuck is wrong with you, girl?"

"Why?" I was asking as if I hadn't heard the people yelling or felt their desperate attempts to intervene. I had been utterly zoned out, oblivious to the chaos around me.

Frustration simmered within me as I wondered why these strangers had interfered. They didn't know me, and at that moment, it felt like everyone hated me.

Denise took me to our cell, insisting that we needed to talk. Conflicted, I followed her, wondering why these people cared when everyone else seemed to revel in my possible demise. In the cell, Denise closed the door.

I felt like a little child again, when you get caught stealing from the cookie jar. When Denise finally spoke, tears streamed down her face, and her voice quivered with anguish. Her questions echoed the sentiments that ricocheted within me. "What's wrong with you? How could you do that to me?" In her eyes, I saw a mixture of pain, confusion, and genuine concern.

I remained silent. What was I supposed to say? Denise's emotional turmoil intensified. "You are a fighter and a survivor. Why, how can you not see this? I know I don't know you long time, but I can see it, you are so strong, this place isn't your end, don't let it be. Cassie, right now I know this is hard, but you need not give up, not now, not ever, you can do good here, you can find yourself here. There are people who care for you."

I still sat there, with nothing to say, I didn't know what to say, because right now, I didn't want to make someone else feel better about my situation. She didn't know me. She didn't know all the years of pain and suffering that was coming undone. Of course, I rarely showed emotion for anyone to actually realise *I was dead inside*. But, seated beside her, guilt washed over me as she spoke of the impact I had on others. Her words had cut through the numbness, forcing me to confront the consequences of my actions.

Yet again.

After hours of introspection, I ventured outside for fresh air, Denise at my side. Her concern was palpable as she questioned whether I would succumb to another impulsive decision. Determined to be strong, I nodded, resolved to believe that life could improve, even in the suffocating confines of prison. This wasn't the end of me, this wasn't where, after everything – I cave. The judgmental stares around me became irrelevant.

Life, for better or worse, would go on.

What Else Could Go Wrong?
28 May 2017

The aftermath of the leaked photos had unleashed a storm of unwanted attention. Guards attempted awkward interactions of women yelling at me in the passageways, pushing me around, inmates aimed smartphones my way in the corridors trying to take photos, and journalists besieged me with persistent calls, leaving their numbers and notes with guards. Even Denise became a person for their inquiries.

Frustrated, I made it clear that I had no interest in engaging with the media. The last thing I needed was for this debacle to haunt me indefinitely. The situation, far from calming down, escalated.

Scott was coming with a media outlet while my mother was coming with another, amplifying the chaos.

Caught in the crossfire, I navigated conflicting agendas. It seemed like my loved ones couldn't even agree on a lawyer. It felt like a circus was forming while I was torn in the middle with no clarity on my case or who was properly representing me. All the while my "partner" and my mother were at logger heads.

The core question haunted me.

What were they even *doing* in Colombia? I mean, if they had just travelled to the other side of the world to bicker like children, they could have just done it over the phone.

I could comprehend Scott's reluctance to involve her to some extent. Yet, in the midst of all the chaos, I questioned why they couldn't set aside their differences *for my sake.*

It appeared that those close to me had signed deals with different media outlets and not really understanding my hell.

The director of the prison had reached her limits, fed up with the escalating chaos that seemed to orbit me like a dark cloud. She used her phone to translate to me. Personally, addressing me, she pleaded for my cooperation, begging me to avoid interactions with the media as it only exacerbated her struggles. "You mustn't talk about what happens behind that door Cassandra, we need no more trouble."

Respecting her plea was easy – dealing with the fallout was not.

An interview, apparently by me, had aired on the radio, triggering a frantic search for a contraband phone. It was chaos. Alarms rung everywhere. Guards were everywhere as the search went on. One guard ended up with a gun held to my face. Panic welled within me. I hadn't spoken to anyone, I didn't do this and now I was at the centre of another storm, yet again and blamed for a situation I didn't create.

The guard's expression dripped with disdain. Denise whispered, "That guard doesn't believe you don't speak Spanish." I was surprised at this comment, did people really believe this? Did they think I was *enjoying* not understanding anything? "Until the elusive phone surfaces Cassandra, your life will be a living hell", Denise translated for the guard.

Stunned, I protested, "I didn't do this! I haven't spoken to anyone. I don't even know what interview you're talking about or what phone." To my surprise, Denise remained silent, leaving my pleas unheard. Why wasn't she helping me? She always helped.

We walked back to our cell; she was oddly quiet. Then Denise confessed to initiating contact with a man who wanted to reach me. "I'm sorry Cassie but I did this, I spoke to someone and said you had asked me to speak on your behalf. I wanted to make people understand what is really going on behind that blue door, and you are the only one the media wants to hear."

I was seeing red, she *used* me, she was no better than anyone else abusing my situation. "Why would you do this? How many times have I said I don't want to be in the media, and you go and do this?" I had no more words, just anger. She had used my name in an interview, intending to shed light on the reality behind prison walls. The collateral damage became clear: I was blamed for a search I had no part in, an interview given on my behalf and my credibility tarnished, well, not that I really had much but now I had none left at all.

The aftermath was a nightmare. Guards ransacked our cell twice a day, uncovering nothing. They were on a hunt for the phone that I had supposedly used to give the interview. Denise, infuriated, fought to reclaim order amid the wreckage yet, I had no interest. As I stepped out of my cell, deliberate bumps and spiteful cries of 'sapa' followed. A once-friendly woman screamed accusations, followed by a sharp slap across my face. The spectacle drew an audience, eagerly awaiting my response, but I refused to give them the satisfaction. I wasn't a fighter, and I definitely wasn't violent, and this place wasn't going to turn me. Denise, however, confronted the accuser, escalating the conflict. Unable to understand, I interposed myself, only to receive another blow, this time it wasn't a slap, I was punched in the face. I felt blood dripping, and I dragged Denise away, I wondered why she sought confrontation.

"Why not? Did you have a guilty conscience?" she asked. The chaos deepened, and tensions simmered.

Later, Denise proposed involving our embassies to combat perceived discrimination. Despite my internal resistance, I agreed; perhaps official intervention could provide some semblance of order. As I reached out to the Australian Embassy, closed for the day, tensions flared again. Denise, called in her embassy, it seemed her solution for everything was to hide behind her embassy, something that I wasn't really sure was worth involving at all, I mean what could they do? I watched her when the lady who had hit me was back, yet this time she wasn't looking at me, but at Denise. She shoved Denise, who hung up the phone call.

The guards began yelling at the women, I could only imagine what the woman was saying but her enraged tirade left everyone silent. Denise and her adversary exchanged glares, resuming their tasks as the guards withdrew. Denise, seemingly oblivious to the chaos she had unleashed, led me back to the trashed cell. My annoyance grew. I was taking the blame for a mess I didn't create. Yet, I couldn't sustain my anger toward

Denise for long. Amidst the chaos, she explained the guard's frustration, emphasizing the inevitability of searches.

All of this could have been avoided.

The next day arrived with a lingering tension. It was exhausting to try and be accepted or at least not bullied. Unexpectedly, a call echoed through the prison corridors, "Cassandra Sains ...... Cassandra Australia," beckoning my attention. No one could pronounce my last name and although my situation was hard and painful, hearing people try to pronounce my name always made me laugh. Descending to investigate, I discovered a guard awaiting my presence. She merely nodded at me, an unspoken knowledge of 'no English'. Perplexed, I followed the guard to the front, where a surreal assembly awaited. My lawyer stood there, flanked by Hana, whom I hadn't met. Apparently, she was now my translator, and behind my lawyer, unfamiliar faces whose purpose remained a mystery. What was going on and why were they here? Surely not, am I really getting out? I wasn't quite sure why it was the first thought that came to me but naturally, there was always going to be some sort of hope lingering in the background until being sentenced.

"Cassandra, these are the investigators who work for your prosecutor, they have come to take an official statement from you and ask questions." It became apparent that the prosecutor's investigators were present, and the time had come to strike a deal.

"Cassandra this is important. You tell them everything that happened to you, they can help you and this will help you with whatever sentencing you're going to receive." I nodded, not yet comfortable around this person who I had only just met.

The atmosphere around me seemed charged with anticipation. Being out the front of the prison and in the offices didn't mean that I was hidden from the other inmates, it seems that they too were allowed out the front to help with cleaning and maintenance type jobs. Guarded gazes from fellow inmates hinted at an unspoken curiosity. I wondered if I was being watched or if they were just curious. The enigmatic figures on the other side of the table introduced themselves courteously, their intentions veiled beneath the surface.

"Who are you, and why you?"

"What happened to you when you arrived in Colombia?"

"Who else is involved?"

"Where did you meet Wendy?"

The gravity of the situation was palpable; deals were in the making, alliances shifting like sand beneath my feet. A lunchtime interruption offered a brief respite.

As I returned to the Patio, eyes followed me with heightened interest, and whispers trailed in my wake. I felt like everyone knew what I was doing and who I was speaking with.

I sought solace in the confines of my cell, possibly the only place where I now felt safe. Denise, ever inquisitive, probed for details.

"Where have you been? I looked for you everywhere and no one know where you were, where did you go?"

I withheld the entire truth, revealing only that my lawyer had visited. The flicker of doubt in her eyes intensified my growing distrust.

As the clock ticked towards 2:00 pm, the call beckoning me downstairs jolted me from my silent contemplation of what was going on, although I still hadn't managed to shake that question.

The mysterious negotiation resumed, delving into potential outcomes. The investigators advised caution:

"You must not trust anyone in there, you are not safe Cassandra from what we understand, you are surrounded by people who wish to cause you pain and suffering. You must maintain allegiance with your current legal counsel, trust no other." The meeting concluded abruptly, leaving me bewildered.

As the guard announced dinner, a frosty stare accompanied her words. Had I transgressed some unspoken rule? There was nothing left to say, I was a prisoner, and the truth was, I wasn't safe anywhere.

Descending into the prison's heart, I sensed an unusual chill in the air. The guard's dismissive demeanour struck me as peculiar. Alone,

I ventured into the familiar territory of the Patio, seeking refuge. A guard, stationed at the desk, eyed me with curiosity.

Suddenly, the Patio door swung open, and the guard ushered me back inside, a silent escort back to the cell. The door closed, but not locked – an unsettling deviation from the routine. The prison walls, silent witnesses to my every move, harboured secrets and uncertainties that lingered in the air. The air in the cramped cell hung heavy with tension as I stealthily entered, hoping to avoid unwanted attention. Denise, engrossed in conversation with two unfamiliar faces, initially failed to notice my return. However, when her eyes finally fell upon me, a dramatic gasp escaped her lips, drawing the focus of everyone in the room.

"Oh, Cassie! Where have you been?" Denise exclaimed, her voice a crescendo of false concern. "I've been looking for you everywhere yet again." The room seemed to pulse with anticipation as if the mere mention of my absence had set off an invisible alarm.

Frustration bubbled within me as I concocted a fabricated narrative about a clandestine meeting with my lawyer, emphasizing the secrecy of our discussions. "So are you getting out? Are you getting a deal? What did you talk about? You shouldn't get a huge sentence. I mean, I got caught with more than you and I got less than six years."

With practiced nonchalance, I retreated to my bunk, feigning sleep by pressing my face against the cold, unforgiving wall. My heart raced, a rhythmic drumbeat accompanying the chaotic thoughts swirling in my mind. When would the prosecutor's investigation unfold? Would the truth, like a phoenix, rise from the ashes of deceit? Would everyone finally fall from their high horses and pay the ultimate price for what they had done to me? I sure hoped so. Maybe they could taste just a spoonful of the pain and the suffering that I had so far endured.

As I navigated the crowded passageway, on my way to dinner, I turned to close the door and tie it shut when a sudden, vice-like grip seized the collar of my shirt. I was violently yanked backward into the metal bars. I wasn't sure what had hurt more, the sudden clothes lining with my jumper or the metal bars that had been slammed into my head, as if caught in the merciless jaws of some unseen beast. Panic surged as I struggled for breath, the woman was onto me, one hand around my throat.

Gasping for air, I dared to turn and confront my assailant, my eyes widening in shock. I tried to push her off, she was too strong. The woman, I had seen her before, in the food run, morphed into a malevolent force. Her fingers clamped my throat tighter. She pulled me up ever so slightly just enough to slam my head back into the floor. A sinister whisper, laden with menace, echoed in my ears as she admonished me for not heeding prior warnings. The eyes that met mine burned with an intensity that sent shivers down my spine. The woman, releasing her grip, issued a final warning – words dripping with malice – before delivering a swift, calculated kick to my stomach. The force of the impact resonated through my body, each throb a reminder of the brutality inflicted upon me. Wincing in pain and gasping for breath, I retreated to the relative safety of the cell, each step an agonizing journey. Climbing to my bunk, I cradled my aching stomach. The charade continued as Denise re-entered the cell, her obliviousness to the ordeal I had just experienced adding another layer of surrealism to the nightmarish tableau.

The next day Denise, vigilant as ever, relayed a cryptic message – "Cassandra, you're leaving Patio Five."

The guards awaited me at the gate.

Denise, a whirlwind of efficiency, directed me to pack my belongings hastily, affirming that time was of the essence. My possessions were unceremoniously crammed into clear plastic bags, not that I had much as it was. Denise orchestrating the chaos with a sense of urgency. In the midst of this whirlwind, she fixed me with a gaze that harboured genuine concern. "Call me," she urged, an unspoken plea for reassurance. I was terrified, I hated the idea of continuously having to fit in, everywhere I go I was the new woman. It was horrible.

Denise carried the bag laden with my meagre belongings. The curious glances of my fellow inmates trailed us. The guard, silent and enigmatic, unlocked the gate. Denise, a reassuring presence, handed me the bag.

The guard led me, bag in tow, along an unfamiliar path, each step amplifying the drumbeat of anxiety in my chest. Hope flickered briefly when the prison exit loomed, only to be extinguished as the guard veered toward an overlooked corner of the compound. Panic surged. A clandestine exchange ensued, culminating in the revelation of an obscured area with locked gates and dimly lit cells.

Cell door number twelve beckoned, and as it swung open, curious faces peeked from adjacent cells. Confusion and fear mingled as the guard ushered me into the concrete confines. There was nothing in here, no light, no mattress, no blanket, no nothing. The unfamiliar voices mentioned a name – 'Lina'. The cell, stark and devoid of comfort, echoed with the metallic clang of a slammed door. I was alone, I was actually alone for the first time since being arrested and I wasn't sure how this made me feel. Darkness enveloped me, and the realization set in – I was imprisoned in a lightless cell with no mattress, alone with my thoughts – isolation. The cold concrete embraced me, tears flowing freely as I grappled with the desolation that this ominous cell promised. Weeks of suppressed emotion, easy to burst. In the suffocating silence, the weight of solitude pressed heavily upon my shoulders, and I wept for what felt like an eternity, trapped within the chilling grasp of my own despair. I was allowing myself to feel and it wasn't a nice feeling.

Patio Seven
10 June 2017

Sleep, though fitful, eventually claimed me, but nightmares stirred me repeatedly, drenching me in sweat and trembling fear. I wasn't sure how many more nights I would be able to handle like this one.

Morning brought with it the hum of conversation, and I realized my cell door was ajar. I thought I was in isolation. Uncertain if this was a temporary liberty for the contada, I hesitated. A pang of discomfort radiated through my body as I rose; the unyielding bed had taken its toll. Questions lingered – why this separate Patio, and what made it distinct from the others? Standing amidst unfamiliar faces, suspicion etched on their expressions, no-one looked happy to see me there whilst I scanned the petite, living room-sized space. A robust woman with short hair caught my attention; an unspoken authority emanated from her. Her disdainful gaze unsettled me, triggering my over-thinking tendencies. Sensitivity was my Achilles' heel.

The guard from the previous night accompanied by two other guards, conducted the headcount. Lines dissolved, and the woman with the short hair engaged in conversation with a select group. Their collective stare turned toward me, an unspoken verdict rendered, intensifying my isolation. "Don't worry about me, ladies," something I wish I could have voiced but couldn't.

As the word 'contada' echoed, I emerged from the shadows, reluctantly joining the communal assembly. The confined space fostered an air of tension; unfriendly glances followed me. The rotund woman's eyes, brimming with disdain, dissected me. Overwhelmed, I sought solace in the anonymity of the back of the line. The cell door beckoned, and

I retreated, attempting to escape the scrutiny that clung to me like a persistent shadow. Behind closed doors, their words reached me – 'sapa' a term familiar from my turbulent past seemed to keep following me, 'Sapa' meant snitch. The knot in my throat tightened, threatening tears, but pride restrained the vulnerability. I sought refuge in the solitude of my cell, closing the door to shield myself from their judgment. They didn't even know what had happened and yet, I was in the wrong already. Prison codes – you don't break them.

Hours blurred into a surreal passage of time as I stewed in my isolation. A knock disrupted the desolation; I initially dismissed it as an error, I doubted a guard would knock to come in and well, I didn't know. Persistence compelled me to answer, revealing a lady whose smile contrasted the ominous atmosphere. Lina, was a tall curvy lady who was fluent in English, introduced herself, triggering a realisation – was she the woman referenced the day before? Wariness lingered as Lina inquired about my well-being and offered helped. Wrestling with trust issues, I hesitated but acknowledged her presence. Inquiries poured forth – the nature of my relocation, the animosity directed my way. Overwhelmed, I questioned my own resilience, doubting my ability to withstand this. I don't know why, something told me I couldn't trust her, but I was certain that I was just imagining things.

Amidst my internal tumult, the door knocked again. Opening it, I encountered the woman with short hair who had looked at me nastily this morning.

Lina spoke: "Cassandra, this is Alejo. She kind of runs the Patio, I guess you could say." Great, I had *already* made an enemy with the person who ran the Patio.

Disgust marred her expression, intensifying my confusion and resentment. Lina mediated a conversation, translating my concerns and Alejo's cryptic responses.

"We don't like snitches in this patio, we don't want you here and we will make sure you don't stay." Alejo's words sunk in. She was friends with Tahlee. "You need to watch your back, here no one will protect you, as you can see, guards don't hang around much." Something could happen to me, and no one would know for hours.

As days unfurled within the confines of Patio Seven, a tentative routine emerged, shrouded in the dim light of a solitary bulb. Lina, a fleeting beacon of assistance, appeared one day bearing a light globe, a token of illumination (literally) in the otherwise shadowy realm. "You need light in here. It's very depressing." She said. The catch of the light was a debt owed in phone cards, a currency of communication within the prison walls – something that I lacked. So, I was left owing Lina, 'money'.

Thoughts of my father, a looming presence in the recesses of my mind, gnawed at me. The anticipated disappointment, the fear of his disapproval, added a layer of torment to my already fragile mental state. I wondered what he was thinking, what he would say to me. Loneliness festered in the absence of human connection. I longed to have a friend. I even thought about Wendy and that for months I thought I had found myself a true friend and possibly girlfriend. Trust, a currency devalued by betrayal, left me ensnared in my thoughts.

The suffocating silence of the cell was shattered by the sound of my name, uttered with concern. Lina called out to me. A heavy sigh escaped me as I acknowledged her call. Lina entered, her eyes reflecting genuine worry, a stark contrast to the indifferent walls that enclosed me. Her words unfurled like a lifeline, a lifeline I wasn't sure I deserved. The guard, a distant observer in this bleak theatre, had shared a disquieting revelation – a nocturnal symphony of my screams and anguished repetitions of "no, no, no." A chorus of my own torment that I was oblivious to, or perhaps, desperate to ignore.

I met Lina's gaze, my eyes mirroring the confusion that brewed within me. Why had Denise never mentioned this? Did she choose silence as a form of self-preservation or ignorance? My mind swirled with questions, but Lina's presence demanded a response. I explained it away as mere nightmares, a triviality I assumed would dissipate with time. But Lina, once a healer in another life, saw through the facade. Her words, "You're fighting a losing battle on your own here, if you don't face what's eating you from the inside out, you won't last, you are in so much pain, I can see it in your eyes, in your body language the way you don't make eye contact, the way you flinch at everything. You find a way to make peace with yourself because in here, you are all you have, if you don't like yourself, you may as well just give up now." Now, when you are ready, we are waiting here in the Patio, because you may feel alone but we all do, so we make do."

She took a seat on my mattress, the worn fabric sagging under the weight of unspoken truths. Lina, the compassionate doctor relegated to the stark reality of prison life, urged me to confront the spectre of trauma that haunted my restless nights.

"I have ... um ... nightmares about some things that happened to me before ending up here. I haven't dealt with what happened and maybe this is why I keep dreaming about it, reliving it."

"Oh, I think something very bad happened to you and you need to speak Cassandra, otherwise, it will end with you here and this place takes enough lives without adding yours to it. I'm sure what happened was horrible, but you need to get past it, you are not alone here."

I couldn't bear to meet Lina's eyes, for within them, I feared the reflection of my own brokenness.

"Thanks, but it's something I have to get over on my own. I will be okay. I can do this," I said, something I was yet to actually believe.

My lawyer, a consistent beacon in this desolation, brought morsels of hope with each visit. "We must accept a deal, I'm sorry but here no ah, important if you are innocent, the ah, drug was in your bag, so you pay the price." I was so sick and tired of hearing the same thing, I realised this, I needed to pay time for having a part in this, YES I get it, but what about *everyone else*? What about what *they* did to *me*? They destroyed my fucking *life*, and they get ... *what*?

Repetition became the anthem of Patio Seven – a cycle of monotonous routines and uncertain tomorrows. Phone calls from Mum and Scott that were supposed to serve as tenuous lifelines to the world beyond my cell were conversations that I could have gone without, constant comments about how hard *his* life was and how *he* couldn't handle it, that *he* wasn't ok.

Scott's complaints about Mum faded into background noise, but the calls at least offered a semblance of connection. Each ring signalled progress – brought me a day closer to freedom. Yet, a fateful call shattered the fragile equilibrium.

Then came the sensationalist news.

"You're a prostitute?" The words, confronting yet questioning.

"Is that you in the photos?" Another question was thrown at me when I didn't answer.

"What is all of this? This will destroy any deal you're after. You do know this don't you?"

"I'm not a prostitute." The truth was, I knew this day was coming, this was maybe Wendy's doing – I was sure of it. She was trying to destroy any chance of me getting a lesser sentence.

The headlines branded me a prostitute, a label that fuelled the dormant flames of anger within me. Why did they persist in tormenting me? The cruelty seemed boundless, a relentless assault on my already fractured identity. Having stepped into Club 220 had been my only secret and it was out. I lingered by the phone, emotions swirling within. Scott's call, once anticipated for reassurance, failed to materialise. The isolation of the cell comforted me, and a sense of powerlessness settled in. The distorted truth peddled by the news eroded any semblance of control, leaving me stranded in a narrative not of my own making.

Days slipped by – a blur of confusion and resentment. Mum's updates, a bitter reminder of the world's perception, stoked the embers of self-hatred.

"Everyone is against you now. Everyone is judging you – social media is being cruel and its everywhere. Some 'Pamela' has come out talking about you and it's not great. Your lawyer said it's not good – this is very damaging. Everyone has said you deserved what's happening."

I had nothing to say, I would just sit back and listen to what was being said, I had time to vent and be angry, I had time to deal with this – I had so much time. It was ironic that I was now so calm, but I think it was because I knew one day, Wendy and all those behind this, would get there's. Karma is such a bitch, and she would take care of this.

Seeking distraction, I diverted my energy towards learning Spanish. Lina's cautionary tales of legal pitfalls for non-Spanish speakers echoed in my ears. Determined to navigate the legal labyrinth, I enlisted Lina's help to scour the library for Spanish learning materials. Learning a new language in the stark confines of prison proved to be a formidable challenge. Nevertheless, armed with determination, an updated dictionary, and a stack of Spanish learning books, I embarked on this arduous journey. If I couldn't control the narrative woven by others, I could, at least, strive to comprehend the language that held the key to my legal fate.

The prospect of owning a phone in prison presented itself as both a necessity and a potential source of risk. The allure of consistent communication with my family outweighed the reservations about the potential consequences. Judy, one of the other inmates in Patio, seemed to be the one with access to contraband items.

She offered me a deal, was willing to sell me a small touch phone at a 'favourable' price of 700,000 pesos, approximately $300.

Cautiously considering the offer, I sought counsel from my mum.

"I need a phone, I need to have contact with you guys about my case and I don't have access to phone cards here, not only that – it costs, like, 30,000 pesos for a 5-minute phone call, it would work out cheaper." Although she didn't say no, the loud sigh announced the annoyance of the expense.

After securing Mum's 'approval', I found myself oscillating between the practicality of the phone and the apprehension of potential repercussions. A few hours of contemplation later, Judy approached me for a decision. Accepting the offer, I committed to obtaining the phone, albeit with lingering doubts about its long-term implications, but that wasn't important in that moment. Concerns about payment logistics surfaced, prompting Judy to direct me to Lina, who, with her seemingly altruistic nature, agreed to assist. This collaboration raised suspicions, hinting at hidden motives within the intricate dynamics of prison life. Nevertheless, fuelled by the desperate need for connection, I embarked on the journey to acquire both the phone and a SIM card.

Days passed; negotiations unfolded. I finally got the phone. However, as I clutched the device in my hands, a disconcerting revelation emerged. Lina, the supposed ally, began asserting possession over the phone, using it freely during both day and night. My attempts to reclaim what was rightfully mine were met with a demand for repayment, an unexpected twist in an already complex saga. Frustrations boiled over, and I confronted Lina, expressing the injustice of paying for a phone I scarcely used. In response, she conceded to return the phone but insisted on a fabricated debt owed to her. The revelation of Lina's duplicity shattered the trust I had placed in her. As the truth unravelled, it became apparent that Lina had orchestrated a scheme, not only appropriating the money meant for my TV, but also pilfering additional funds for personal use. The realization left me incensed, and I sought solace in revealing her deceit to another inmate who I had become quite close with, Elsy in the Patio.

"Yo, ah money to Lina para television and ah, phone." I tried to brokenly explain what had happened. "Como así Cassandra – you ah, dar money a Lina? No, no, no. She ah, ladron. Mmm, she robber." Realising what she was saying sunk in, shit. Lina stole from people, and I walked right into the trap.

Elsy, a trusted companion, joined me in exposing Lina's betrayal, and Judy corroborated the theft by revealing she had only received 300,000 pesos for the phone. The magnitude of Lina's deception, totalling 700,000 pesos, was laid bare for all to see. Although justice within the confines of prison proved elusive, the collective awareness of Lina's actions served as a small consolation. Judy, recognizing my innocence in the matter, assured me that I wouldn't be held accountable for the stolen money. The aftermath of the revelation left me wiser but scarred, a testament to the harsh lessons learned within the unforgiving walls of Patio Seven. The fleeting trust I had in others crumbled, replaced by a sobering awareness of the cutthroat dynamics of prison life. Not only that, I also still hadn't learnt not to trust everyone.

The pivotal moment arrived when my lawyer, presented the plea deal for my consideration. 72 months in prison – no chance of parole or benefits. To my bewilderment, the existence of this deal had caught me off guard. The lack of communication and transparency in the process added to my frustration, and the fact that my lawyer arrived without a translator heightened my suspicion. When was this all agreed too? Why hadn't anyone spoken to me lately about this? Refusing to sign anything without a clear understanding, I sought assistance within the prison to unravel the complexities of the presented deal. Elsy – she tried to convince me that it was a good deal, "Tomar el acuerdo and you go, bye bye." Yet, it wasn't that simple. I didn't care about doing the time, well that's not true, I did but I wanted these other people to get their fair share too. Despite reservations about divulging personal matters, I couldn't afford to be ignorant of the terms. Lina, stepping forward to translate, became my reluctant ally in deciphering the legal jargon.

As the details unfolded, my outrage intensified. The proposed deal outlined a six-year prison term with a fine, devoid of any mention of the circumstances leading to my incarceration. No investigation, no information, and the assertion that I had provided no assistance. The glaring lack of clarity fuelled my frustration, and I directed my incredulity towards my lawyer. The lawyer, entrusted with safeguarding my interests, failed to provide a satisfactory explanation. "What the hell is this?" "You said I was most likely looking at four years. What happened? Why is there no investigation, what is this? I'm not signing this. I won't. I cant."

"Cassandra, this is what they give, you must accept, or you get 30 years, what you want? 30? Don't risk it, forget about the others."

How *dare* he tell me to forget about the others! I wasn't tormented, manipulated, tricked and raped for nothing, I would make them pay, even if it was the last thing I would do. I would risk the 30 years for it. Instead, he touted the deal as the best I could hope for, claiming that my mother herself had pleaded for this arrangement with the prosecutor. His insistence, coupled with the suggestion that refusing the deal would disappoint many, reeked of manipulation. The final blow came with the ominous assertion that not signing would likely lead to 'regret'.

Overwhelmed by conflicting emotions, anger, and a sense of helplessness, I succumbed to the pressure. The pen met the paper, and I begrudgingly signed the deal. The act symbolized a reluctant acceptance, a compromise with a system I deemed corrupt. In that moment, the weight of acquiescence settled on my shoulders, and I couldn't shake the feeling that, by signing, I had somehow validated the injustices I had endured. The internal struggle persisted as I grappled with the aftermath of my decision. Questions lingered: Could I challenge my own lawyer? Was there a way to navigate this labyrinth of legal complexities? The frustration and resentment simmered beneath the surface, fuelling a determination to one day have the opportunity to tell my truth, to speak up for myself against a system that seemed determined to stifle my voice.

Unsolicited Interview
10 July 2017

As part of a media deal which had been arranged as an exclusive interview. Something that I hadn't really agreed to do was the prospect of a *60 Minutes* interview.

Despite the reluctance, I found myself thrust into the spotlight, a place I never desired nor welcomed.

Nervousness consumed me on the day of the interview, what could I say? What was I allowed to talk about? I was about to have my first hearing in days, and I knew that I wasn't allowed to speak about my case – with anyone.

The uninvited intrusion of the media into my life, coupled with the scrutiny of strangers, fuelled my frustration. I resented the attention; this wasn't the kind of fame I sought. I despised the idea of being in front of a camera, facing an interrogation about events I couldn't fully discuss due to the ongoing legal proceedings and a warning from my prosecutor.

As the minutes crawled by, I received assurances that everything would be okay. However, the reassurance did little to quell the knots in my stomach. I couldn't stomach food that day; my nerves wouldn't allow it. When the guard came for me at 2:00 pm, she made light of my new-found 'fame,' a jest that only heightened my discomfort.

Led to a room reminiscent of earlier interrogations, I felt the weight of unpleasant memories. To be honest, I didn't know much about the deal to do this interview.

As the camera crew prepared, the host from *60 Minutes* greeted me amicably, a stark contrast to the looming dread I had anticipated. The facade of friendliness, however, soon shattered as the interview began. The promised laid-back atmosphere vanished, replaced by an interrogation that left me feeling more like a spectacle than a person. The heat of the lights intensified the discomfort, both physically and emotionally. I felt like the host refused to let me speak, his insistence on a narrative that suited an agenda really fuelled my anger. I felt cornered, my attempts to explain drowned out by a predetermined script aimed at making me appear unhinged. Which, well, I probably was – who wouldn't have been! Nearly three months in prison and not one day went by when it was any easier.

The questions about my mobile phone became a focal point, and my genuine confusion and frustration were overshadowed. The fact that I couldn't recall the passcode, combined with the unexplained failure of the police to unlock it, painted me as careless and evasive. The interviewers seemed determined to depict me in the worst light possible. Upon the interview's conclusion, the host reverted to the friendly demeanour I had encountered initially, leaving me emotionally bruised. Walking back with the guard, she noticed my anger and offered solidarity.

"Mmmm, I no speak, much English ah but he is very mean he not know what this place is like, we have very very bad people here."

Alone in my cell, the interview took its emotional toll. How dare I be set up for something like that! Why would anyone allow this to happen? I refuse to take part in anything else.

My desire to scream, yell, and cry simmered beneath a veneer of composure. Watching the aired interview later only deepened my despair. I saw a version of myself that, divorced from context, invited harsh judgment. The comments from supposed friends and family on social media further wounded me. People thought I didn't see what was said, but I did. I must admit, it did hurt more than I expected it too, but I also knew that I would never forget those who turned their backs on me.

The aftermath saw professionals analysing my every gesture:

"She is moving her arms too much. It's a sign of lying."

"Those red rashes on her chest, those are due to lying."

Everything about me, branding me a liar based on nuances that had innocent explanations. The pervasive judgments and insults from those who claimed support tore at my already fragile emotional state. The inability to correct the narrative, to defend myself against the onslaught of negativity, became an enduring struggle. I would have loved to say "Yes I move my hands a lot when I talk, why? I don't fucking know! I just do it." Red rash? Yes, I suffer from anxiety and when I get hot flushes, nervousness, anxiety – that's what happens! The wounds inflicted during that interview echoed long after the cameras stopped rolling. I knew that no one was ever going to believe me.

I should have given up.

I should have just accepted it then.

Raqueta
9 September 2017

It was Saturday, Saturdays marked the days that men could visit, often my inmates would have others look out for them while they would have quickies, but this wasn't a conjugal visit, just an ordinary day behind prison walls, marked by the routine of inmate visits and the clandestine indulgence of alcohol within the confines of the Patio. The secret of smuggling in contraband became apparent to me when a bag fell from the roof, a mysterious delivery that hinted at the covert operations within our prison community. Chaos unfolded three days earlier, with a bag landing near the prison phones, and the voice calling out for Sandra or Sof, revealing yet another player in this underground trade.

As the day unfolded, the atmosphere in the Patio became increasingly charged. The first signs of trouble emerged when the guards, seemingly oblivious until then, decided to conduct a search. Panic rippled through the Patio; the call of "They're coming" echoed, triggering a frantic rush to hide, dispose, and erase any evidence of the forbidden revelry. Elsy, perceptive to my innocence, pulled me aside, forewarning of the impending storm.

The guard's entry into my cell was unexpected, catching me off guard. The realization that the women were unaware of the impending search left me powerless to warn them. The guard grabbed a fist full of hair and dragged me out into the Patio, I stood witnessing the chaos unfold, the very fabric of our daily existence unravelling.

The directive to evacuate the Patio during the search resonated with a sense of violation. Guns pointed in our direction, we stood with our hands on our heads. The guards' actions, invasive and ruthless, painted a grim picture of the power dynamics within the prison walls. The Capitan's authoritarian presence intensified the atmosphere, exacerbating tensions that would reverberate for days.

The human rights representative's futile plea for involvement during the search highlighted the skewed balance of power. The Capitan's arrival further tainted the already compromised situation, setting the stage for a sequence of events that would leave an indelible mark on the inmates' psyche. The search, exhaustive and ruthless, spared nothing. Phones were ripped from walls, personal spaces violated, and the aftermath resembled a war zone. The arbitrary nature of the intrusion was evident in the desecration of personal belongings, an assault on the little semblance of normality we clung to.

Amidst the wreckage, the directive to undergo blood tests, a crude attempt at determining alcohol consumption, added a surreal layer to the unfolding drama. I wasn't worried at all, yet Jan – one of the twin sisters who was also in Patio Seven had consumed a ridiculous amount of alcohol and was withheld for further testing. The Capitan's callous response to the plea for a restroom underscored the dehumanizing aspects of the prison system. The night descended, shrouding the Patio in darkness as the guards extended their search to the roof. The ominous sight of a ladder raised unsettling questions. Jan's return, now handcuffed and defiant, hinted at the chaos beyond my immediate sight. Shit was about to go down between the inmates.

Then there was the Capitan's unusual summoning of Emily. Emily was the patio's known snitch, inside and outside prison she was very powerful and respected, she was a mafioso's daughter. Locked up for life, she had been in prison since her 18th birthday and would probably never get out. The crimes she committed – kidnapping, extortion, torture, murder. His family was and is the first original mafia family in Colombia. However, along the way, she began snitching to get guards to act in her favour, she had outside food, art supplies, clothes, technology all entered in by the guards and she would snitch other inmates too. She loved the drama, loved getting into fights then playing the victim, to sit back and see what would happen to the rest of us. It added a layer of intrigue, leaving us in suspense. The guards' departure, laughing and conversing, left us to grapple with the aftermath, our cells in disarray, and the unspoken threat of further repercussions.

Contada marked a moment of reckoning, a sobering realization of the toll exacted by the search. The guards' callous treatment, the trampling of personal effects, and the lingering fear of retribution set the stage for the inmates' collective response. The clean-up, an act of resilience, sought to restore a semblance of order amid the chaos.

The aftermath of the search laid bare a web of tangled emotions and simmering tensions within Patio Seven. As the inmates grappled with the intrusion, the drama unfolded with a raw intensity that mirrored the complexities of prison life.

The guards' decision to ban Jan and Lily from having visitors for a month was a punitive measure that further fuelled their resentment. The sisters, seething with anger, found themselves at odds with Emily, who appeared unscathed by the search. The perception that Emily's cell had been left untouched cast a shadow of suspicion over her, igniting a spark that would kindle the fires of animosity.

The tension escalated when Jan, driven by a potent mix of intoxication and fury, embarked on a destructive mission. The echoes of porcelain plates, glasses, and mugs shattering against walls reverberated through the Patio. Emily, seemingly retaliating for the destruction of her art supplies, unleashed a counterattack, hurling everything within reach into oblivion.

The guards, passive spectators to this chaotic ballet of destruction, stood by, a testament to the selective nature of authority within the prison walls. The inmates, divided by loyalties and grievances, navigated the fallout of this clash, their allegiances shifting like sand in the ever-shifting winds of prison politics.

Amidst the wreckage, a dichotomy emerged. Some, like Alejo and me, sought solace in cleaning up the debris, a futile attempt to restore a semblance of order to the chaos. The smell of spilled alcohol, broken belongings, and shattered camaraderie lingered, a pungent reminder of the fragility of alliances within the prison walls.

The drama, however, transcended the physical realm. Jan's cry of "*Dónde está la sapa?*" (Where's the snitch?)" echoed through the Patio, a desperate attempt to unmask the perceived snitch in their midst. The search for a scapegoat intensified, adding a layer of paranoia to the already charged atmosphere. The fear of betrayal, real or imagined, rippled through the inmates, leaving a trail of suspicion in its wake. The guards' intervention during Jan's rampage was a fleeting moment of authority, a reminder that even in chaos, their control remained absolute. Yet, the inmates, resilient and defiant, found ways to resist. The refusal to be drawn into the drama unfolding between Jan and Emily became an act of rebellion, a silent protest against the arbitrary nature of power within the prison.

As the night wore on, and the echoes of shattering glass subsided, the inmates returned to their cells. The clean-up, an act of defiance against the chaos, continued. My cell, like many others, bore the scars of the search – photographs torn from walls, belongings scattered haphazardly – a stark reminder that within the prison's rigid order, a silent battle for dignity and autonomy persisted. The drama, far from being a fleeting spectacle, left an indelible mark on the inmates' psyche. The fear of the unknown, the shifting dynamics within the Patio, and the looming presence of a new Capitan intensified the undercurrents of unrest. The inmates, bound by the shared experience of survival, grappled with the aftermath, each one carrying the weight of their personal dramas in the unforgiving landscape of prison life.

The night brought an unexpected turn of events. Apparently, being the newest edition to the patio, they presumed I didn't share the same hate for Emily in this moment for the search, maybe they thought I understood what it was like to be labelled a snitch. But I wasn't about to say no, I mean, who was I to say no? This wasn't my house. Relocating for the night, a temporary reprieve from the brewing storm, marked a shift in alliances.

The next day dawned early, the guards demanding a swift restoration of order. The clean-up, a collective effort, sought to erase the traces of the turmoil that had gripped the Patio. Contada became a measure of resilience, a testament to the inmates' ability to endure and rebuild, even in the face of adversity. The revelation of the search's findings exposed the extent of the clandestine activities within the Patio. The confiscated contraband, from hidden alcohol to forbidden items, drugs, Botox injections for the ladies who couldn't live without it, phones, knives, among other items like brand new clothing, shoes ready to sell inside. It all painted a vivid picture of the subversive underbelly thriving within the prison walls. The presence of twenty-nine mobile phones, a staggering number, fuelled speculation and paranoia.

The installation of security cameras, a symbolic response to the breach of security, marked a new era within the prison. The investigators' scrutiny, the filling of the tunnel, and the subsequent media coverage propelled the inmates into an unwanted spotlight. The ripple effect of the search reached beyond the Patio, triggering a chain of events that would redefine the inmates' relationship with the prison administration.

The Unveiling of the Trials and Understanding the Sentencing
The First Day of the Trial
26 July 2017

The day I had dreaded for weeks finally arrived. The hearing was set for 3:00 pm, and the morning was spent in a poignant exchange of words with my mother. My lawyer's visit followed a brief encounter laden with unsolicited advice. His words carried an unspoken directive: accept the plea deal. The weight of the suggestion left me seething, as if innocence or guilt mattered little in the grand scheme – they just wanted a quick resolution, consequences be damned.

"Cassandra all you have to do is say you accept and its done – remember, think of everyone who is close to you, this is the best thing for you and them," my lawyer told me.

"I'm not sure if I can do this, I know I signed but I keep going over and over it again in my head and I can't. This isn't fair."

My lawyer's departure prompted a call to my mother, a call that only fuelled my frustration. She, too, echoed the sentiment that accepting the deal was the safest route, an assertion that grated against my sense of justice. The looming threat of a 30-year sentence in Colombia's formidable prisons hung over me, but I couldn't fathom succumbing to a fate I didn't deserve. Was no one interested in seeing Wendy or Carlos behind bars? Did no one not care about what they had done to me? The day crawled by, every passing minute stretching into an agonizing eternity. Lunch arrived, but my stomach refused, tied in knots of anxiety. My Spanish, a feeble comfort, had improved, yet the complexity of the impending trial left me restless and uneasy.

I waited to be called, patience slipping away like sand through my fingers. A nap, an attempt to hasten time's crawl, proved futile. The guards finally summoned me, and, in a moment that felt both sudden and long-awaited, I found myself standing at the threshold of inevitability. The front of the prison greeted me, a departure from the familiar confines. Other women eyed me with a mix of curiosity and judgment, their conversations revealing whispers about the mysterious 'gringa.' A body search, the clink of handcuffs, and I was told to wait − a few minutes stretched into an eternity as anticipation gnawed at me. Layla, one of the guards, returned, hinting at the need for extra security. A disconcerting revelation, and I boarded the van, alone with my thoughts. The streets of Bogotá, glimpsed through barred windows, blurred in my periphery. Layla's mention of threats and the necessity for added security elevated the stakes, reminding me that my ordeal had transcended personal struggle.

The courthouse loomed ahead. Outside I could see hundreds of cameras and people standing there, but out of all the people, one person's face stood out, Carlos was there.

It was like he could see me, he stood there, just watching as the van pulled into the carpark. What was he doing here? My translator Layla's reassurance offered a glimmer of solidarity in the face of the unknown. As we entered the courthouse, the atmosphere shifted. Cameras, reporters, and unfamiliar faces turned the trial into a circus. What the fuck was going on here? The realization that my private ordeal was now a spectacle gripped me with anger and vulnerability. My lawyer, Hana, and my family, sat amidst the unfamiliar faces. The prosecutor's stern gaze hinted at the adversarial proceedings ahead. A new presence, a translator with uncertain linguistic prowess, added an unexpected layer of complexity. You would think they could have found a decent translator but well, it was better than nothing. The judge's entrance marked the beginning. The prosecutor laid out charges, painting me as the mastermind of a global conspiracy. Every accusation, each charge, felt like a blow to my defence. The narrative unfolded like a malevolent script, casting me as a puppeteer orchestrating chaos across borders, a mastermind of a huge organisation. It was a surreal moment, detached from the reality I knew. The prosecutor's office translator, a questionable choice in linguistic proficiency, struggled to convey the nuances of the proceedings. His faltering translations cast a veil of uncertainty over the already tense atmosphere, leaving me to decipher distorted renditions of my fate.

My lawyer's intervention, a timely correction of the translator's missteps, showcased a rare display of solidarity. The judge, stern and unyielding, absorbed the unfolding drama with a practiced demeanour. As the prosecutor pivoted toward the plea deal, a Faustian bargain hung in the air. The weight of guilt, a burden I vehemently rejected, pressed down on me. The language barrier, an insurmountable wall at times, made every word a potential pitfall. The prosecutor's argument unfolded; each assertion delivered with a calculated venom. She painted a picture of me as the linchpin of an elaborate criminal network, weaving a web of deception that spanned continents. Every piece of evidence presented felt like a betrayal, an intricate mosaic designed to condemn me. Yet there was no actual evidence to back up what they were saying.

The charges, far-reaching and ominous, seemed detached from the reality I knew. The prosecutor's impassioned delivery struck a chord, not because of the validity of her claims, but because of the harsh reality that these allegations, no matter how baseless, held the power to shape my destiny. The courtroom, a theatre of judgment, held its breath as the prosecutor wove her narrative. The weight of the accusations bore down on me, a suffocating force that demanded a response. As I sat there, absorbing the onslaught of words, a resolve simmered within me – a determination to defy the narrative being spun, to stand firm in the face of orchestrated adversity. The judge's gaze, penetrating and inscrutable, sought a reaction. The translator incompetently stumbled through the prosecutor's fervent delivery. My lawyer's stern expression mirrored my own inner turmoil, a shared acknowledgment of the uphill battle we faced.

The plea deal, the prosecutor's pièce de resistance, loomed ahead. A choice, presented as a lifeline, dangled before me. The weight of the decision, the consequence of accepting or rejecting this Faustian bargain, pressed down on me. The judge, turning his attention to me, posed the pivotal question.

The courtroom held its breath.

I, fuelled by a surge of defiance, I uttered a resounding ...

"No."

The ripple of astonishment and whispers cascaded through the room, momentarily unsettling the meticulously constructed facade of the trial. A recess ensued, granting a temporary reprieve. Layla's words of commendation echoed, offering a rare glimmer of support within the cold confines of the courthouse.

"You're doing great Cassandra, I'm sorry you're going through this, I hope you get out. Don't let these guys get away with doing this to you."

Back in the holding area, I navigated the sea of emotions that surged within me – relief, uncertainty, and a lingering sense of the unknown. The judge's return heralded an unexpected turn of events. The trial suspended; a respite granted for a thorough examination of evidence. My lawyer, Orlando's reassurance, a lifeline in the uncertainty, hinted at the arduous path that lay ahead. Escorted back to the van, I grappled with conflicting emotions, the weight of impending judgment echoing in my mind.

Within the confines of my cell, I dissected the day's tumult, contemplating the consequences of rejecting the path of least resistance.

As sleep claimed me, the trials of tomorrow, the weight of impending judgment, waited patiently for their turn. In the cocoon of sleep, dreams and fears intermingled, weaving a tapestry of subconscious anticipation. The night unfolded, a silent prelude to the continuing drama that awaited me when the sun would once again cast its light on the prison's unforgiving landscape.

The Second Day of the Trial – The Verdict?
9 August 2017

Today, the judge's decision would ring through the courtroom, dictating the course of my future. Fear gripped me, but I wouldn't allow it to surface. Strength and a well-worn poker face were my armour. The afternoon sun painted the courtroom in a harsh light as the guard called my name. Unprepared for whatever awaited, I navigated the familiar routine of paperwork, signatures, and an obligatory body search. The van, a vessel of uncertainty, awaited. This time, Layla was absent, leaving me surrounded by unfamiliar faces. Security, a silent but imposing presence, hinted at the gravity of the situation. I had been studying the Colombian law book like crazy, knowing it was the only way to keep up with everything going on around me.

Arriving at the courthouse, the guards, startled by the presence of news crews, questioned, "That's for you?" I nodded, a silent admission to the unwelcome attention. Opting for a discreet entrance through the parking lot, we dodged the prying lenses of the media. The sanctuary of the waiting room beckoned, shielding me momentarily from the storm outside. The courtroom, a vast expanse filled with cameras and reporters, loomed ahead. Anger bubbled within as I faced the unwarranted intrusion. My lawyer, Hana, occupied her seat, providing a familiar anchor in the sea of unfamiliarity. I locked eyes with each in turn, drawing strength from their silent support. The guard, a momentary barrier against the intrusive cameras, unshackled me. Greetings exchanged, I smiled at my mother, a façade of assurance for her benefit. I felt she wanted me to accept a deal. If only she knew how much I was actually struggling. The guard's nod signalled the impending proceedings. I turned, ready to face whatever fate awaited, I would take it as it comes, I was strong. I could do this.

The translator, an unwelcome déjà vu, greeted me. Across the room, the prosecutor and her mysterious companion took their places. The judge's entrance, a prelude to the unfolding drama, commanded silence. We stood, a collective breath held, as he settled into his seat. The stage was set.

Identifications completed, the judge delved into a meticulous dissection of the evidence – or lack thereof. He lambasted the prosecutor for negligence, citing the failure to investigate alternative suspects and the dismissal of crucial evidence. The accusations, a damning indictment, hung in the air. The CCTV footage, a potential lifeline, was dismissed due to alleged malfunctions, which meant the prosecutor never even looked for the street footage. The prosecutor's blatant disregard for my written confession, signed and dated in her investigators' presence, drew the judge's stern rebuke. Questions about my phone, its messages laden with threats, raised eyebrows and tempers. The prosecutor's audacious claim that I refused to cooperate with unlocking the phone elicited shock and anger. That did not happen! Lies hung heavy in the air, and my face burned with a mix of indignation and frustration. My lawyer's swift denial that this was true echoed my own disbelief, probably the first words he had spoken all this time. The judge, a stoic figure, observed the theatrics with a measured gaze.

As the judge continued, my attention wavered. The translator, an afterthought in my focus, struggled to bridge the linguistic divide. The hours stretched, an endless procession of legal intricacies. Panic gripped me as I realized the implications of a flawed translation reaching Australian ears. In other words, I was screwed. Seriously! How could a prosecutor's office not afford to pay a decent translator who could actually translate to the level required. The judge, mercifully, announced his decision. A small victory, he declared, rejecting the plea deal and granting 90 days for the accusatory process to begin. Part of me was so happy – everything I had said all along was true, these people needed to investigate, and they would find the real criminals. The courtroom exhaled, tension lifting on my half of the room, however the cameras and reporters slamming false information to their viewers:

"Plea deal rejected due to much evidence against Cocaine Cassie."

"Cocaine Cassie to face life in prison."

Honestly, it was so frustrating hearing it all and not being able to say or do anything. Nothing more I would have liked than to be able to stop and say "Hey, have you ever thought about actually reporting the truth, or I dunno, something that people are actually interested in seeing?"

The judge's gaze met mine, a moment of shared understanding. It was a win, small and scary as I was now back to facing a huge sentence. Stunned, I turned to my lawyer, seeking clarity. Mum's expression betrayed her fears, but I clung to the judge's words about the prosecutor's negligence. A victory, my lawyer assured me, but a daunting journey lay ahead. I wasn't about to let anyone destroy my small win.

Back in prison, the weight of a further impending trial settled, and the promise of a visit and planning for the fight that awaited me, brought a glimmer of hope.

Handcuffed once more, I faced the onslaught of questions from reporters. Although anger always seemed to fill me when I had to walk through these vultures, this time I didn't care. Misconceptions swirled, fuelled by a flawed translation. As I passed the seething prosecutor, our eyes locked. Defiance burned in my gaze – I wasn't defeated, not today. The echoes of the judge's admonishment lingered, a reminder that the fight was far from over. I could do this.

Shadows of the Legal Dance
20 September 2017

Moving forward with the trials proved to be a labyrinth journey, a relentless pursuit of justice obscured by legal intricacies. The prosecutor's reluctance to proceed stemmed from an apparent lack of preparation, a failure to delve into the judge's directives. Yet, this was only one layer of the complexity. I wasn't sure if this was a good or bad thing anymore, yet only time would tell what would happen to me.

A revolving door of prosecutors became an additional hurdle. Each change in legal representation reset the clock, granting them the liberty to request more time to scrutinize the case. The law, a double-edged sword, mandated a 90-day limit for formal charges. Beyond this threshold, parole beckoned until accusations were officially pressed. Days ticked away, exceeding the mandated count as weekends and public holidays fell by the wayside. Trips to the courtroom were a tumultuous affair. Days within the prison's confines would momentarily yield to the promise of legal proceedings. Removed from the familiar confines of the Patio, I navigated the gauntlet of exiting prison, only to find myself ensnared in a cage for hours. The anticipation would crescendo, only to be shattered by last-minute cancellations. The ordeal, a disheartening cycle, painted each trip with frustration and discomfort. The guards, often callous and brusque, manifested a harsh reality, tight handcuffs left bruised wrists, a tangible reminder of my status as a criminal. Did I not deserve basic human decency?

On day 87 of the legal proceedings, an unexpected summons disrupted the routine. A call to the front gate for remission, a signal that an unannounced hearing loomed. Anxiety gripped me; questions swirled.

Did my lawyer withhold this information intentionally? Would I face the legal labyrinth alone? Urgently, I beseeched Mayor Nancy to alert my lawyer, a desperate attempt to bridge the information gap.

The guard escorting me was Tahlee's sister. I didn't think I would ever run into her, stupid I know, but here we were.

Yay.

Her demeanour, a mix of disdain and aggression, surpassed any previous encounters with other guards. Being pushed around, handcuffs so tight, that bruising and blood surfaced, bruised wrists, baton beatings and being thrown to the ground marked the journey. I guess she was getting even for Tahlee. Arriving at the courthouse, a shared cell with curious glances awaited. Silently, I rejected small talk, my mind consumed by unspoken fears. The absence of prior knowledge fuelled a storm within me. Why was I unaware of this hearing? Doubts about my lawyer's actions gnawed at the edges of my thoughts. Today, the shadows of uncertainty danced in the harsh light of legal proceedings, casting doubt on the path ahead.

Leaning against the cold, indifferent walls of the unfamiliar holding cell, I observed with trepidation as fellow inmates were selected one by one for clandestine proceedings. This courtroom, a stark departure from the usual backdrop of my hearings, injected an extra layer of unease into the already tense atmosphere. Panic clung to me like a relentless shadow, fuelled by the uncertainty of whether my legal representation would materialize, and the disquieting possibility of enduring this ordeal without defence. Each tick of the clock intensified the anxiety gnawing at my core.

The room, filled with a constant hum of foreign voices, seemed to amplify the isolation I felt. As the term 'gringa' punctuated their conversations, I sensed the weight of their collective gaze, an unwelcome reminder of my foreign status. Yet, I resolved to remain impervious to their glances and whispers, focusing solely on stifling the rising tide of panic within. The passage of time, marked by the agonizing wait, stretched into an indeterminate void. Hours slipped away as the questions multiplied in my mind. What if my lawyer failed to appear? Could they subject me to this ordeal without proper legal representation?

The uncertainty clawed at my composure.

In the midst of the restless atmosphere, the term 'gringa' surfaced multiple times, a linguistic barrier crumbling as my fellow inmates chatted amongst themselves. The foreign language became a barrier, an insurmountable wall that severed me from the vital information exchanged in hushed tones. I was left in the deafening silence of anticipation. As the room remained cloaked in ambiguity, the collective murmurings veered into the uncharted territory of speculation. Determined to unravel the mystery shrouding my fate, I decided to break the uneasy silence. A passing guard, leading another inmate back to the cell, became an unwitting recipient of my inquiry.

"Guard, do you know if I will be having a hearing today?", I asked in Spanish.

The room plunged into an abrupt silence, even the guard registering shock. The revelation that I understood a bit of Spanish seemed to catch them off guard. The guard shook her head, confirming the cancellation, leaving me in a state of disbelief. The mistreatment I endured under the watchful eye of a callous guard was for a hearing that wasn't going to happen. Why hadn't they disclosed this from the beginning?

The aftermath of this revelation unfurled a disheartening reality. I wouldn't return to the prison until all the other inmates had their turn, subjecting me to a purgatory of discomfort. The urgency to use the restroom clashed with the indignity of an exposed toilet, exacerbated by its proximity to the men's waiting cell. Looking at the toilet I remembered my near miss back in the men's holding cell and I looked away, I could hold onto my pee. The predicament intensified the curiosity of fellow inmates. Instead of hostility, they offered apologies and sought to understand my presence. Sharing my story, they empathized, revealing the unfortunate commonality of such experiences within these prison walls. The guard, harbouring a palpable disdain for me, exacerbated the situation. As sandwiches were distributed to others, she singled me out, claiming there weren't enough for me. I refrained from complaint, but the unexpected solidarity among inmates confronted the guard. Threats of retribution through formal reports stirred unrest among them.

Despite their kindness, I urged them to let it be. I was, uninterested in further complications.

The mistreatment I endured at the hands of the guard unfolded like a cruel drama. She wielded her authority with a malicious glee, pushing me around, making snarky comments, and ensuring that the handcuffs clamped around my wrists were painfully tight. Bruised wrists and demeaning treatment marked my journey through the maze of the courtroom. Yet, in the face of this cruelty, I chose to endure in silence, my spirit unbroken. Curiosity brewed among the inmates, prompting an explanation for the guard's hostility. I told them about her sister, Tahlee. Tahlee it seemed, was a divisive figure within the prison, owing money and sowing discord among inmates. The revelation that she labelled me a snitch, while being one herself, added a layer of irony to the situation. Amidst these revelations, a fellow inmate, aware of my new-found understanding of Spanish, urged me to share the truth of my story. A surprising wave of encouragement followed, challenging my preconceptions. Yet, I hesitated, content with the solitude and the partial understanding that surrounded me.

The unexpected distraction offered by these conversations left me in a conflicted state. The cancellation of the hearing evoked relief, yet the complexities of my life within these prison walls lingered. As the guards returned, securing us together once again, the journey back to prison commenced. Annoyance and relief coexisted as the familiar walls of confinement welcomed me back, sparing me the presence of the guard who had made my day unbearable.

The Illusion of Justice
10 October 2017

The day of reckoning unfolded as I was summoned to the prosecutor's office in Paloquemao, an unusual occurrence that piqued my curiosity. The guards were instructed to uncuff me, leaving me alone with the prosecutor and my lawyer. A surreal moment ensued as the prosecutor, sporting a sly smile, initiated a conversation. His condescending remark about my youth and naivety left me momentarily speechless, prompting a restrained smile in response.

The air was charged with an aura of trepidation as I prepared to delve into negotiations surrounding a deal that carried the weight of my freedom.

The prosecutor laid out the terms, echoing a familiar refrain that had been orchestrated by the initial prosecutor. A sense of curiosity gnawed at me, and I sought insight into the alleged evidence tying me to the activities. To my surprise, the prosecutor unveiling an investigation by the Australian Federal Police.

As the details unfolded, a wave of indignation surged within me. The AFP's so-called 'investigation' had pinpointed my friendship with David, a police officer who had selflessly aided me in communicating with my family during the initial stages of my ordeal. How ridiculous can this be? The absurdity of the situation struck me – accused of 'association' with someone who had offered me assistance mere days after my arrest. The prosecutor's approach mirrored the systemic corruption that plagued the Colombian legal landscape. By recycling the same plea deal, it became evident that the pursuit of justice remained elusive. The prosecution's refusal to conduct a thorough investigation perpetuated the charade, keeping me entangled in a web of dubious accusations.

Stubbornness, a trait that had both its merits and demerits, became my ally in the quest for justice. Refusing to concede ground when innocence was at stake, I harboured an unyielding determination to expose the fallacies surrounding my case. The prosecutor's recycled plea deal echoed a blatant disregard for the judge's directives and an insistence on maintaining the illusion of justice.

The prosecutor's narrative unfolded, weaving a tale of inevitability – a coercive plea deal presented as the sole option. His assertion that the trial's duration could span two arduous years further fuelled the pressure. The revelation that, even if acquitted, the time spent languishing in prison wouldn't be deducted from my sentence, *contradicted Colombian law*. An unexpected turn shifted the conversation toward a disconcerting truth – the prosecutor's admission that *the legal system thrived on convictions, regardless of innocence*. The revelation cast a pall over my hopes for a fair trial, exposing a callous disregard for truth and justice. In the ensuing dialogue, the prosecutor attempted to manipulate my emotions, invoking familial ties and insinuating that accepting the plea deal was a benevolent choice.

After he had said his peace. The prosecutor left the room.

The prosecutor's exit heralded a moment of despair, compounded by a revelation that struck at the heart of my defence – the disappearance of my phone from evidence. It had been settled that I would accept the deal if I was given a chance to open my phone, a phone that had been left in the hands of a not-so-trustworthy Sergeant. I watched and listened as my prosecutor and lawyer began talking very fast, and then I heard it. The phone was gone, it went 'missing' from evidence when the judge asked for a further investigation. The realization that crucial evidence had vanished, coupled with the prosecutor's nonchalant attitude, sparked a surge of anger and helplessness. How does that even happen? Where had it gone? Who has it?

Upon my return to the prison, the weight of the compromised legal system pressed heavily on my shoulders. The disheartening encounter left me yearning for solitude, a respite from the isolation that echoed the pervasive corruption veiled within the folds of Colombian justice. As the echoes of the prosecutor's words reverberated within me, I grappled with the harsh reality that justice remained an illusion, an unattainable ideal within the confines of a corrupted system.

A Surrender to Circumstances
16 October 2017

The day loomed, pregnant with the weight of decisions that would shape my destiny. The anticipation of a hearing to accept the pre-agreement stirred restlessness within me, rendering sleep an elusive luxury. As dawn broke, I found myself engulfed in a sense of foreboding, a prelude to the tumultuous events that awaited.

The prosecutor's pre-emptive measure to expel all media from the courtroom hinted at a perceived threat to my safety. Whispers of an alleged betrayal, a supposed exchange of information for leniency, painted a distorted image of my intent. The reluctance of my lawyer to unearth the truth before a sentence perplexed me, fostering a growing suspicion that elements beyond my comprehension were at play. The veiled agenda of the prosecution, ignoring evidence and bypassing due diligence, hinted at a system where justice bowed to expediency.

The day unfolded with an oppressive atmosphere, my stomach rebelling against sustenance as anxiety overshadowed hunger. The impending hearing cast a shadow, amplifying the disquiet that had become an unwelcome companion throughout my ordeal. As the clock relentlessly ticked away, my fellow inmates, voices tainted by the bitter reality of a skewed justice system, that to the initial plea deal might have spared me this agony. Upon the call of the guards, a shroud of nervousness enveloped me. The bus ride to the courthouse carried an air of secrecy, underscored by a guard's ominous warning about the gravity of the situation. The prosecutor's alleged contact with the Mayor fuelled speculations about undisclosed threats, leaving me to grapple with the unsettling uncertainty. The courthouse, an arena of conflicting emotions, presented an unusual tableau. The bus navigated into the parking lot, an exception to the norm, and a heightened sense of vigilance permeated the air. Unease lingered as guards scrutinized their surroundings, a tangible manifestation of the perceived peril accompanying this pivotal hearing.

Escorted into an unfamiliar room, smaller than its counterparts, I found myself at the mercy of a proceeding that transcended the routine. My lawyer, wearing a reassuring smile, inquired about my readiness – an inquiry met with a nod, concealing the maelstrom of conflicting emotions within. The choice that lay ahead, fraught with consequences, forced me to confront the stark reality of navigating a system seemingly indifferent to the pursuit of truth. Seated before the judge, the familiar ritual commenced, yet the stakes had risen. The judge explained the agreement between the prosecutor and my legal representation, but my thoughts were consumed by the gravity of the decision awaiting me. The change in judges, a shift in perspectives, clouded the path ahead, fostering a sense of apprehension. A surge of panic gripped me, constricting my breath as the judge's inquiry pierced the deafening silence. The decision, an irrevocable crossroad, beckoned me to either accept a plea-deal synonymous with surrendering my innocence or confront the looming spectre of a potential life sentence. The weight of responsibility pressed upon me, the burden of safeguarding not just my fate but the well-being of those who cared.

A million thoughts collided within, rendering words elusive. Faced with an unenviable choice, I grappled with the desire for personal vindication against the compulsion to shield loved ones from the spectre of a prolonged legal battle. The microphone, a conduit for a fateful utterance, hung heavy in the charged air as I surrendered to circumstances. The acceptance of the plea-deal echoed through the room, sealing my fate in a compromise with truth. I had accepted that it didn't matter how little I had known about the drug trafficking plot, it was time to accept my responsibility in it all, all I had wanted was for a proper investigation to take place, but it didn't matter anymore.

I surrendered. I accepted the plea deal, the very same one that I had once rejected. What choice did I have? It seemed someone was always one step ahead of me. Someone didn't want me getting out.

The judge, with a terse acknowledgment, set the sentencing date

– 1 November 2017 – a mere two weeks hence. The air, thick with the resonance of a choice made under duress, foretold a narrative etched in the annals of a justice system that faltered, leaving the quest for truth in its wake.

Sentencing
1 November 2017

D-day arrived, casting a shadow that stretched beyond the confines of the courtroom. The anticipation of media vultures, hungry for a spectacle, added an extra layer of tension to the already fraught morning. The weight of the impending sentencing pressed on me, rendering food and drink tasteless as my stomach churned with anxiety. The prospect of facing the public eye on this defining day left me sick to the core. The call came swiftly, and soon I found myself handcuffed and ushered onto the bus. Another inmate, oblivious to the gravity of my thoughts, chattered incessantly. My mind, however, was preoccupied with the tumultuous journey ahead, a journey through a sea of reporters and flashing cameras.

As we reached the courthouse, the spectacle outside revealed yet again a familiar face that sent shockwaves through me – Carlos, a face from a past I had hoped to leave behind, the face that I saw every night, in my nightmares, a face that still haunted me. Panic gripped me. What was he doing here, lurking in the shadows? The chaos outside intensified as guards grappled with the unexpected media frenzy. The familiarity of faces and a surge of panic distracted me from the impending trial. Separated from my fellow inmates, I was confined to a small cell, my security tighter than ever. The guard's attempt at reassurance fell on deaf ears as I grappled with the impending storm. The judge's entrance marked the commencement.

Standing before the judge, the weight of the plea deal's acceptance bore down on me.

The judge's words, cold and decisive, announced a six-year prison sentence.

"Cassandra Sainsbury – Resident of South Australia – Australia. 22 years old is hereby sentenced to 72 months in prison where she will not have access to parole, she will not have access to any beneficial to leave prison until said 72 months have been served in full. Furthermore, Miss Sainsbury must pay a fine to the people of 400 minimum Colombian salaries or its equivalent."

400 salaries?

Did I look like I had a casual $150,000 to pay this fine?

Shit.

A wave of disappointment eclipsed any tears; disappointment in a legal system that had failed to serve some sort of justice, disappointment in the prosecutors and lawyers who prioritized expediency over truth. My lawyer's jubilation added insult to injury. His job was done, while mine had only just begun.

The courtroom held a stifling silence as the reality of my fate set in. A decision made in the name of expediency had irrevocably altered the course of my life. The judge's departure left me to grapple with the numbness that accompanied a sentence delivered without mercy. In the aftermath, I pondered the duration of my lingering in the courtroom, contemplating the absurdity of the media circus.

Unexpectedly, the prosecutor approached, his words slicing through the air.

"Cassandra, my dear, you did the right thing," he remarked callously.

"You'll be out in two years max. Don't worry, little one."

Did he not just hear what the judge said? No parole, no nothing, I mean it was *his* plea deal after all.

The insinuation of tearing me apart hung in the air, leaving me seething with anger. His assurance of a brief imprisonment, his nonchalant dismissal of the circumstances, only fuelled my indignation.

The guards, sensing my vulnerability, finally intervened. The prosecutor's departure provided scant relief as my lawyer bid farewell, leaving me to grapple with the reality of my choices.

The return to the prison was a tumultuous journey through a sea of reporters, the media's relentless pursuit leaving me battered and bloodied. A brief respite within a waiting cell allowed the guards to strategise, their concern evident in the absence of a protective vest. The impending exit required a human barrier, a shield against the prying eyes and opportunistic intrusion of the media. I looked in the crowd, searching for the face that haunted me, but I didn't see him, where had he gone and why did he show up? To make sure I had signed the deal? I would never know.

The guards, their protective instincts heightened, offered a modicum of solace. As I navigated the throng of reporters, a shove from behind sent my head colliding with the bus, blood staining my forehead. Frustration surged within me, a desire to confront my assailant squashed by the slamming bus doors. Inside, the guards grappled with the aftermath, cleaning my wound, expressing regret for their inability to shield me adequately. The journey back to the prison was a conversation tinged with disdain for the media's tactics, a sentiment that veered dangerously close to generalizations about foreigners. Upon my return to the prison, an unexpected meeting with the Mayor Nancy unfolded. Her apology, laden with genuine remorse, hinted at the futility of protection in the face a media onslaught. Yet it wasn't her fault. I didn't blame them at all. Besides, I'd had worse beatings.

Back in the Patio, the isolation I sought was elusive. The weight of judgment from those around me, the mixed emotions of friends and family, left me in a state of emotional turmoil. Alone, I succumbed to tears, the weight of six years settling heavily on my shoulders. Nancy's attempt at reassurance did little to alleviate the inner conflict.

Should I have fought for the whole truth? Because I wanted the full truth too. The prison walls seemed to close in, suffocating me with a sense of hopelessness. The barrage of hate, both from strangers and those close to me, added another layer of pain. The realization that I had signed away six years of my life, for something that I deemed myself responsible for. The story of a troublemaker, a life disrupted by judgment and false accusations, fuelled my despair. Yet, amid the darkness, a flicker of resilience emerged. The time ahead, however daunting, would become an opportunity for self-reflection and growth. The commitment to use this experience to become a better person, to defy the narrative imposed upon me, became a source of strength.

I would make it through this, I was more than capable of that!

Unforgiving Judge
30 November 2017

In Colombia once a circuit judge sentences you, your case is then passed onto a judge who is now in charge of your release from prison and accepting any discount, good behaviour or anything else. It's called an 'Executing Judge.' It made things all very confusing, it seemed like in this place they liked have so many different judges.

This judge, an enigmatic arbiter of my destiny, would scrutinize my behaviour behind bars, deciding if any glimmer of redemption existed in my story. The prospect of this meeting weighed heavily on me, a cloud of uncertainty casting a pall over my already turbulent prison life. Alejo, with her proficiency in Spanish, accompanied me, a decision prompted by the concern of an older inmate in our Patio. Scepticism lingered in my mind – was this genuine assistance or a ploy to gather gossip? Regardless, we ventured to the next building, where my judge presided, the air thick with anticipation.

As I entered the room, the judge's disdainful gaze swept over me, signalling an ominous beginning. Her eyes, filled with an unsettling disgust, foreshadowed a challenging encounter. The judge, stern and unwavering, inquired about my proficiency in Spanish. I admitted to understanding fragments, relying on Alejo for translation. The judge's nod conveyed a cold acknowledgment.

The interrogation commenced; each question delivered with a measured intensity. How many drugs were in my suitcase? How long had I been incarcerated? Alejo faithfully translated, yet I couldn't shake the bewilderment. Hadn't the judge received my detailed paperwork? The realization struck – each judge managed a multitude of cases, armed only with the basics. My assumption that they were privy to the intricacies of my case crumbled.

The prosecutor's promise of a shortened sentence unravelled. The judge, armed only with scant information, offered no reprieve. The truth hit hard: my prosecutor's assurances were built on a foundation of half-truths. Anger surged within me. The disappointment in my lawyer, complicit in these falsehoods, added another layer to my disillusionment. The judge's verdict was a cold pronouncement:

"Tough luck. You have a six-year sentence to pay, and you're not getting out any sooner, no matter what you do."

Her words echoed in the room, shattering any hope I clung to. The prosecutor had made sure that I wouldn't get out any sooner, it was almost like they wanted me to stay put. No amount of rehabilitation, good behaviour, or commitment would alter her stance. The judge, unmoved, declared the inescapability of my full sentence. The weight of six years pressed upon me; a sentence that now seemed unyielding.

I longed to argue, to plead my case, but the reality was stark – I had no recourse. A tear betrayed my stoic facade, but I swiftly wiped it away. I refused to show weakness to a judge who seemed determined to break my spirit. Keeping my head down became my only strategy, a silent plea for a change of heart that seemed unlikely. The meeting ended abruptly, and Alejo signalled it was time to leave. Back in the Patio, I sought solitude in my cell, only to find Alejo trailing behind. Annoyance flickered, but I bit back my words. She revealed something:

"Don't take it personally, she lost her son to drugs and well, you're a 'cause' of death in her eyes. Maybe you can request a new judge?"

I shook my head, I would take this as it was, if this was the judge I was given, there was a reason for it, something this place was teaching me was that everything really did happen for a reason.

This added a bitter layer to my frustration. Judges were supposed to be impartial, yet this one harboured a bias rooted in personal tragedy. Although, I understood.

Having now received the judge who has the ability to grant me parole and having found out that she is biased, which meant that getting parole wasn't going to happen, she made it clear I would pay the full six years in prison.

Alone again, I wrestled with unanswered questions, the injustice of an impartial judge weighing heavily on my mind. Alejo's revelation lingered, an unsettling truth about the uneven scales of justice. My need for composure became paramount; losing control was not an option. I had to be strong, resilient, proving it to myself each passing day. In the face of an unforgiving judge, I sought a silver lining, a reason to endure. Everything happened for a reason, or so I told myself.

It hurt to think that this prison was my home now because I honestly didn't see myself getting out anytime soon.

The Birthday Raid
December 2017 – January 2018

In the desolate confines of the prison, where time seemed to lose its normal rhythm, special occasions were mere reminders of a life left behind. The calendar marked Christmas, New Year, and my birthday with the same indifference as any other day. Yet, as the date of my birth approached, a peculiar unease settled over the prison, casting a shadow on the otherwise mundane routine.

Christmas arrived, a day that felt eerily like the one before and the one to follow. The air was thick with depression, a collective melancholy permeating the atmosphere. I hadn't really had family around for Christmas in some time so to say that it was extremely hard, that would be a lie, however it was hard to be there and not try to have some kind of Christmas spirit. Some chose to sleep through the day, a desperate attempt to escape the grim reality. I didn't blame them, although I wasn't from here and I was yet to experience what Colombians were really about, I could see that the holiday season was a very big deal to these people. Family was and is everything to them. I opted for a quiet day, seeking solace in the pages of a book that I was trying to practise reading and the respite of sleep, trying to convince myself that it was just another day. The truth, however, lingered, unspoken but palpable – the festive season was a cruel mockery behind bars. I watched as we all came together for one meal, making do with the food we received for the day and making some weird mixture of rice with whatever else was served. The food was shit. Who were we trying to fool? But it was the way we all came together to share a moment, to not feel so alone, together.

As my birthday approached, a peculiar unease settled over the prison, casting a shadow on the otherwise mundane routine, yet a faint hope flickered. Perhaps, this day would be different. Maybe just wishful thinking. I decided to start it on a different note, reaching for my mobile phone to connect with my mother. But even in this small act of defiance against the prison norms, a foreboding feeling crept in – an intuition that something ominous awaited. Speaking to my mother, I sensed an impending shift, a disturbance in the routine.

"Happy Birthday, Babe. I hope it's a good day. What are you doing?"

"Sitting in the patio, everyone is watching TV or eating breakfast. Today is a public holiday in Colombia so usually nothing happens today. It's a nothing day – literally."

My mother continued to talk to me about unimportant topics, I guess she tried to make me feel better, it was my first birthday behind bars, yet speaking to her didn't make me feel better, I was always constantly reminded that she hadn't been around for years, so many birthdays I had on my own. Almost like life has prepared me for being alone.

"Ah, Mum, I have to go, I don't know why, but something doesn't feel right. I need to hide my phone and I think I'm just going to lay down and read or something." Just like that, I turned off my phone and I began hiding my phone. It wasn't the greatest hiding spot, wrapped in a sock and hiding inside a hanging jumper in the patio. I knew one day it would be found, but as long as it wasn't found in my cell or on me, that's all that mattered.

A gut feeling urged me to conceal my phone, a habit formed out of necessity. The sense of paranoia wasn't unwarranted, and soon, the prison echoed with the sounds of running feet, an unusual occurrence on any day.

Curiosity overcame caution, prompting me to investigate. As I stood up, a guard loomed in my doorway, shouting for me to vacate my cell. Here we go. The running had not been a false alarm; something significant was underway. The guards systematically invaded each cell, wreaking havoc as they tore through personal belongings, dismantling shelves, ripping mattresses, and desecrating whatever possessions we held dear.

This wasn't a routine search; it was a raid, meticulously executed on a day when mobile phone usage was expected, on a day like my birthday.

The realization struck – a Captain named Dave, wearing a smug smile, had orchestrated this display of authority. His threats, previously dismissed as empty, had materialized into a calculated crackdown.

The Captain's demeanour exuded satisfaction, his plan unfolding as expected. He meticulously scrutinized every cell, demanding permission letters for possessions like special dietary food, TVs, tables, and chairs. While the scrutiny was understandable, what came next left me in disbelief. Captain Dave delved into the food brought by visitors, casting aside what he deemed unacceptable, throwing the food on the floor, stomping all over it without a care in the world. The arbitrary nature of his actions revealed a personal vendetta, likely stemming from a prior altercation with an outspoken lady in the Patio. His wrath spared no one, and as the raid unfolded, it became evident that the Captain harboured a grudge against our entire Patio.

Phones, alcohol, 'medication' like Botox injections and things that the rich girls decide they can't live without in prison – I think they hadn't grasped where they were exactly – and various contraband were confiscated, laying bare the darker underbelly of prison life, things that I still hadn't realised they could get in here. It seemed when you had money, nothing was off limits. Captain Dave, standing before us, announced the consequences – no visitors for a month, a prohibition on food deliveries, and the removal of all unapproved items, including tables and chairs. His declaration underscored an unwarranted hostility towards our Patio. I didn't take it personally, I knew exactly where I was and I never seemed to complain about anything, I was in prison. After all, what was the point in fighting it?

When my turn came, the Captain questioned the origin of my foreign food. The embassy would often bring me in a couple of snacks from Australia and some dietary foods, they were always allowed to do so, but it could only be a couple of things in each 6-month visit. I explained that it was brought in by my Embassy in our most recent visit. He requested to see the paperwork and proof that I was actually a foreigner (Funny, huh? As if he couldn't tell) before allowing it. I was never rude to the guards or any commanders, I was merely a number in this place that had to do as told, I had no rights and I never forgot that. As the Captain stripped the Patio of everything not sanctioned, my mind flashed back to the first major search I endured in this very Patio. It had been similar but this time, the Captain had been angry, almost like revenge, I wonder who had upset him.

After the raid had finished, we were left with a huge clean up, I retreated to my cell, where I was reminded, there were no joyful moments here, there were no 'try and make it special'. There was just you, a number and in prison, that was it. On the day that I had planned to stay in my cell, buried in my paper-thin blanket, crying, Captain Dave left an indelible mark, turning my first birthday in prison into yet another ordeal.

Forbidden Connections – Navigating the Complexities
February 2018

In the confined world of prison, where every action is scrutinized, and rumours spread like wildfire, unexpected connections can be both a source of comfort and a cause for concern. My interactions with Jane, one of the prison guards, blurred the lines between friendship and something more, leading me down a precarious path.

Jane's attempts to get closer to me were evident. She brought chocolates, engaged in conversation, and showed a level of attention that couldn't be ignored. The whispers and sidelong glances from fellow inmates fuelled speculation, and I, in turn, began avoiding Jane. A harmless crush had the potential to jeopardize everything I had worked so hard to build – trust, respect, and a reputation as someone who wouldn't compromise their principles.

One day, as we were being locked into our cells, Jane surprised me with a casual remark about waiting to use my phone. Panic surged through me; she had unknowingly hit the nail on the head. However, I dismissed the notion, assuring her that I didn't possess a phone. In that moment, the unspoken boundary between us became painfully clear. The following day, Jane's behaviour shifted. She seemed to be avoiding me, and oddly enough, that suited me just fine. The less attention, the better. But then, an unexpected twist occurred. A fellow inmate, someone I barely interacted with, called me into her cell. Closing the door behind me, she handed me a phone number, revealing that Jane had asked her to pass it on. The clandestine nature of the exchange left me dumbfounded, realizing the potential consequences of such a connection.

The decision to act on Jane's number weighed heavily on my mind. The risks of pursuing any form of friendship with a guard were clear, but the allure of connection, especially in the isolating environment of prison, was undeniable. The internal debate intensified, mirroring the external drama that was sure to unfold.

Eventually, curiosity got the better of me, and I sent Jane a message. What began as a discussion about English lessons, something she genuinely wanted to learn, soon evolved into something more *personal*. The conversations became a lifeline, a daily ritual that transcended the confines of our roles as guard and inmate. As the dynamic shifted, it became apparent that Jane harboured feelings beyond friendship. Her genuine concern for my well-being was a stark contrast to the complex web of emotions entangling us. I questioned why she settled for a connection she couldn't fully embrace, but the answer remained elusive, lost in the shadows of secrecy.

My dependence on our conversations grew, despite the risks involved. The contrast between the safety of our virtual connection and the potential dangers of real-life repercussions was a constant inner struggle. I couldn't deny the warmth and attention Jane provided, a stark contrast to the emotional void I had experienced since a previous heartbreak from many years ago, my first unofficial girlfriend. Yet, the looming question persisted:

Why choose a connection behind bars over a tangible relationship outside?

It was a puzzle I couldn't solve, and perhaps one I wasn't meant to. As the entanglement deepened, the realization dawned that this forbidden connection, while providing solace, held the potential to unravel the fragile stability I had fought so hard to attain. The complexity of emotions within the prison's walls mirrored the intricate dance of secrecy and risk that defined our unconventional relationship.

As the prison walls enclosed us, months had passed since Jane and I first started talking, the tangled web of relationships and rumours grew more intricate, weaving a complex narrative that blurred the lines between truth and deception. My connection with Jane, the prison guard, was tested when whispers of her involvement with another inmate reached my ears. Jane had warned me about the rumours that circled her, cautioning that people would claim to have relationships with her.

"People are always trying to destroy anything I have. Other inmates always say that I hit on them, that I flirt, but I swear I don't," she said.

As the entanglement deepened, the realization dawned that this forbidden connection, while providing solace, held the potential to unravel the fragile stability I had fought so hard to attain. The complexity of emotions within the prison's walls mirrored the intricate dance of secrecy and risk that defined our unconventional relationship.

Still, I endeavoured to maintain trust, hoping that Jane wasn't playing a double game. Technically, we didn't have anything, but I would have hated to know that she had a girlfriend while confiding in me; it just wouldn't have been right.

A revelation came when Jarrah, my crazy cellmate, eagerly shared news about her cousin, who happened to be Jane's girlfriend working in the prison's hair salon. "Jane has a girlfriend, you dirty faggot. Why don't you try and get one that doesn't have a girlfriend already?" The revelation struck a nerve, triggering a mix of anger and hurt. I had asked and given Jane many opportunities, and she had denied everything.

Jarrah, thrilled with her new dirt, spilled the beans about Jane's secret relationship, complete with affectionate messages and voice notes. The proof was undeniable. I was left grappling with the emotional fallout. Jarrah told me to stay quiet, fearing that confronting Jane might lead to trouble. But I couldn't hold back and confronted Jane, demanding the truth. Jane continued to deny everything, saying the evidence was just the product of an obsessed person. The frustration was unbearable. Here I was, staring at undeniable proof, while Jane kept lying to my face.

Things got real when Lisa, Jane's girlfriend, confronted me during a medical appointment. "Who the fuck do you think you are? Talking to MY girlfriend? Fuck you and find your own fucking girlfriend." She slapped me and told me to stay away.

Shocked and confused, the painful reality hit me hard. I was just a pawn in a drama I knew nothing about. I distanced myself from Jane, determined to move on. Despite her attempts to reach out, leaving messages and notes, I resisted. Her apologies and explanations felt hollow, drowned out by the weight of betrayal.

Curiosity got the better of me, and I finally confronted Jane again.

"Jane, can I ask you something? Please be honest. I won't get angry, but I'm really confused right now. You're free to have a girlfriend and all, but you told me you didn't. Is it true you have one in prison, another inmate?"

"Of course it isn't true. Remember I told you women would do this? I warned you!"

Her excuses shifted from blaming Lisa's obsession to expressing regret and a longing to reconcile. I remained firm, unwilling to accept her lies. As the drama unfolded, Jarrah told me Lisa was blaming me for Jane's alleged breakup. I refused to take responsibility, knowing the lies and deceit weren't my fault.

The Unlikely Alliance
April 2018

In the months after the birthday raid, a strange metamorphosis occurred within the prison walls. Captain Dave, the once-hated enforcer, seemed to shift his stance toward me. I didn't understand why, what had I done that made me stand out? It was an unexpected turn of events, one that left me perplexed as to his motives and the implications it carried. I was already studying a nursing degree from within the walls and would often get called out for exams and practical sessions, but this was a whole new level.

Why was he being nice to me?

The Captain, who had previously exhibited nothing but disdain for our high-security Patio, began frequenting it more often. I wondered if he was trying to make people too scared to have phones or whatever it is they would do in their cells. His presence, once a harbinger of trouble, now signalled a peculiar interest. He sought me out during these visits, engaging in small talk that only deepened the mystery of this new-found connection. He would always ask how my studies were going, talk about my case, talk about the educational system that the prison had. While he extended an air of camaraderie, the alliance he seemed to be forging stirred tensions among my fellow inmates. They interpreted our interactions as collusion, a perception I struggled to dispel. My inmates thought I may have been snitching on them, or causing some commotion but it wasn't the case at all.

The truth was, I maintained a level of respect for Captain Dave, not out of allegiance but out of a pragmatic understanding. In the confined, unpredictable world of prison, showing defiance to authority only invited trouble. Unlike some in Patio Seven, I recognized the boundaries of control within these walls – our actions were the only realm we governed.

There were only consequences for breaking the rules, hence why we were all here to begin with. Captain Dave's unexpected overtures didn't stop at casual conversations. Several times, he summoned me from the Patio to the Command Centre, presenting me with tasks that further blurred the lines between inmate and authority figure. I found myself assisting guards with English homework, translating for newcomers, and, most intriguingly, acting as a liaison for foreign ambassadors. One particular occasion stood out. A delegation from China and Japan arrived to study the Colombian prison system. The Captain, eager to present a polished image, orchestrated a facade of order and prosperity. I spent nearly a whole day translating, subtly veering from the dictated script to offer a more comprehensive view.

Despite the orchestrated display, I couldn't help but shed light on the flaws and corruption within INPEC – Colombia's prison correctional system. These guards were fresh out of school and into a job that they knew they could easily exploit, asking for money to smuggle in mobile phones, drugs – even weapons. They would turn a blind eye on guards raping inmates or being accomplices in other inmates raping and assaulting us. It's very unfortunate that these guards live off of the money they make off the inmates. One aspect I highlighted, however, was the abundance of opportunities for inmates to earn sentence reductions. This was true and I loved that there were so many opportunities, it was also a huge distraction for anyone who worked. I emphasized the various vocational programs – hairdressing, nail salons, teddy bear making, and more – that provided a pathway to shave time off their sentences. The discount system, effective in its redistribution of opportunities, allowed those nearing release to benefit from the available programs.

These interactions not only showcased my language skills but also provided a glimpse into the potential for personal growth within the confines of the prison. I relished the chance to meet new people, break the monotony of prison life, and, unbeknownst to the Captain, build a foundation for my future aspirations. However, this alliance with Captain Dave proved short-lived. Within three months, his actions would catch up with him. Violations of human rights, denial of medical appointments, reduced food rations, and mistreatment during searches painted a grim picture. His reign ended abruptly, exposing the dark underbelly of his leadership. The perceived friendship between us, which had already stirred suspicion, now brought its own set of challenges. Rumours circulated, accusing me of being an informant or secretly colluding with the Captain. In truth, my motives were far simpler – I aimed to leverage these opportunities to secure a role as an English teacher in the prison school, a small step towards reclaiming a sense of purpose within the confines of my sentence. I hadn't been interested in anything else other than that, it was one thing to be studying and advance towards a career in nursing that I wasn't sure I was even going to use but I wanted to teach English, and the only way to get my foot in the door, was to have the right connection.

El buen Pastor corridor. "The calm before the lock down."

Prison patio.

The dreaded prison blue door that haunted me.

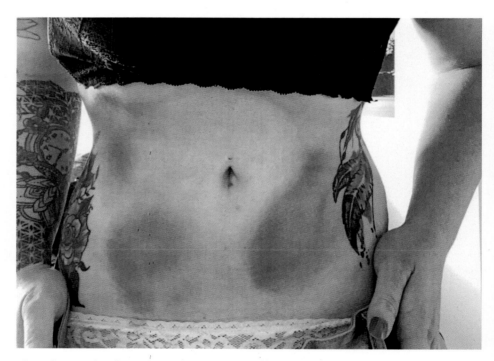

The aftermath of another prison beating.

Crystal and me on New Year's Eve 2019 our last get together before I was released. This was in our cell we called home.

My arm tattoo represents the time it was when I was released from prison – 11.29 pm.

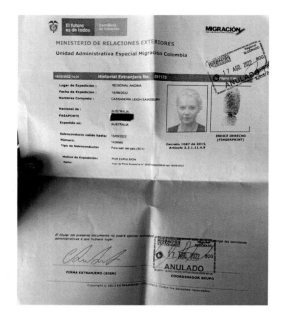

Document of legality in Colombia. End of sentence from Migration. 16 August 2022.

Three ex-inmates and me at a get together in Aug 2021 Bogotá.

Andi and me at the Foundation Event for Second Chance Foundation. I was managing the event. February 2022.

Andi and me with of Andi's friends, 2021.

Meeting with Foundacion owner for ex-convicts, organising free English courses in 2021.

Crystal, Dako, Jei and me – my Bogotá friend group. Motorbike ride up to the viewing point of Bogotá, 2021.

Me and Layla – my emotional support when I got out of prison, she is my everything, 2020.

Post-PTSD body – becoming proud of myself. September 2023.

Getting to know each other, 2021

Tato and me in a small town while travelling in Colombia, July 2021.

Wedding Day, 19 March 2022

A Punch from the Unexpected
April 2018

Within the confines of the prison Patio, an arena pulsating with its own rhythm of conflicts and alliances, tensions simmered beneath the surface. It wasn't unusual for women to clash, I mean, just imagine hundreds of hormonal, depressed, angry women all stuck together – would you go crazy and explode? The collision of disparate lives within this confined space often led to eruptions, and that day was no exception. Despite my innate aversion to discord, a peacekeeper by nature, I had never ever been violent, the volatile environment of the prison rendered such aspirations implausible. Living in close quarters with a diverse array of women heightened the probability of confrontations, and on that particular afternoon, the air crackled with an unexpected hostility.

Lunch had come and gone, leaving behind a deceptive calm, this was usually the time most of us would either sit and read, write or knit and others sleep, that belied the tempest brewing beneath the surface. The tranquillity that usually accompanied the afternoon hours was shattered when a dispute erupted between Jan, Lily, and an elderly inmate. Now, we already know that Jan had a bit of a crazy side to her – no one had forgotten her outburst with Emily. Lily was her twin sister and let's just say, she was no better than Jan. The scene unfolded like a discordant symphony, and I, against my better judgment, chose to step into the maelstrom.

The elderly lady, driven by a surge of animosity, targeted Jan and Lily with unwarranted aggression. My Spanish wasn't perfect and even on a good day I couldn't understand Lily and Jan properly. In a feeble attempt to diffuse the situation, I positioned myself between the warring parties, an ill-fated mediator caught in the crossfire. The decision to intervene proved misguided, as the elderly woman, with surprising vigour, launched a punch directly at my face and followed it up with a second punch.

What!

A collective gasp echoed through the Patio as time momentarily froze. Stunned by the unexpected blow, I stood in silent disbelief. A 74-year-old woman had just punched me, not once but twice while I attempted to lend a helping hand.

What the actual fuck!

The irony of the situation lingered in the air, thick with a mixture of shock and incredulity. Everyone stood there, watching me, wondering how I would react, wondering if this would be the day I would retaliate. Regaining composure, I uttered, "Well, that's the last time I try to help anyone. What a joke," before retreating from the chaotic tableau. The force of the punch reverberated through my jaw, leaving me both physically and emotionally bruised. The mirror, a reluctant witness to the incident, reflected the immediate aftermath – a face already bearing the tell-tale signs of a bruise. It wasn't unexpected. My skin had always been prone to quickly displaying the aftermath of physical encounters. In the solitude that followed, I grappled with the surreal nature of the situation. A senior citizen had inadvertently become the assailant, and I, the unintended victim.

Taking refuge in a painkiller and deciding to focus on my studies, the solace of a book, I mulled over the bizarre turn of events. The irony of being assaulted while attempting to mediate a dispute wasn't lost on me. The incident, though peculiar, resonated with a deeper frustration. All I had sought was to extend a helping hand, yet I found myself nursing the consequences of that goodwill. At the time, the incident failed to evoke amusement. Instead, it fuelled irritation, a testament to the unpredictability of prison life. When recounting the episode to my mother, I downplayed the severity, emphasizing the accidental nature of the blow.

"I got punched in the face by an old lady. Not once, but twice."

"Why? What did you do to her?" Mum questioned.

"I didn't do anything to her. I was just trying to help. Why would you just assume that I did something to an old lady? She's 74, Mum, I'm not going to fight a 74-year-old."

Cellmate or Hellmate?
June 2018

Jarrah, in her fifties, short, dark skinned arrived with a peculiar backstory. Fresh from a liposuction surgery, she didn't look it. She was still quite big. She was placed under scrutiny to ensure the completion of her post-surgery massages. The guard, with an air of nonchalance, informed me that she would be my new cellmate. As I looked at Jarrah, a strange sense of unease crept over me. There was something about her that didn't sit right, and I fought against the instinct to judge too quickly. Who was I to judge right? Setting aside my reservations, I assisted her in settling into the cell, providing her with the personal hygiene products she lacked, it wasn't like I had heaps to spare, but one thing I had learnt here, is that we can all use some help. It was an act of solidarity, reminiscent of the kindness I had once received in this unforgiving environment. My friend suggested we invite Jarrah to join our mealtime gatherings – an invitation-only affair in the prison hierarchy. No one would sit where they weren't invited. Despite my reservations, I agreed, attempting to ignore the uneasy feeling she stirred within me.

To my surprise, Johana, a high-profile figure known for her connections to a notorious cartel, sought out Jarrah. Something else that added to my uneasy feeling. Their lengthy conversation behind the cell door raised my concerns.

Johana later warned me about Jarrah:

"Cassandra, I don't mean to scare you, but she isn't a good person, be careful. She worked with my brother, and she was his right-hand man and she snitched. She tried to have him killed. Cassandra, you're not safe with her. Don't trust her."

As night fell and the cell door locked, the reality of sharing space with this enigmatic woman sank in. My anticipation for a peaceful night waned; Jarrah's presence hinted at impending turmoil. She, however, seemed desperate and vulnerable, shedding tears over her inability to contact her family. Something that I could relate too, how could I judge her if I didn't know her. Her pleas for assistance with a phone call raised an internal conflict within me. Should I trust her?

Reluctantly, I allowed her to use my phone, but not without setting strict conditions. The limited time frame was non-negotiable, a precaution against potential misuse. As she made calls to her family, requesting an array of personal items, I couldn't help but wonder if she comprehended the gravity of our surroundings.

The uneasy truce shattered when she made a pointed remark about my supposed involvement with a guard, insinuating an illicit connection.

"I saw your message to a guard. Johana told me you are a guard's girlfriend. You better not fucking snitch on me, bitch."

What the fuck just happened?

"I am no one's girlfriend. You haven't even been around me for two hours to know anything, I don't snitch and I'm not the guard's girlfriend. Understood?"

The strained conversation reached an abrupt halt, signalling the beginning of what promised to be an uneasy coexistence.

As the night settled over our confined space, I braced myself for the challenges that sharing a cell with Jarrah would undoubtedly bring. Of course, I got put with a psychopath.

Of course.

The origin of her animosity would remain a mystery to me. Perhaps it was resentment from being placed under my supposed guardianship upon entering the prison. Or maybe it was something deeper, linked to her troubled past or familial connections.

Jarrah's hostility manifested most prominently in her homophobic slurs and derogatory comments about my sexual orientation. Her words were sharp, designed to cut deep, and her disdain for me seemed to intensify with each passing day.

"You're a faggot, diseased and sick. God does not need someone like you here. I was sent here to take care of sick people like you and stay the fuck away from me, don't even look at me."

I reacted:

"Please don't come in here, pretending to know me or anything about me. If I'm gay, that's my business. It's not like I'm interested in you. Get over yourself. You're not every gay woman's desire, or any. Yuck."

It wasn't often that I would need to react, I would ignore her but nearly every second day being told that I'm a sick faggot it was exhausting and hard to deal with.

The situation later escalated rapidly, reaching a point where her threats took on a sinister tone.

"I will end you. Do you not know who I am and who I work with? You won't ever leave this place. I will pay to make sure you can never leave. You're a dirty faggot who deserves to rot in this place and I will make sure. God has sent me to take care of you."

Other days it would be: "The day you step out of prison, you're a dead woman. I will have my men waiting for you. They will take you and torture you until you beg them to end your pathetic life."

The catalyst for a full-blown confrontation came when Jarrah, in her relentless pursuit of making my life unbearable, spread malicious rumours about me throughout the prison. She had told everyone that I was snitching on them, that I had planned with Jane to get everyone's phones taken, that I was organising raids in her patios. The once-friendly faces turned cold, and the curious glances turned accusatory. The insidious nature of her lies cast me into a state of isolation, a pariah within the very community I had sought solace in. Confrontation became inevitable.

One day, things changed, and it was no longer just words. Jarrah, driven by a violent rage, showed her true psychotic side, attacked me within the confines of our cell. I wasn't sure what had actually upset her enough to do this, but it wasn't entirely unexpected.

But it was still a surprise.

Pushing me against the wall, elbow lodged in under my neck, leaving me no way to defend myself while gasping for air, she began kicking, punching, chocking me.

I dropped to the ground; she sent two full-bodied kicks into my stomach. As blows were exchanged, another inmate intervened, pulling her away. Blood trickled from my mouth, a testament to the brutality of the encounter. Jarrah, undeterred, continued her barrage of insults even in the aftermath.

"See! You're fucking miiiiiinne!!! Just wait until no one is around to help you. You won't leave this place alive!"

Shadows of Surveillance
June 2018

Glancing outside my cell, I was confronted by the ominous presence of the INPEC Special Ops crew. Panic gripped me; my phone, an illicit lifeline, lay exposed on my bed. Shit. I couldn't get caught with this. In a frenzied attempt to conceal it, I stashed the device in a black bag, disguising it among bags of cereal knowing that it would be no match against the special operations. It was impossible that they wouldn't find it. The impending cell search was imminent, and I needed to act swiftly.

Jarrah looked completely unfazed by what was outside. Did she know something?

The guard, seemingly complicit in the unfolding drama, knocked on each cell door, providing a momentary reprieve before the inevitable intrusion. It was an odd act of kindness that she had done. We were herded outside, made to wait in the cold, hands above out heads, uncertain about the nature of this Special Ops search. The very mention of 'Special Ops' hinted at a severity that left us uneasy. This patio had received some nasty searches, but never before from Special Ops.

Once back in our cells, one by one, we were each summoned, invasive strip searches and metal detector scans ensued, each inmate subjected to scrutiny. You were told to strip naked, squat down and cough. Once they were happy, we were sent out with our clothes in hand, forced to get dressed in front of everyone. The Special Ops crew, armed with advanced technology, targeted specific areas where contraband might be concealed. It became apparent that they suspected either fraud or illicit activities orchestrated from within, which seemed to go on more often than not.

As the minutes turned into agonizing hours, the uncertainty of the situation loomed large. I waited for my phone to be found, I knew the hiding spot hadn't been good enough. Phones, USBs, CDs, and even a DVD player were unearthed – a motley collection of contraband that puzzled even seasoned inmates. Who had a DVD player? The guards, expecting a day off as a reward for each find, displayed a mix of anticipation and disappointment as the haul was revealed. Amidst the chaos, I couldn't shake the fear that my concealed phone would be discovered. The longer the search persisted, the more apprehensive I became. To my relief, I was not called out for the contraband, leaving me to wonder whether they had overlooked it or if it had been stolen during the search. This too has happened. Guards would sometimes pocket any phones and resell them inside the prison to other inmates. Good business I guess.

Jarrah, my enigmatic cellmate, maintained a watchful gaze throughout the ordeal. She was behind this, she had to be. Suspicion lingered between us, the unspoken question of whether the other had emerged unscathed in the search. As we returned to our cell, the aftermath of the Special Ops operation left its mark – a shattered pot plant, broken drainpipes, and a palpable sense of violation. Everyone's items all thrown out into the patio. They were all mixed together. In the following days, the prison echoed with whispers of lost phones and confiscated contraband. Patio Seven always seemed to be the topic of conversation when it came to the searches that were done. The destruction left in the wake of the search prompted a collective decision to transform the Patio into a 'spotless haven'. Yet, beneath the surface of this collective effort, a sense of caution prevailed. In the solitude of my cell, I dared to check the concealed phone. It was still there. I had been lucky. I hadn't yet lost a phone; I knew that one day I would. It was impossible that I would last years with the same one. The day I lose my phone, I would have to learn to live without one.

The Night of the Blade
July 2018

Jarrah and I had managed to ignore each other most of the time, yet I knew she was waiting for the perfect moment, just the right guard to be on shift.

The recent confrontations and Jarrah's escalating threats had transformed our cell into a battlefield, and I found myself on the front lines, bracing for an attack that seemed inevitable, she had me on edge, every night. I couldn't sleep, I was in a constant state of stress. This woman was out to kill me.

The metallic clinks of distant gates and the muffled sounds of nocturnal activities served as a disconcerting lullaby. The guard had left. It was often that the guards would leave us unattended.

Suddenly, the silence shattered like fragile glass. It was Jarrah, her eyes ablaze with a manic fervour that sent chills down my spine. In her hand gleamed a makeshift weapon – a crude, serrated knife fashioned from materials scavenged within the prison's hidden corners. She had gotten her hands on a knitting needle, yet this one had a filed edge on it. The world seemed to warp around me as she lunged forward, her every movement a distorted dance of malice. Instinct propelled me backward, but the confined quarters offered no escape. The narrow bed became both my refuge and my prison as I desperately sought a means of defence.

Jarrah's attacks were relentless, fuelled by a fury that seemed to transcend reason. The blade danced perilously close. Fear and adrenaline intermingled in me, heightening my senses to a surreal degree. The metallic tang of blood lingered in the air. I felt the sudden surge of pain each time the needle was pushed into my abdomen, legs and arms. I couldn't stop her, she was crazy, and I had no strength, I was certain that this was the end, I wouldn't survive this attack. I closed my eyes. I remember wanting it to end, for the pain to go ...

I fought for survival, my body moving on instinct, evading the frenzied strikes with a mixture of agility and sheer luck.

The sounds of the struggle reverberated through the prison walls, a discordant symphony of chaos. Shouts and echoes cascaded through the corridor, an eerie accompaniment to the life-and-death struggle transpiring within the cell. Guards, alerted, approached cautiously, unsure of the scene that awaited them. As the seconds stretched into an eternity, the tide began to turn. Jarrah, consumed by her manic assault, failed to notice the approaching guards. The cell door burst open, flooding the room with blinding light. I wasn't capable of keeping my eyes open. The guards, faces etched with a mix of urgency and apprehension, swiftly intervened, separating us in the nick of time. Bloodied and battered, I was ushered out of the cell, leaving behind the stifling confines that had become a crucible of violence. I held my abdomen. Jarrah, subdued and overpowered, was led away in handcuffs, her crazed protests fading into the distance:

"She started it. She came after me!"

"Crazy bitch!" I wanted to respond but I had no voice, no words.

Bloodstains adorned the floor.

Jarrah had managed to stab me at least three or four times.

Five times.

One in my forearm. Three times in my stomach. Once in my thigh. The stab wounds weren't huge due to the size of the weapon, but they were two to four centimetres deep.

The Unforgiving Dentist's Chair
August 2018

The aftermath of the violent encounter with Jarrah left me physically and emotionally bruised.

It was impossible to believe that even after her crazy outbreak, we weren't separated. I wondered what she had told the guards that night. The echoes of that night lingered in my bones, a constant reminder of the perilous dance I had engaged in to preserve my existence within the prison's unforgiving walls. In the days following the incident, the prison's response was swift and unyielding. The guards, clad in stoic indifference, escorted me through the corridors to a destination unknown. I asked continuously where I was going, and one merely responded – "Check-up."

Eventually, we arrived at a nondescript door bearing a small, weathered sign that read 'Dentistry'. Dread settled in the pit of my stomach like an anchor as the door swung open, revealing a stark, clinical room. A dentist's chair stood at the centre. I hadn't asked to go to the dentist. In fact, I didn't need the dentist. I didn't know what was going on. Why was I here? I tried to question the guards, but they didn't respond.

Seated in the dentist's chair, I was acutely aware of the sterile environment surrounding me. The dentist, a figure shrouded in a sterile mask and gloves, peered over me with a clinical detachment that sent shivers down my spine. Without a word, the procedure began. The dentist's actions were methodical, deliberate. It wasn't merely about dental hygiene; it was an act of retribution.

The pain was excruciating, a symphony of agony that resonated through every nerve. I tried to get up and push the dentist's hand away, but the guards held down my arms. I moved my head from side to side trying to get away from the drill in my tooth, but someone now held my head in place. Tears began to fall down my cheeks, the dentist's motions seemed choreographed, as if extracting a pound of flesh for every ounce of rebellion. The metallic taste of blood seeped into my mouth, a cruel reminder of the violence that had transpired in the cell.

I was being tortured.

It was a macabre form of discipline, a reminder of the prison's absolute authority. My pleas for mercy fell on deaf ears, drowned out by the mechanical drone of the drill. As the minutes stretched into an eternity, I felt the insides of my teeth being hollowed out. The dentist's impassive expression betrayed no hint of remorse, a job done.

When the ordeal finally concluded, I was left battered, broken, and transformed. The dentist, satisfied with the macabre performance, ushered me out of the sterile chamber, leaving me to grapple with the physical and emotional remnants of the punishment.

What the hell had just happened?

Was that even legal?

Could they *do* that?

"Think twice about telling someone Cassandra and you'll be back here before you can say 'help'." The guard whispered to me. Jarrah was behind this.

Fucking bitch.

What else was she capable of doing to me? I didn't want to find out, not anymore.

As I staggered back to the familiar confines of my cell, the pain in my mouth mirrored the ache of my stab wounds and my empty thoughts, a silent reminder that within these walls, resistance came at a cost, and justice bore the face of a merciless dentist.

The corruption inside the prison. It's one thing to hear about it, and one thing to live it. Guards would cover each other's back while they would pick their next victim. You weren't safe anywhere in the prison, and the rules state that no men can enter into a women's prison, but they do, they have others vouch for them and this is how the next tormenting moment of my life started.

In Patio Seven, we had another full-on search after my stabbing incident, they were coming in to find any possible items that could be used as a weapon. I was still quite crippled from the stabbing, and I couldn't react or anything else quite well, and to be honest it wasn't something that I thought I had to be worried about until this day. I knew that I already had issues with a male guard who tended to be there whenever we would have to do full body searches and today wasn't an exception. We were being called into closed cells for strip searches, to make sure we had no hidden weapons, I believe it was only women guards doing the search, like it should be. But you wouldn't believe my shock when I walked into the cell. They had the male guard. I looked back at the door, wondering how long it would take for me to get away if I needed too. This man had a sick and twisted look in his eye, he's one of those people that make you feel uncomfortable with just one look.

The guard demanded I face the wall, hands up and that was a struggle, I placed them where I could and I felt him uncomfortably close, I could hear his agitated breathing, I tried to block it out and find out a way to make this search go by quickly. The door was open, I was sure nothing could happen until I heard him yell, door. And I saw it being closed.

I hoped this wasn't what I thought it was, but ...

The guard yelled at me to strip to my underwear for the search. I shook my head, there was no need, I didn't have anything, although at this point, I wish I did. I turned and faced him and said "No".

I walk to the door, and I tried to push it open, but it wouldn't budge, it was locked. He repeated, pants and jumper off – I did as I was told and again, he told me to face the wall hands up, I did as I was told, I knew what was coming and I wanted to stop it but how? How do you stop this? He did the search and I thought it was over, he was respectful, until he wasn't. I felt sudden pressure against my upper back, and I couldn't move, he plastered me against the wall, and I was limited because of my wounds. I felt him pushing my legs apart and pulling my underwear to one side, and I felt the pain of him forcing something inside me. It was hurting so much, again I could hear his breathing, I remembered all the pain and suffering I had endured up until now and I didn't want to be a victim anymore. Ignoring my pain I managed to lower my arms and elbow him and it forced him to stumble back. I ran to the cell door and started to bang at it like crazy, someone had to hear me. Sudden pain made me scream. He pulled me back with a fistfull of hair and he pushed me to the floor as he tried to unzip his uniform, I tried to squirm away, I was crying I didn't want this, and then I heard running and a guard suddenly opened the cell door, he told the male guard to get up and I scrambled to my feet, I ran, some of my stitches had opened and I was bleeding everywhere. I went to my cell, no one came to see me and when I tried to report the guard, I was told that I had *provoked* him, that it was *my* fault and that they would make sure that it would affect my good behaviour if I tried to report this anywhere else.

This place of helplessness was a place all too familiar, I found myself hurting all over, I had a crazy cellmate who tried to kill me, and a lifetime of trauma, I knew that tonight the nightmares would come back but tomorrow would be another day. I would get through this night as I had done with so many others.

The Games of Lenny's Vengeance
October 2018

Life within the confines of the prison's Patios were a tangled web of alliances and animosities, a delicate dance where every step could lead to unforeseen consequences. It was hard, no one ever talks about how hard the people are, not the actual life. If I thought Jarrah was a formidable adversary, Lenny proved to be an entirely different breed – the kind of adversary who thrived on manipulation, money, and an insatiable desire for control. It seems, no matter what, someone always hated me in here.

Lenny was someone who I had avoided from Day One. She was bad news. Tall, long black hair, extremely transformed face due to surgery and fillers. She was scary to look at. Her liposuction was quickly wearing off.

My inmates naturally took to me, I wasn't mean to anyone, I enjoyed trying to teach my peers English.

So, Lenny's enmity toward me, birthed from some twisted sense of entitlement, manifested in a relentless pursuit to tarnish my reputation within the Patio's social fabric. It was a vendetta fuelled by resentment, a venomous cocktail that bubbled beneath the surface, waiting for the opportune moment to strike. She liked being the centre of attention and unfortunately, she wasn't.

Lenny's narrative cast me as a privileged interloper, an outsider who hadn't paid the supposed entry fee.

"She paid to get into this patio. She isn't meant to be here. She isn't under threat from anyone. She made a deal with Mayor Nancy to snitch on us."

Despite her persistent attempts to tarnish my standing, I held my ground. I refused to succumb to the chaos she tried to instigate, one bully was enough for me, Jarrah's twisted forms of harassment and torture were teaching me to hold my ground and be strong.

But Lenny was just getting started.

Johanna's request for personal training became the catalyst for Lenny's descent into avarice-fuelled madness. When she learned of our sessions, jealousy ignited within her like a fever. In Lenny's world, apparently money had always been the solution, the universal lubricant that could smooth any transaction. She was 'rich'. This meant, in her eyes nothing was out of reach even 'friendships'. However, I was an immovable force, immune to the allure of her ill-gotten wealth. Money wasn't a selling point for me. There wasn't enough money in the world that would want me to have her as an 'ally'.

Lenny wanted me to be her personal trainer too, offering double what Johana paid. But she was unable to comprehend a world where her wealth held no sway. She didn't realise that Johana wasn't paying me to train her. It was something that I was doing because I enjoyed it. So I declined, and in that moment, Lenny's animosity escalated.

Another orchestrated raid on my cell revealed her desperation, a ploy to tarnish my image, to expose me as a rule-breaker. Yet, the guards found nothing, and I emerged unscathed. The victory, however, was short-lived.

Lenny, unrelenting in her pursuit of vengeance, resorted to the lowest form of betrayal – snitching. She pointed accusatory fingers, directing the guards to the supposed location of my concealed contraband. Yet, with snitching on me, she had just made a whole patio furious with her.

As the guards combed through my belongings, I felt a surge of anger, an indignant fire that threatened to consume me. But the universe, in its twisted sense of justice, intervened. My phone was discovered, but not in my possession, saving me from the repercussions of a bad behaviour report. However the phone was confiscated, the only thing that made me feel a little better was that I hadn't received a bad behaviour report because it hadn't been found with me, meaning Lenny still didn't get what she wanted.

Undeterred by her failure, Lenny approached with a malicious glee, taunting me with her victory. "How are you going to talk to your family now huh? Do you want me to help you get a phone? Sorry, but I won't help you." Yet, her triumph was short-lived.

Her comment actually made me smile.

I turned and replied:

"Oh Lenny, if you think your money will get people to actually like you, you're wrong. You will never have any real friends. You're pathetic, just like your murder money."

She threw a punch. She managed to hit my nose and blood spilled – a futile attempt to break my spirit. But the laughter that escaped my lips in that moment was a testament to my resilience. I didn't have to retaliate; I wouldn't go down to her level. The guard's refusal to indulge in her theatrics delivered a blow to Lenny's inflated ego, exposing her as the architect of her own downfall. The games of vengeance she played were a mere sideshow in the grander theatre of prison life.

Every day I was learning to be stronger, to stand up for myself. The games of Lenny's vengeance were mere echoes in the vast expanse of my prison existence, fading into insignificance in the face of a more profound struggle for survival. I didn't know how I had managed to survive so much and still keep going, but I would. This was my living proof, that I could survive it all.

Into the Depths of Patio Six
November 2018

As the sergeant delivered the abrupt news of my relocation, I found myself thrust into a whirlwind of uncertainty yet again. The abrupt packing, the unfamiliarity of what lay ahead, and the tears that threatened to spill ....

Patio Seven, with all its complexities and conflicts, was suddenly a thing of the past. Lenny, Jarrah and a part of myself were left in that patio. Moving forward was the only way out of this place.

The sergeant, sympathetic to my predicament, offered a quiet apology and insight into the power plays at the heart of my sudden relocation.

"I'm sorry Cassandra, but you'll be better here. No nasty women in here, and you will have more freedom, you will see. This isn't a bad thing, even though it might seem like it is." I nodded, she was right, everything happens for reason. I had to embrace change.

The influence of money, the currency of power within the prison's walls, had orchestrated my departure. Lenny, with her wealth as her weapon, had wielded it.

The transition into Cell 23 of Patio Six marked a descent into an environment that defied the very essence of humane living.

The first jarring revelation was the absence of a bed. No concrete bunk, no rudimentary sleeping platform – just an empty void space. Black mould grew on the walls, and a horrible smell hung around. The lady who accompanied me, seemingly nonchalant in the face of such conditions, offered a half-hearted explanation about bed frames fashioned from patio findings. Crates and pieces of wood were what everyone seemed to use in this patio. The stench of humidity permeated the air. The lady's casual mention of a water leak added a layer of despair to my already unsettled emotions. The cracks in the walls hinted at the structural neglect that defined this forsaken corner of the prison.

The dampness, like a persistent spectre, clung to every surface.

The absence of a bed, the oppressive humidity, and the ominous cracks in the walls were tangible manifestations of the dehumanization that prisoners endured.

I settled into the dismal reality of Cell 23. The night that followed was an exercise in endurance, tears silently mingling with the palpable dampness that clung to the air. It was a night spent grappling not only with the physical discomforts but also with the emotional toll of being relegated to a space that seemed designed to break the spirit.

It's Just Stress
17 November 2018

November 17 marked a day that would unravel a nightmare I never saw coming. The celebration of a new system granting inmates genuine graduation certificates was underway, a glimmer of achievement in the confined world we inhabited. Watching my students receive their diplomas, I felt a sense of pride in the difference I had made, oblivious to the impending storm that was about to engulf me. As the ceremony unfolded, an ominous sensation gripped me. Cold shivers sent tremors through my body, and a sudden fever seized me. What the hell was going on? The pain in my stomach was excruciating, a stark departure from the usual digestive discomfort I had endured in prison. I had been grappling with irritable bowel syndrome, navigating a treacherous terrain of dietary restrictions, but this was different – this was torment. I pushed through the discomfort for my students, I had to be there for them, they were so proud of themselves, and I wanted to be there. We had all worked hard for this!

The following day, my condition worsened. A dash to the toilet became a desperate race against the uncontrollable. Diarrhoea struck with unrelenting force, and I convinced myself it was a passing ailment, a consequence of something disagreeable I had eaten.

Days turned into weeks, and my feeble attempts to seek help from the prison medical staff were met with dismissive diagnoses of stress. "It's just stress dear. It's a stressful time for your internals." Bullshit. They attributed my deteriorating health to the approaching holiday season, a convenient excuse that denied the severity of my situation. My weight plummeted at an alarming rate. I shed 8 kg in the span of a week. I became a ghost of my former self. I was losing weight far too quickly. I feared that this was the end of me. I had survived crazy bitches yet at the end of the day, a damn tummy bug would be the end of me.

Visits to the medical facility yielded the same diagnosis – stress. They handed me pills, claiming they would curb the diarrhoea, but the remedy proved more malevolent than the ailment itself. The pills triggered a cascade of worsening symptoms, including relentless vomiting. The prison walls closed in on me as I endured a relentless assault on my body. Desperation drove me to explore alternative remedies from fellow inmates. An old lady suggested a concoction of hot Coca-Cola and bicarbonate soda promised relief from the relentless diarrhoea. While sitting on the toilet, the old lady handed me the drink and it was *absolutely disgusting*. Who would even think of these things? The vile brew failed to abate my suffering. My body continued its revolt, and I found myself in a vicious cycle of agony.

Then one night I collapsed on my way to the toilet. Awakening in the prison's emergency room, I discovered the depths of my degradation. I had become a mere wisp, weighing less than 50 kg. The haunting scent of impending death clung to me. It had taken just over a month for 30 kg to disappear and yet, the prison medic continued to say I was stressed. Bullshit! I knew it was something else, after all I was studying nursing, I mean I was no doctor, but I had more knowledge than they belittled me to think.

In late December, the embassy's intervention finally shattered the façade of medical neglect. Witnessing my emaciated state, the embassy representative was appalled. The dire reports provided by the prison were exposed as egregious lies. The prison had been registering that I was fine and had been properly attended and was on the mend to recovery. It was a turning point that initiated a semblance of urgency in my medical treatment. Despite the embassy's involvement, my suffering persisted. I was transferred to a hospital. Handcuffed to a hospital bed, I underwent a battery of tests, endured IV lines, and was force-fed in an attempt to restore my failing health. Days turned into an agonizing blur of sleeplessness, nausea, and the relentless cycle of vomiting and diarrhoea. The prison guards would neglect to take to me the toilet so I would shit myself at least two to three times a day. It was humiliating.

The hospital staff, perplexed by the enigma of my illness, injected me with special medications aimed at healing my battered intestines. It was a trial-and-error process that, against all odds, showed signs of progress. The medicine began to take effect, slowly but surely arresting the relentless onslaught on my body. Eleven excruciating days later, I emerged from the hospital, a frail spectre of the person I once was.

A Ray of Opportunity
December 2018

Patio Six, with its dreary confines, ironically opened a door to unexpected possibilities. The sergeant had been right, maybe there was more freedom here. Amid the dilapidated cells and the lingering scent of despair, a short, enthusiastic lady approached me with an unexpected proposition. She asked if I would be interested in becoming an English teacher for fellow inmates in the school that I had once visited. The prospect intrigued me, and as the details unfolded, it became apparent that this could be more than just a new role – it was a chance to alter the course of my time behind bars. Studying nursing had kept me busy, and a part of me urged to not be stuck in a Patio anymore, I wasn't the same scared girl I was when I arrived, I felt like I could handle anything. I mean, shit, how many beatings, stabbings had I had?

The lady emphasized that my proficiency in Spanish, albeit basic, would be sufficient for communication, as the classes themselves would be conducted in English. I met her surprise at my new-found Spanish abilities with a sense of pride. Yes, I could communicate, and yes, I was ready to embark on this unanticipated journey as the first native English teacher in this corner of the prison. I had done well to manage this language.

While the thought of interacting with inmates who might have been part of past conflicts instilled a tinge of apprehension, I recognized the growth within myself. This was an opportunity to not only impart knowledge but to defy the shadow of fear that had loomed over me in previous encounters. The decision to embrace this role was not solely a means of gaining time off my sentence; it was a conscious choice to contribute positively to the lives of those confined alongside me.

I envisioned a classroom where language became a bridge, connecting individuals with aspirations beyond the prison walls. Education, I believed, was the most potent tool for transformation, and here I was, offered the chance to wield it. A chance to do more.

As the days unfolded and the classes began, I threw myself into the task with unwavering dedication. The dynamics of the Patio started to shift. I found solace in the act of teaching, and the gratitude reflected in the eyes of my students became a beacon of hope in the midst of adversity. Although I had previously taught English to my inmates it was never in a school. It wasn't recognised as an official job or discount. This is definitely something new now. I would now have my own classroom although I would be out and about with the very same people who had once raped, assaulted and beat me up.

Reflecting on the tumultuous journey within these prison walls, I found myself standing at a crossroads of transformation. I've witnessed both the darker and brighter facets of humanity. There's a new-found maturity etched into the lines of my story, a willingness to confront my own errors and defects. I've learned that resilience isn't just a shield against external challenges; it's a force that shapes the self from within.

A Prison Event
December 2018

In the peculiar world of prison life, I found myself thrust into an unexpected opportunity: a Madonna tribute event featuring the classic 'La Isla Bonita.' I grew up with a Madonna-loving mom, so I knew a few tunes. But of all the songs they could pick, it had to be one I'd never heard! And let's not forget, I have a raging case of stage fright, and being the centre of attention is about as appealing to me as a toothache. As I reluctantly navigated through learning the song, the prison committee (yes, there's a committee for everything) assured me that I had a 'nice voice.' Frankly, I wasn't convinced, but hey, if they were happy, I was willing to roll with it. I agreed to this madness, but the catch was, since I didn't even know the song, cue a crash course in 'La Isla Bonita,' where the committee members, with glistening eyes, taught me the tune as if I were the Madonna prodigy they never knew they needed.

On the day of the grand event, I was led to the supposed iconic dress that Madonna wore in the music video. I was mentally preparing myself for a sassy red number, and what do I get? A long, black, sparkling concoction that could only be described as fashion's misguided attempt at a tragic romance novel cover. I looked like I was auditioning for a low-budget vampire movie rather than a Madonna tribute.

The makeup artist decided that orange was my colour. The fake mole resembled a misplaced chocolate chip. My hair, subjected to gallons of hairspray, was lifted into a side ponytail that screamed '80s aerobics gone wrong. I stared at myself in the mirror, wondering if Halloween had come early to prison this year.

As I made my way to lead the parade, dressed in an outfit that would make even Madonna cringe, I felt like I was on a collision course with the absurd. The heels were a size too big, the dress too long, and my stage presence was more awkward penguin than pop icon. And just when I thought it couldn't get worse, the dress snagged on a rogue nail, and I found myself doing a not-so-graceful faceplant. Awkward silence followed before erupting into laughter.

Yet amidst the chaos, something magical happened. Laughter became our shared language. I invited fellow inmates onto the stage, and suddenly, we weren't just prisoners; we were a bunch of misfits sharing a moment of sheer ridiculousness. The camaraderie, the shared glances of "Can you believe this?" – for a brief moment, we weren't defined by our mistakes or circumstances.

Creating Opportunities
January 2019

Becoming an English teacher in prison was a twist in my story I never saw coming. I never thought I would be a teacher. It became a profound chapter in my life. The barrage of questions from the inmates was like a flood, a deluge of curiosity that went beyond grammar and vocabulary. They wanted to know about me, my experiences, and later the intricacies of the English language that often go unnoticed by native speakers. I became the English teacher everyone wanted to have. I was listed the teacher with the most attendance in prison, which had never been seen before.

I was making a difference in the lives of these women.

The experience was challenging and rewarding. I anticipated that teaching would be a distraction, a way to make time move faster, but it turned out to be a journey of personal growth. Stepping into that role was like being the new kid on the block, with everyone eager to connect, to unravel every nuance of my existence.

Terrifying?

Absolutely.

Necessary?

Without a doubt.

Despite my past ordeals, I was fortunate not to encounter hostility among my students. The inmates were welcoming, and as I navigated this new role, I learned about the two-faced nature of prison dynamics. Gradually, I evolved into the 'cool teacher,' not because I was lax in my approach – far from it. My teaching style was interactive, engaging, and tailored to adults in a prison setting. They appreciated the break from the monotonous routine, and I found satisfaction in helping them grasp the complexities of the English language. Teaching English wasn't just about conjugating verbs and expanding vocabulary; it was about bridging gaps, breaking stereotypes. I studied my own language to be ready for any question thrown my way, a commitment I hadn't anticipated. In a place where authority often meant condescension, I made a conscious effort to treat everyone with respect and equality. Other teachers would often treat their students as if they were below them, I refused. I was there to uplift.

My approach won the respect of many inmates. I shattered their preconceptions, proving that education could be a collaborative journey. In a system where English learning was a luxury, I introduced an accredited course with an English institute called the Michigan Language School, but the course was more than just language – it was empowerment. Here in Colombia, English-speaking individuals were a rarity, often limited to those who could afford expensive courses, leaving many excluded. The idea of providing a genuine opportunity to learn English, free from exorbitant fees and indifferent institutes, was a game-changer. Teaching these women wasn't just about conjugating verbs or mastering tenses; it was about giving them a chance to rewrite their stories. They saw this as a once-in-a-lifetime opportunity, a lifeline that could lead them to a future beyond the prison walls. The admiration in their eyes mirrored the transformation within me, a testament to the resilience of the human spirit even in the most unlikely of places. I suddenly became the go-to person for everything in prison, judge petitions, legal documents, writing letters. I would always help anyone in any way I could because one thing I reminded myself from day one – don't ever feel sorry for yourself because there will always be someone who is going through something ten times worse.

A Brief Moment of Hope
April 2019

A proposal came from the Director of an English school outside the prison walls. This visionary Director saw the potential for a genuine English language course within the prison, leading to the coveted certification in English language skills – a treasure in the Colombian context. Excitement rippled through the prison corridors as the prospect of a *real* English school, complete with authentic textbooks, certified teachers, and the invaluable presence of a native speaker, loomed on the horizon. The proposal wasn't just about learning a language; it was about crafting a tangible skill that could be wielded as a powerful tool upon re-entry into society.

Eager to contribute to this transformative initiative, I took on the role of the coordinator for the English course. This meant more responsibilities, but it also afforded me the privilege of engaging with influential figures like the Director of the prison. The initial scepticism among prison staff lingered, a cautious reaction rooted in the history of projects starting strong and fizzling out in the face of challenges. Nevertheless, the Director and I forged an agreement: I would take charge of the course, and when needed, he would facilitate the logistical support. I envisioned this English course as a Rubik's cube of change – a puzzle that, once solved, would alter the trajectory of these women's lives. The goal was clear: equip the students with a skill that would transcend the prison walls, providing a tangible advantage in a society where such opportunities were hard to come by.

As the course kicked off, the enthusiasm among the women was palpable. Workbooks and textbooks were received like precious gifts, and their commitment to homework and class attendance exceeded expectations. Despite the additional workload, as I juggled the responsibilities of coordinator and teacher, I relished every moment. It was a labour of love, a testament to the transformative power of education. The ripple effect extended beyond the prison walls. The contacts I established through this endeavour might bear fruit, offering me a contract to work with the school upon my release. The prospect of a job waiting for me outside assuaged the fears of post-prison life, providing a new-found confidence in my ability to support myself.

However, the euphoria was short-lived. After three months, the course encountered insurmountable hurdles. The guards posed obstacles, restricting the women from attending classes and impeding the Director's efforts to bring in workbooks. A series of seemingly minor issues snowballed into a barrier that shattered our dreams. As I informed the women that the registered English course was coming to an end, a heavy sadness settled in the room. This opportunity, once seen as a lifeline, was slipping away. Undeterred, I tried to explore alternatives within the education program, but bureaucratic resistance prevailed. The powers-that-be deemed it a waste of resources, dismissing the transformative potential of education.

The heartbreak was profound. Yet, amidst the disappointment, a resolve ignited within me. I knew that upon my release, I had to channel every ounce of effort into making these opportunities accessible to the women who believed in the worth of such skills. The journey to bring education into the heart of incarceration was fraught with challenges, but the flame of possibility still flickered, ready to be reignited beyond the prison walls.

Prison Drink
July 2019

Two sisters, known for their outgoing demeanour, had extended an invitation to their makeshift celebration in my next-door cell mate's cramped quarters. This wasn't something I would generally join in on, but it was these moments that made me feel like a normal human being every now and again. You know, having a harmless drink and a chat in prison – totally normal.

Entering the cell, a peculiar aroma greeted me – an unsettling blend of liquorice. Suppressing my aversion to the smell, I found myself facing a shot glass filled with a mysterious clear liquid. It certainly didn't carry the fragrance of plain water, but in the spirit of adventure, I tossed it back. Heck yeah, I was fitting in, finally! The taste was nothing short of repulsive, a fiery journey down my throat that left me questioning the wisdom of my impulsive decision.

"Oh my god, this is disgusting!" I spat out in English, and everyone looked at me and burst out laughing – "watcho what?" They replied pretending to speak English. As the conversations unfolded, the sisters regaled the gathering with tales of their lives beyond the prison walls. Others chimed in, sharing snippets of their daily existence within the Patio. The shots continued to flow, and an entire two litre bottle of the enigmatic concoction vanished, though its effects on me were not immediately apparent. I maintained my composure, chatting with the eclectic group of women, oblivious to the impending storm brewing within.

The call of nature struck suddenly, and I stood up with the confidence of sobriety. Little did I know, the alcohol had done its work. Dizziness and a heavy head accompanied me to the toilet, but it wasn't until I felt the desperate need to vomit that the full force of my condition hit me. In my haste, I couldn't reach the toilet in time, and the passageway became an unfortunate canvas for my alcohol-induced masterpiece. The clean-up that ensued was a stark reminder of the unwelcome consequences of my brief foray into the world of prison revelry. The lingering smell of vomit served as a testament to the unexpected turn of events. As the others concluded their gathering, the realization dawned upon me – it was time for contada. Panic set in. I reeked of alcohol. Hastily changing my shirt and liberally applying deodorant, I wasn't sure if it would help, I hoped against hope that it would be enough to conceal the indiscretions of the night. Although I didn't have the right mindset for prison, I found everything somewhat funny.

The guards initiated their head count. I felt another wave of vomit approaching, and with a desperate rush, I made it to the toilet just in time. My cell mate, seemingly unfazed by my ordeal, inquired if I felt better.

"Never drinking that shit again," I declared.

I made my way back to my cell where I found an empty container. I don't know when, but I fell asleep with my head in the container.

The subsequent morning greeted me with a cricked neck and a throbbing headache. I could just imagine what the guards must have thought to do a routine check-up and see me out cold, head in a container. I smiled at the thought. The cold shower offered a semblance of relief, but a full day of English classes loomed ahead. It made me feel like a normal human on the outside, working through a hangover. I soldiered through, teaching with an uneasy stomach and a new-found appreciation for the simplicity of my mouldy mattress.

Shadows of Betrayal
August 2019

In the confined world of the prison Patio, where camaraderie could be a thin veneer for hidden agendas, I unwittingly walked into a web of obsession and deceit, yet again. Elly, a seemingly innocent student, had crossed the line between friendship and fixation. I should have recognized the signs sooner – the lingering glances, the persistent presence – but I believed, perhaps naively, that a genuine friendship could exist within these unforgiving walls. Months had passed since our initial interactions, and Elly's intensity had only grown. She shadowed my every move, a silent sentinel waiting for me to emerge from class. Invitations to lunch became increasingly insistent, culminating in a disturbing encounter within the confines of her cell.

As the door closed and she secured it, a sense of foreboding crept over me. Elly's gaze intensified, and her intentions became clear. She stated I really like you. I want to have something with you. I have a girlfriend, but I can keep a secret if you can." She wanted more than a friendship and she wanted a possession. I, however, could not reciprocate those feelings, and I made it clear it was not for me.

"Elly, I'm sorry, but this isn't happening. I'm not interested in you like that. I'm really sorry." I genuinely felt bad.

The rejection didn't sit well with Elly. In the confined space, her demeanour shifted from intense infatuation to a dark determination. Panic set in as she barred the door, a realization dawning that escape was not an option. Her demand for more became a demand I couldn't meet, and I recoiled as her desperation turned into aggression.

The struggle was fierce, a macabre dance in the dimly lit cell. She forced herself upon me forcing her hand down my pants and forcibly pushed her fingers inside me, I screamed in pain. The pain was searing as her nails dug into my flesh, and I felt the warmth of blood on my skin. In that moment, I grappled not only with physical agony but with the harsh reality of betrayal. It all happened so quickly, almost like she had been planning it precisely, it was scary. As I pushed her away, the room felt like a cage, a witness to the shattering of trust. Her bloodstained fingers and that sinister smile haunted me, leaving an indelible mark on my psyche. In the aftermath, I stood there, feeling stupid and vulnerable – betrayed not just by her, but by my own misplaced trust.

Regret washed over me like a tide. How had I allowed myself to become ensnared in yet another twisted game? The realization of my own vulnerability was a bitter pill to swallow, and I vowed, with a new-found fire, that this would not happen again. I confronted Elly, warning her of the consequences should she dare to come close to me again.

"I will have to tell the guards, Elly. You need to leave me alone. You're becoming very possessive and it's frightening. Don't make me report this."

I wasn't a fighter, but I wouldn't allow this to happen. She understood that I was serious as she backed away from me.

Kitchen Drama
September 2019

The prison hummed with its usual cacophony of voices and clanging metal.

The Health Department, a spectral force of cleanliness and order, materialized in the prison's midst for an unannounced inspection. The news rippled through the cellblocks like wildfire, spreading anticipation and dread in equal measure.

As the inspectors delved into the bowels of the prison, they unearthed a grisly find in the kitchen that left even the most hardened inmates aghast.

Decomposed meats.

Rotting dairy.

Fruits and vegetables that had long abandoned their prime adorned the prison's daily meals.

The kitchen was promptly declared a public health hazard. The shockwave reverberated through the prison's corridors as the news of the condemned kitchen reached every cell. The clanging of metal bars echoed a discordant tune, as the reality sank in – the kitchen was shut down until further notice.

Panic set in among the inmates, especially the women and children, as hunger became a real concern.

The prison, however, responded with callous indifference. A lockdown was enforced. The authorities seemed indifferent to the plight of those they confined. Requests for a solution to the meal crisis were met with bureaucratic inertia, leaving the inmates stranded. Prison shops were forcibly closed, we were told that they would not allow us any access to food until the lesson was learnt, *to be happy with what we were given or go without.*

Two days passed. The Director, an embodiment of unyielding authority, obstinately refused offers of food donations. In her eyes, the inmates deserved the agony they were enduring, the consequence of daring to expose the putrid underbelly of the prison's kitchen.

On the fourth day, fights erupted in the yards, fuelled not only by the gnawing hunger but by the despair that clung to the air like a suffocating mist. The guards, armed with batons and an authoritarian mandate, descended upon the tumultuous scene. A forced lockdown ensued, confining the inmates to their cells.

They locked us down, stopping us from moving and making us even hungrier. They didn't seem to care about our suffering.

Fights broke out in the yards. It wasn't just hunger that made people fight, but also the hopelessness that hung over everything. Guards came with batons and forced everyone back into their cells. I found myself entangled in a brawl, an unintended consequence of the chaos that unfolded around me. A commanding officer, a wielder of unchecked power, revelled in the opportunity to exert his dominance. His blows rained down upon me, an orchestration of pain conducted with sadistic precision. Amidst the blows, he leaned in with a sinister whisper, "Women shouldn't have a voice in my prison. Before you leave these walls, I'll ensure you learn a lesson you won't forget." I was on the cold, unforgiving floor, a casualty of a system that had forsaken its duty to protect. The hunger that clawed at my stomach was now eclipsed by the ache of a battered body and a spirit teetering on the edge of despair. In the prison's shadows, where cruelty reigned supreme, the fight for survival took on a new, ominous form.

After days of the inmates protesting and demanding basic human decency, the prison finally came to an agreement with the health department, and they had agreed to open the kitchen again on the condition that weekly inspections would be granted. This was never going to happen, we all knew that when the prison wants to hide something or keep people out, they could. Within the week, the food had returned to its regular state, mouldy and inedible.

On My Way Out
December 2019

The anticipation of freedom lingered in the air as I observed the bustling line-up outside the judge's office. Curiosity led me to investigate, and the person in charge informed me that my turn was next. Reluctantly, I approached, knowing all too well the repetitive nature of our conversations.

However, now, with nearly 60% of my sentence served, perhaps the dynamics had shifted.

As the last person wrapped up their discussion with the Judge, the office overseer ushered me in. The Judge eyed me with a subtle surprise, noting my new-found ability to converse in Spanish. It was a momentary departure from the impersonal exchanges we had shared before. I took a deep breath and began recounting the details of my sentence, the job offer awaiting me on the outside, my exemplary behaviour, and my participation in various prison events. To my astonishment, the Judge's demeanour softened, and she seemed genuinely attentive. I delved into the incident that led to my imprisonment, and a flicker of sadness crossed her face. It was an unexpected response from someone I had always considered a distant authority figure. She inquired about my current status, asking if I was still participating in educational programs. I affirmed, mindful of the ticking clock toward the 60% mark.

In a surprising turn, she encouraged me to start organizing the paperwork for my conditional release, a significant departure from her usual position. She instructed me to submit everything promptly, assuring me that she would evaluate the situation. Grateful for the unexpected support, I pledged to compile the necessary documents and expressed my appreciation. However, as I immersed myself in paperwork organization, a realization struck – I was two months shy of completing the required 60% portion of my sentence. A dilemma unfolded before me, questioning whether it was prudent to submit the paperwork prematurely. Despite the eagerness for freedom, I decided to wait. Prudence dictated my actions, ensuring that when the time came, my request would align with the legal prerequisites. It was a decision laden with patience and foresight, a gamble on delayed gratification over potential regrets. After having spent 34 months in prison so far, what was another two months when I knew in the long run, would work out in my favour.

At the end of January 2020, I had finally fulfilled the time required to officially ask for parole, and now, without hesitation, I sent off my final request to the Judge.

Regrets
December 2019

In quiet moments of reflection, something that I have a lot of time for, a heavy cloak of remorse envelops me, a shroud woven from the threads of regret and self-awareness. The faces of those I have inadvertently hurt parade before my mind's eye, each expression etched with the pain I played a part in causing.

I hadn't meant to hurt anyone.

Although I was not close to him, my father was someone who played on my mind often. I knew that my whole family had been put through an ordeal and it was not fair on him or those close to me. It's a haunting gallery of mistakes, and I am the reluctant curator, forced to confront the consequences of my actions. Guilt, like an uninvited guest, settles in the chambers of my heart. The weight of knowing that my choices, whether born of ignorance or a momentary lapse in judgment, inflicted wounds on unsuspecting souls is a burden too profound to bear lightly. I am haunted by the echoes of their suffering, the silent cries that reverberate through the corridors of my conscience.

I should never have come to Colombia, I should never have had been here, yet I was, something that, although I hated every single living moment of it, there was a reason for all this happening to me. But I still hadn't discovered it. But I needed to know. Why do fucked up things like this happen to people?

I find solace in the determination to evolve, to emerge from the cocoon of remorse as a better version of myself. It's a journey fraught with humility, an acknowledgment that the road to redemption is neither swift nor effortless. With each sincere apology for the pain and suffering

I had caused those around me and each act of kindness, I strive to mend the fractures I inadvertently caused.

In the realm of remorse, there exists a glimmer of hope – a hope that my evolution can contribute to the healing of those I've hurt. It's a humble plea for forgiveness, an earnest desire to rewrite the narrative and, in doing so, create a future where empathy and understanding prevail.

Marina – Another Challenge
January 2020

It all began innocently, a casual meeting in the Patio, connected by the thread of a mutual foreigner friend.

Marina was just another face in the crowd at first, tangled up in a mess of relationships and drama. She had a girlfriend, Sonia, whose jealousy was so intense that she saw me as a threat. But Marina's love life was already a disaster. She confessed she had another girlfriend outside the prison. "I have a girlfriend outside. She looks after everything I want and need. It's easy to manipulate her. She knows that when I get out, I'll be all in for her. She's my world, I think." Hearing this made me sick.

What a shitty person.

I tried to keep things casual, but Marina had other ideas. She wanted to learn English, so she joined my group lessons. But rumours started spreading through the prison, whispers about us being involved. Scared of the fallout, I ended our lessons.

Things exploded when Sonia punched me in the face in the education building, leaving me with a bloody nose. She accused me of stealing Marina from her. I hadn't done anything. We were just friends. After all the drama with Jane and Elly, I didn't need any more chaos.

In vulnerable moments, Marina told me about her tough life. "My mother is really sick in Venezuela, and my baby sister needs help. I would steal to sell things for money to provide for them. I was the only income, and now they have nothing. I need help. What can I do in here?" I felt sorry for her and gave her some money, even though I didn't have much myself. She knew exactly how to pull at my heartstrings.

But soon, her true colours showed. She played mind games, created drama, and became so possessive I felt like I was suffocating. She proposed to me in public, and I reluctantly agreed just to avoid embarrassing her. I knew she was toxic, but I was trapped. I was nothing but a dollar sign to her.

At first, Marina's intensity seemed like passion. But it quickly turned into aggression. She became violent. The first time she hit me, I was in shock. The sting of the slap echoed in our shared space.

She apologized, saying, "I'm so sorry, Cassie. I swear I can be better. I will change. I need you in my life. You have helped me more than anyone else. I need you." I believed her, hoping it would be different next time. It never was. She was scared I'd stop helping her.

The prison walls felt like they were closing in on me. I was a captive audience to her horror show. My emotional and physical well-being were the casualties. She threatened to end her life if I tried to leave. I didn't know if she was serious, but I couldn't take the risk. Every day was a tightrope walk between false calm and inevitable storms. Her possessiveness turned our space into a battleground. The isolation of prison made me feel even more trapped.

The bruises faded, but the scars remained. The outside world seemed like an unattainable dream. I tried to voice my pain, but she gaslighted me. Her apologies were rehearsed, and her promises were empty. I yearned for escape, not just from prison but from *her*.

The breaking point came when she drew a makeshift blade on me. Jealousy was her poison. I held up my hands to defend myself, and she sliced my hand open. It wasn't the first time she hurt me. She'd choked and punched me whenever she saw another woman talking to me. I was a teacher. I helped other inmates, and they sought me out. This put me in constant danger with her. It was then that I realized I couldn't stay trapped in this cycle any longer. I had to fight for my freedom.

Leaving prison wasn't just about physical freedom. I needed to free myself from the emotional chains Marina had wrapped around me. I craved peace, self-discovery, and healing – difficult to manage when I kept getting attacked and wounded.

Covid Riot
March 2020

While incarcerated, we diligently kept ourselves informed about the evolving situation of Covid in China. The prevailing consensus was ominous – the potential impact on Colombia could be catastrophic. The medical services in the country were already lagging behind, and the prison system, characterized by its careless attitude, appeared utterly unprepared. My concerns extended beyond the nation at large; I was more apprehensive about the vulnerability of the prison environment. With no real medicine and the absence of diligent doctors, the prospect of Covid infiltrating any of the Colombian prisons spelled disaster. Just as I had barely recovered from a near-death experience due to my stomach condition, the looming threat of Covid intensified my desperation to escape this perilous setting. Within the prison, Covid dominated conversations. We anticipated its arrival, though the precise timing remained elusive. Reports of growing cases in Colombia, escalating by tens of thousands daily, fuelled anxiety. Understandably, fear bred irrational behaviour among the inmates. Outside the prison walls, families of prisoners took matters into their own hands, pleading with the government to intervene. They desperately sought to shield their loved ones from the potential ravages of the virus, recognizing that anyone entering this harsh environment would emerge forever altered.

Then, a glimmer of hope flickered on the horizon. The Colombia magistrates explored options to safeguard the prison population. A purported project emerged, suggesting that those who had completed a significant portion of their sentences would be granted early parole. Others with specific sentences might find themselves on home detention until the virus ran its course in Colombia. However, progress was sluggish, giving the impression that it was a media stunt designed to pacify families and prisoners rather than a genuine intention to follow through. Meanwhile, Covid tightened its grip on Colombia, claiming lives by the hour. The first cases of Covid within the prison became a stark reality. One Friday afternoon, a rumour circulated that all prisons would unite in protest. The objective seemed clear – to exert pressure on the government, which the rumour alleged was denying treatment to those succumbing to the virus within the prison walls. Initially sceptical, I dismissed the idea as mere hearsay. However, as events unfolded, it became evident that the protest was more than a rumour. The atmosphere within the prison became charged with an unexplainable fear that gripped everyone.

It was Saturday evening, Patios Two and Three ignited the protest after catching wind on the radio that other prisons had already begun their demonstrations. And just like that, it was 'go' time. Each Patio rallied at the bars in every passageway, fervently shouting for the project to be granted for releases, banging their food containers in unison. It was a peaceful protest, driven by the shared desire to survive the looming threat of the virus. While this wasn't my first protest in this prison, having been actively involved in the last one over the kitchen incident, this time, I hesitated. Considering my proximity to earning parole, I grappled with the ethical dilemma of leaving and leaving others to confront the aftermath.

Initially, the protest seemed harmless, a peaceful expression of our desperate situation. However, the atmosphere shifted when Special Operations guards arrived, preparing for a potential riot. The prisoners were incensed because, truth be told, they hadn't initiated any destructive action *yet*. The mere presence of these guards signalled an imminent escalation. Reports on the radio indicated that men's prisons were spiralling out of control.

Smoke began emanating from cells as mattresses were set ablaze and tossed into open areas. Despite the heightened aggression, it remained somewhat manageable until the radio broadcast the news that some men had escaped during the riot, only to be fatally shot by the guards. Outrage spread through the prisons – the guards could have incapacitated them without resorting to lethal force. The women, now fuelled by extreme aggression, provoked the guards to react. Patios Two and Three were subjected to gas, and the air resonated with the cacophony of banging objects and agonized screams. In the midst of this inhumane chaos, I found myself in a particularly tumultuous Patio. Devoid of any objects in my hands, I observed the unfolding tragedy. Being the sole blonde in the facility, I stood out conspicuously. The Commanding Officer in charge of the operation unexpectedly yelled my name from below. Shocked, I looked down, and he barked, demanding to know what the hell I was doing. I remained silent – what could I possibly say? In an odd twist, he threatened, "I'm coming for you." Fear gripped me as I hastily retreated to my cell, fully aware that he intended to make good on his words.

Within moments, the women in my Patio screamed "GAS!" The guards had unleashed gas bombs into all the passageways. While I didn't bear the full brunt due to being inside my cell, the agony was still unbearable. My cellmates tried to assist with my asthma attack when, abruptly, the guards flung open the cell door and hurled another gas bomb inside before sealing the door shut. We cowered under blankets, attempting to shield ourselves, but the gas permeated everything. Something obstructed the door, trapping us. We were now confined in a gas-filled cell, and the guards were adamant about keeping us there.

This horrifying ordeal felt like hours, but eventually, the door swung open. We were dragged out one by one and made to kneel before the other inmates, guns pointed at our faces. The Commanding Officer issued threats, "Stay the fuck down, we will shoot. Stay down, get the fuck down! Shoot on movement!" warning us against any wrong moves. In my passageway, an older lady struggled to breathe and kneel.

When she attempted to stand, a Special Ops officer, brutally struck her ribs, producing a sickening crunch. In an inexplicable surge of courage, I stood up, pulling the guard away from the old lady. The Commanding Officer got in my face and told me to move and kneel down, I looked back at the old lady now screaming in pain and I shook my head, I looked at him, the man who had once beaten me and told him I wouldn't move, I told him that was enough, he had made his point, but it wasn't enough for him, he hated women standing up to him. The Commanding Officer grabbed a hand full of my hair and in one swift move threw me aside, it hurt but I didn't care, I had to help the old lady, I slowly stood up again and as I'm standing up, something slammed into my stomach, this left me instantly unable to move. He had kicked me and absolutely winded me. I couldn't breathe. With a fist full of my hair, he pulled me up and told me to kneel. In this moment I felt so much hate. The Commanding Officer smiled as he looked at me, this man took so much advantage of his position here, he enjoyed beating the shit out of women. Dragged into our cells forcibly, we were locked in, deprived of food, water, and toilets until further notice – the final words uttered by the laughing Commanding Officer and his cohorts. "You're going to rot in this place Cassandra, mark my words, bitch."

I had done nothing to deserve this treatment. In past protests, I had always retreated when things turned aggressive, yet this man sought any excuse to lay his hands on me. Anger surged within me. As I slowly rose to assess the bruise forming on my body, I vowed not to let him escape accountability. Being a guard was one thing, but this abuse of power was intolerable.

After enduring two days of being confined to our cells without access to food, water, or even basic sanitation, our patience wore thin. Seven of us crammed into this small space, frustrations boiling over. Tuning into the radio, we learned of the chaos that unfolded in the men's prisons during the riot – a grim reality of several lives lost, and others injured, some not even involved in the escape attempt but ruthlessly murdered. It seemed as though the guards revelled in the fear. News of my own ordeal, standing up for an elderly lady, circulated rapidly through the Patios, instilling fear in everyone regarding the Commanding Officer's potential retribution. The prospect of reporting or suing him terrified many, but I stepped forward, ready to endure further beatings if it meant protecting my fellow inmates.

I managed to secure medical attention for the elderly lady, ensuring she received treatment for her broken ribs. At least 65 years old, she faced this ordeal amid the Covid pandemic, a daunting prospect for her recovery. As for myself, I was provided with a cream and a generous supply of painkillers to alleviate the effects of the brutal beating. The imposing bruise on my body became a symbol, along with my other scars, this was added to the list of brutal beatings, but this one was different, this I had earned by standing up for the people who couldn't stand up for themselves. The person who once arrived in this facility, facing threats, stabbings, bullying, and beatings, had transformed into someone willing to put herself on the line for her fellow inmates.

Although a semblance of normality slowly returned to the yard, the prison was far from fully restored. We may not have been locked in our cells, but the scars, both physical and emotional, lingered. I took action by reporting the Commanding Officer to the human rights representative dedicated to the prison system. However, deep down, I knew that this might not yield tangible results. Still, I vowed that it wasn't over. I would confront this man and seek justice. Meanwhile, the grim reality persisted – Covid had infiltrated the prison, and the proposed project for early parole due to the pandemic remained stalled in the courts. It appeared that no one would benefit from the so-called 'Early Covid Release.'

The prison system defended itself, shifting blame onto the inmates, asserting that we had brought the riots upon ourselves, and callously declaring that the men who perished deserved their fate. The government remained silent. Indifference prevailed, and it seemed that no one cared about the harrowing conditions within the prison walls.

Crystal – The Bestie
October 2019 to March 2020

Just when you think you know how life will be, something or someone always arrives to change things up.

For me, that was Crystal. The first day I saw her, she instantly annoyed me. There was something about her that I just couldn't stand. She was standing in the gate to our yard, yelling and carrying on like an idiot to the guards in English. She was extremely tall and had a crazy afro going on. We both looked at each other and she came across as an attention seeker and honestly, I didn't like that. I looked straight past her and asked the guard, in Spanish, to leave, my accent was enough to confuse an English speaker because it came out very naturally by now. I didn't look back as I walked away from her, all I could remember thinking was how annoying!

A few days later, a friend who I often translated for said she had a new friend who spoke English and wanted me to meet her. I was worried because this friend had a knack for finding trouble. To my surprise, it was that same annoying girl. No escaping her now.

She introduced herself as Crystal.

I replied, "Cassandra. Not Cassie. Cassandra."

She smiled and said, "I know who you are. I followed your story from the other jail where I was." That surprised me. She said my story helped her get through her own mess. Crystal had been caught in Cartagena with cocaine and sentenced to five years. She had spent a year and a half in Cartagena before being moved to Bogotá. She hated it here, struggling with the harsh reality of Bogotá's prison life. "I can't handle this place, girl. It's unbearable. How have you managed to be here this whole time? Why do the guards respect you? What did you do?"

"You just do what you're told," I said, "Never forget you're in prison, and the rules and laws are there for a reason. The guards are good with me because I've been through hell and back here. I showed them I'm worth respecting."

Everyone thought I had it easy, but I had just learned to hide it well.

Crystal needed me to survive. She thought prison life was a joke, hadn't really learned from her mistakes, and didn't grasp the consequences of her actions. She was from Miami, from the hood, and was used to dodgy stuff. I tried to avoid her, seeing her as the attention-seeker she was. When she found out I was gay, something switched in her. She started hitting on girls, desperate for attention and not to feel lonely. I understood that loneliness all too well.

Despite my initial annoyance, we became friends. I wanted to help her, teach her to value this time, to be strong without needing drugs to get through the day. Crystal became my escape from Marina. I'd hide with her when things got bad. I wanted her to be better, to survive this place.

We started talking and hanging out every day. Our bond grew in the darkest place of our lives. Crystal was hilarious, sometimes so gullible it made me laugh. She constantly got into trouble with the guards for being loud and rude. She made the last months of my incarceration different. Even though she was always in some kind of trouble, I found myself looking out for her, almost like a mother figure. She'd joke about it, but I made sure she was okay, had food, was mentally stable, helped her with her release – everything.

Life with Crystal broke my routine. Looking after her gave me something I hadn't had in a long time: a friend. I laughed again, felt a bit of joy in the darkest of places. We were so different, but we found a great friendship. I felt my age again, something I had forgotten.

I only had six months with Crystal before she got parole. I knew I'd miss her, but I hoped she'd get her life together.

We made so many plans. "Girl, I'm going to start recording music again. We're gonna be such great friends! I'll wait for you on the outside so we can hang. Damn, bitch, I know we're gonna be great!" she said.

I loved Crystal to bits and hoped our plans would come true.

Crystal got out on parole in February, and just like that, she left me behind. I tried to call her, but she wouldn't answer. Sometimes she seemed annoyed. Eventually, I stopped trying. I missed her a lot, but I had to understand.

This place wasn't worth remembering.

Prison Release
27 March 2020

The anticipation of freedom, an emotion I thought I had lost touch
with, gripped me as I navigated the intricate web of bureaucracy that
governed my release from prison. Amidst the turmoil within the prison
walls, I had almost forgotten about my parole application. Yet, on that
fateful Monday morning of March 27th, the call to my favourite judge's
office altered the trajectory of my life.

Dialling the number became a routine, a ritual fuelled by desperation
and hope. The assistant on the other end, recognizing my voice from
countless calls, delivered news that felt surreal.

"The judge has granted your parole," the assistant declared matter-
of-factly.

A cautious excitement overcame me as he explained the necessary
steps. A $2000 caution fine stood between me and freedom, a sum that,
once paid, would set in motion the wheels of my release. The information
hung in the air; a moment frozen in disbelief.

"What? Really? Are you kidding?" I uttered, questioning the
authenticity of the unexpected reprieve, but the assistant had no reason
to lie to me. His job entailed conveying both the good and the bad. I hung
up the phone, still in shock.

Walking into my cell, I chose to keep the news to myself for a moment.
I needed time to process the gravity of what was happening. The cell, my
confined space for so long, felt different that day. Sitting on my bed,
I pondered the enormity of leaving a place that had become a hauntingly
familiar nightmare.

I shared the news with Carina. A mixture of emotions played across
her face. 'I'm leaving you," I tearfully confessed. Leaving behind
individuals, each with their stories of suffering, posed a dilemma. The

joy of personal liberation clashed with the weight of abandoning those who had become a part of my journey. Strangely, happiness wasn't always the response to news of someone leaving prison; here, departures were tinged with complex emotions. With the outside world in turmoil, the clock became my adversary. Each passing moment influenced the pace of my liberation.

I relied on Crystal, who had already tasted freedom, who had finally answered my calls. The outside world was elusive for me, and the time zone difference hindered direct communication with those who could help. Crystal, despite occasional frustration on my part, became my lifeline, my sole connection to the world beyond prison walls.

As I awaited Crystal's help, conflicting emotions intensified. The prospect of leaving conflicted with the bond formed within the prison community. I had earned respect and assumed the role of a support system for my fellow inmates. Whether writing petitions, letters, providing English lessons, or sharing whatever I had, I became a lifeline for those in need. Leaving meant severing these ties, a bittersweet departure from a makeshift family. The bureaucratic hurdles, exacerbated by the onset of a global lockdown, added to the urgency. The Judge's office transitioned to virtual operations, threatening to elongate the process if my caution fine wasn't swiftly paid. Crystal, despite my occasional impatience, worked diligently to facilitate the payment through my lawyer. The prison adage echoed in my mind: it was easy to get in but seemingly impossible to get out.

The final steps of my release, seemingly straightforward, metamorphosed into a labyrinth of obstacles. Lost paperwork, delayed behaviour reports, and absurd excuses became the norm. The prison system, notorious for its inefficiency, tested my patience in these final moments. As the prospect of freedom beckoned, a new-found anxiety replaced the accustomed calm within me. The prospect of a Friday release loomed, a testament to the sluggish pace of prison procedures. My impending departure didn't go unnoticed. Guards sought my contact for English lessons, and inmates came to wish me luck, accompanied by subtle requests for favours. The weight of leaving, laden with mixed emotions, pressed upon me. I pledged to stay in touch, to offer support from the outside. Yet, the road to freedom, even at its culmination, remained a winding path fraught with challenges. In the confined world of prison, where time seemed to move at its own pace, I prepared to step into the unknown, propelled by the tantalizing promise of liberation.

The clock seemed to tick agonizingly slow as I clung to the hope that this day would mark the end of my incarceration test.

It was now the 3rd of April 2020. It had only been five days since I knew I was getting out. My patience was put to the test. The anticipation was almost unbearable. The guards, undoubtedly weary of my persistent inquiries, may have labelled me as annoying, but I couldn't afford another letdown.

Today *had* to be the day, the day I walked out of the ominous blue door that had loomed over me since my arrival. By 2:00 pm, anxiety and impatience had reached their peak. The deafening silence left me grappling with uncertainty. The elusive moment of signing the parole conditions remained elusive.

I had organized for Crystal to wait, her arrival impending in a few hours, and her steadfast support became a reassuring constant.

Downstairs, as I scanned the familiar faces of the guards, my eyes locked onto Jennifer, a guard who had once harboured disdain for me. Our relationship had undergone a transformation. I had managed to unveil the layers beneath the hardened exterior, and we had developed an unexpected camaraderie. When I approached her, explaining my situation, Jennifer pledged to investigate and returned with a smile, holding the parole agreement that held the key to my freedom. The weight of her words, "Only for you would I delay my early knock off," resonated deeply. It was a gesture that transcended the typical interactions between guards and inmates.

As I sat there, poised to sign the parole agreement, the tangible proof of my impending release, a sense of fulfilment washed over me. Jennifer conveyed the next step – the mandatory Interpol check that stood between me and freedom. Her honesty about the potential delay, courtesy of it being a Friday, underscored the unpredictability of the bureaucratic processes. Gratitude filled me as I thanked her sincerely, realizing that I had come a long way from being the most despised person in the prison three years ago. The journey, marked by adversity and personal growth, had carved a path leading to this moment of potential liberation. In the face of uncertainty, a glimmer of hope flickered, and the camaraderie I had forged within the prison walls served as a testament to resilience and transformation.

The clock struck 6:00 pm, signalling the impending contada, a point after which departures were rare, disrupting the prison's routine. Engrossed in a conversation with Crystal over the phone, the guards at the front provided a disheartening update – the mandatory Interpol check remained incomplete, and the likelihood of my departure that day seemed bleak. Resigned to the familiar sting of disappointment, I accepted the reality, recognizing that this emotional rollercoaster was an intrinsic part of the unpredictable process. This weighed heavily because tonight at midnight Colombia's isolation would start, meaning I would be stuck in prison until further notice.

Calling Crystal back at 8:30 pm, the verdict was clear – today wouldn't mark my liberation.

It was a bitter pill to swallow, but safety prevailed, and she should head home in the late hour. Fumbling with one of the burner phones in the bathroom area, I heard my name being called. Panic surged, and the phone was swiftly discarded. Three guards stood there, one familiar face among them, Paula. Maintaining a casual facade, I greeted her with a nonchalant, "Hola Drago, what's up?" Little did I know that behind her back, she held a white piece of paper that would alter my fate.

The mix of emotions within me was indescribable. Initially, I thought it was a cruel jest, a mind game played by the guards. Paula, realizing I wasn't reacting as expected, declared, "It's time to go, Sainsbury. Move it or I'll leave you in here."

The reality hit, and I blurted out, "No me jodas! – Marica! Me voy!" (Don't screw with me. Oh shit! I'm leaving).

Tears welled up unexpectedly; the flood of emotions overwhelmed me. Hastily bidding farewell to everyone who approached, tears and well-wishes intermingling, I grabbed my bag and stepped out of my passageway into a sea of women. What awaited me was beyond expectation – a throng of hundreds, an emotional chorus of support, hugs, and wishes. The genuine display of affection and camaraderie was something I hadn't anticipated. The weight of the moment, the culmination of years of struggle and resilience, hit me with profound intensity as I navigated through the crowd. The journey toward freedom had reached its zenith, surrounded by the echoes of heartfelt goodbyes and the collective spirit of those left behind.

Walking down the stairs with a cohort of women by my side, the very same individuals who had once made my life a living hell, I couldn't help but smile to myself.

You did it, Cassie. You showed them who you really are.

Exiting the yard, the guards instructed me to leave my bag and proceed to the doctor for a final check, a formality that seemed to stretch into an unexpected three-hour ordeal. Eventually done, I made my way back toward the yard, a route that, during normal circumstances, would be deserted as inmates were typically locked in their cells. Yet, as I passed each yard, I was met with more women wanting to bid me farewell, expressing gratitude for my presence and the non-judgmental support I had offered. In those moments, I realized that my time in prison hadn't been in vain.

I had made a difference.

The guard waiting at the end added a touch of humour, remarking on the unusual sight of a foreigner receiving a 'walk of fame' out of the prison. I thought she was making a sarcastic comment when she stopped walking and turned to say:

"I watched you grow in here. There were times where I thought you would be shipped home in a body bag, especially after the beating you took, but you showed all of us, not just strength and resilience, but you have such a kind heart. Take a look around! You made a difference here. Not everyone does that. Be proud of leaving this place. You have no one to thank but yourself."

Her words left me speechless.

Facing the Commanding Officer, the source of much torment, his initial expression changed as he aggressively approached, demanding to know what I was doing there. In that moment, I resolved to end this chapter. The guards, witnessing the exchange, observed as I stood tall and looked him directly in the face. Speaking quietly but resolutely, I conveyed that my departure didn't signify the end of our problems, and I vowed to ensure he wouldn't lay another hand on anyone in that prison. Surprised, he allowed me to pass, and as I walked away, the approving expressions on the guards' faces hinted at a shared sentiment.

Walking amongst the guards as an equal was a surreal experience. Their hugs and requests to stay in touch marked a stark contrast to the dynamics of the past. Walking out, I spotted Jane emerging from an office, a moment of confusion on her face. With no hard feelings, I smiled and waved goodbye. Even as her girlfriend stood by, a protective figure, I wished them both the best. In that moment, I embraced the idea that everyone deserved a chance at happiness.

In front of the dreaded blue door, the symbol of incarceration for many, I paused to absorb the significance of this moment. This door, bearing the weighty word 'Carcel,' represented the prison, a place that held memories of pain and suffering. As I stood there, I reflected on the scared 22-year-old who had crossed its threshold, contemplating the journey of survival and transformation that brought me to this point. The guard beside me asked if I was ready, and I turned for a final glance at the yards, a silent acknowledgment of the challenges faced and overcome. With a nod to the guard, I signalled my readiness for the next chapter. As I crossed the threshold of that notorious blue door, a torrent of emotions surged within me, a kaleidoscope of self-discovery and pain that had etched its mark over the years of confinement. The air, thick with the weight of the prison's history, suddenly gave way to an overwhelming sense of liberation. Each step outside felt like shedding the heavy chains that had bound my spirit. The first breath of freedom was a paradox, a cocktail of exhilaration and trepidation, as if venturing into an uncharted territory of the soul.

The prison walls, which had served as both witness and warden to my journey, faded away, replaced by the vastness of the outside world. It was a moment pregnant with the realization that survival within those unforgiving walls had sculpted me into a person unrecognisable to the naive 22-year-old who had first entered. The pain endured had become the chisel that carved resilience into my character, forging an unyielding strength that stood as a testament to the depths of human endurance. Yet, the first steps into new-found freedom weren't just a celebration; they were a confrontation with the mental bearings of the past. The scars etched into my psyche were not easily forgotten. The fear of the unknown, the spectre of past trauma, and the haunting memories of a life confined threatened to cast shadows on the brilliance of liberation. It was a delicate dance between self-growth and the lingering pain, a juxtaposition that tugged at the seams of my emotional fabric. In those initial moments beyond the prison gates, I grappled with the paradox of feeling both liberated and burdened. The journey ahead held promises of self-discovery and redemption, yet the echoes of the prison's cold walls reverberated in the recesses of my mind. It was a powerful cocktail of conflicting emotions, a symphony of triumph and tribulation that would resonate within me long after the physical bars were left behind.

Crystal, waiting for me, was playfully interacting with an army guy, a scene that brought laughter amid the tension. I took a deep breath, savouring the taste of freedom. Something once taken for granted had become the most precious and valuable possession, a realization that lingered in the air as I embraced the unknown challenges that lay ahead. Stepping into the realm of freedom was a surreal experience, a sensation that went beyond mere physical liberation. The world, once confined to the rigid routines of prison life, now stretched before me in all its unbridled vastness. It was overwhelming, to say the least, and the cravings of the palate were momentarily overshadowed by the sheer joy of unrestricted movement.

Contrary to the clichéd expectation of indulging in a long-craved feast, my initial desire was not for food but for the simple act of walking freely. I wanted to navigate the streets, soak in the unfiltered air, and relish the new-found autonomy that had become so unfamiliar behind bars. The weight of constant vigilance, the fear of guards, and the confinement to small spaces were replaced by the uncharted territory of open streets and boundless possibilities. However, the ghost of prison habits lingered. The instinct to be cautious, the reflex to adhere to a predetermined routine, and the awareness that consequences could loom around unforeseen corners were ingrained in my psyche. I found myself caught between shedding the remnants of prison life and preserving them as a cautionary reminder of the precipice that bad decisions could lead to.

When the time finally came to break my fast outside the prison walls, it was not with an extravagant spread or a gourmet delight but with a simple pleasure – Domino's Pizza. The BBQ meat lover's pizza, with its savoury flavours, marked my re-entry into the world. The act of savouring each bite was a celebration of taste, a rekindling of the forgotten joy that food could bring. It was a reminder that freedom extended beyond physical boundaries to the sensory realm, where every flavour held the promise of a life unconfined.

In the days that followed, I indulged in the pleasures of new-found freedom cautiously, mindful of the delicate state of my stomach and the need for proper medical attention. Yet, that first night of culinary indulgence served as a poignant metaphor for the bittersweet symphony of liberation – a blend of caution, relish, and the overwhelming taste of freedom.

Nightmares in the Shadows
April 2020

As freedom unfolded its wings around me, a haunting spectre lingered in the shadows of my nights – nightmares that were relentless, each dream a vivid re-enactment of the prison horrors I sought to leave behind. Sleep, once an escape from the harsh reality of incarceration, now transformed into an unwelcome battleground where the ghosts of my past waged war on my fragile peace. The nightmares were meticulous in their cruelty, resurrecting the claustrophobic cell walls, the suffocating stench of despair, and the cacophony of distant cries echoing through the corridors. In the cold sweat of midnight, I found myself back in the prison yard, the weight of confinement settling upon my chest like an oppressive force.

One recurring dream cast me into the labyrinth of concrete passageways, each step heavy with the echoes of prison boots. The haunting silence, interrupted only by the distant sounds of keys jingling and metal gates clanging shut, reverberated through my subconscious. Faces of fellow inmates flickered in and out of focus, their eyes haunted by the same fear that had once gripped me. As the nightmares persisted, their cumulative toll began to wear me down. Sleep, which should have been a respite, transformed into a battleground where my subconscious grappled with the demons of my past. Waking up drenched in fear, my heart racing, I found the line between dreams and reality blurring, the boundaries of my new-found freedom becoming increasingly fragile.

The mental fatigue etched itself into the lines on my face, and the bags beneath my eyes bore witness to the silent struggles waged within the recesses of my mind. In the daylight, I wore a mask of resilience, but the nights betrayed the vulnerability that lurked beneath the surface.

I sought solace in the waking world, attempting to outrun the shadows that pursued me into the daylight. Therapy sessions became a lifeline, a safe space where I could unravel the knots in my psyche, exposing the wounds that festered beneath the veneer of composure. The therapist's office became a sanctuary where words became tools, gradually dismantling the prison architecture within my mind.

Sweet or Sour Freedom
10 April 2020

Navigating the unfamiliar terrain of post-prison life proved to be a journey fraught with unexpected challenges. As I stepped into the world beyond the prison walls, I clung to the belief that anything awaiting me outside had to be better than the ordeal I had just survived. Little did I know that the universe had its own plans, and the pandemic that unfolded would cast a shadow over my new-found freedom.

Securing a teaching job through an outside institute had initially fuelled my excitement and optimism. The prospect of earning a living and engaging in meaningful work promised a departure from the desolation of prison life. However, fate had its own twist in store for me. The day of my parole coincided with the abrupt halt that Colombia, like much of the world, experienced as the pandemic took hold.

From the confinement of prison, I found myself thrust into another form of isolation. The irony of my situation wasn't lost on me – I was free yet confined, liberated physically but restrained by the invisible chains of a global crisis. The abrupt shift from the confined routine of prison to the uncertain stillness of pandemic lockdown left me feeling adrift.

Stepping out of prison into the unknown world beyond was like stepping into a dream of freedom, or so I thought. I was hopeful, believing that life outside those walls had to be better than what I had endured inside. But fate had other plans, and the pandemic hit just as I was beginning to find my footing.

Getting a teaching job was a glimmer of hope. It felt like a fresh start, a chance to leave behind the bleakness of prison. Yet, the day I was released coincided with Colombia's sudden lockdown due to the pandemic. It was a cruel twist of fate. Instead of freedom, I found myself in another kind of confinement.

Ironic, isn't it? I was physically free but trapped by the invisible chains of a global crisis. The routine of prison was swapped for the eerie quiet of lockdown. It felt like being adrift in uncharted waters, unsure of what lay ahead.

Life beyond prison demanded swift adaptation, a feat made all the more challenging by the restrictions imposed in response to the pandemic. The world had ground to a halt, and I felt a sense of stagnation creeping in. The grand plans I had harboured to rebuild my life now faced the harsh reality of a global crisis.

The weight of the pandemic bore down on me like a relentless storm, leaving me scared, angry, and feeling lost. The escalating death toll in Colombia and the struggling health system were constant sources of terror. Thoughts of the prison haunted me, knowing that Covid had infiltrated its walls, claiming lives daily. The inability to help those still trapped within those confines left me frustrated and emotionally exhausted.

Amid the chaos, a bureaucratic nightmare unfolded as immigration remained shuttered due to the pandemic. The promised online portal for visa and permission papers turned into a cruel joke, with endless hours spent in virtual queues leading nowhere. Frustration mounted as I faced the pressing need to legalize my stay in Colombia. The job market, once promising due to remote work opportunities, remained elusive as my lack of paperwork became a barrier.

The frustration was disheartening, and the hurdles seemed insurmountable. Yet, I refused to succumb to self-pity. I was determined to navigate this maze, tapping into my problem-solving skills. The rejection from big companies fuelled my determination rather than dampening my spirits. Undeterred, I reached out to major corporations, offering business English classes and creating tailored courses. Rejections persisted, but I persisted harder.

Approached by English schools, the looming obstacle was my lack of papers. Despite immigration reopening, they obstinately refused my appointment, and I found myself at odds with the law once again. The warnings from the police became a harsh reminder of the urgency to make things right. Enough was enough; I craved the stability of legality. Drawing on my knowledge of the law, I researched and presented my case to immigration, initiating a battle that would last eight gruelling months.

During this time, I became intimately acquainted with the immigration office, earning a reputation for being a persistent nuisance. But I didn't care; the end justified the means.

Finally, after months of appeals, arguments, and standing up to a seemingly impenetrable government department, I received the precious paperwork. I had not only secured my own future but had also paved the way for over 50 other foreigners grappling with similar challenges. The fight had been exhausting, but it reaffirmed my resilience and determination to overcome obstacles, no matter how formidable.

In the new-found landscape of legal possibilities in Colombia, I found myself harnessing the power of my networks, meticulously crafted through university studies, immigration endeavours, legal circles, and English schools. Amidst these connections, a serendipitous opportunity emerged – one that had the potential to redefine my life after a year and four months of freedom post-prison. My foray into the professional world led me to a private school, a gateway to a potential breakthrough. An interview with the school board awaited me, and the prospect both thrilled and daunted me. The self-doubt, a lingering spectre from the past, crept in. Would my experience, my unorthodox teaching methods, and my unwavering passion be enough? The absence of an English degree fuelled my insecurities, but I reminded myself that I was capable of anything I set my mind to.

To my surprise, as I walked out of the nerve-wracking interview, I clutched a contract – a contract offering me the position of head teacher and Year 11 home room teacher. It was a surreal moment, a testament to the unpredictable twists that life can take. I had once again defied my own expectations, determined to shape my life on my terms and not let the shadows of the past dictate my future.

Week one as an official teacher marked the commencement of a chapter that felt remarkably aligned with my aspirations. The students were receptive, my colleagues supportive, and I revelled in the joy of imparting knowledge. My self-imposed pressure to excel stemmed from a need to prove something to myself, an internal dialogue of self-confidence and a determination to believe in my abilities. As the head teacher, responsibilities cascaded upon me, demanding oversight of fellow educators, compliance checks, and administrative tasks alongside my teaching role. Far from being overwhelmed, I found solace in the whirlwind of responsibilities, revelling in the sense of usefulness that had eluded me for several long years.

Yet, the sweet taste of success turned bitter when a fellow teacher, envious of my position, orchestrated a campaign to tarnish my reputation. Gossip and insidious comments led to the inevitable – the school board, swayed by external pressures, had no option but to let me go. The disappointment was palpable, but the resilience I had cultivated whispered that this setback was merely a prelude to something bigger and better. Undeterred, I embraced the next challenge that presented itself – venturing into the world of freelance English teaching. Relief work in schools and institutes became my forte, but it was my foray into business English courses that truly set me apart. My name echoed in the hallways of recognition, a testament to the journey I had undertaken to prove that my past did not define me.

I resorted to a brief dalliance with OnlyFans, born out of societal pressures and financial considerations. I was lacking assistance from my family for income, and I needed to pay for my living expenses. I thought I could do it, everyone already thought I had one so what did I have to lose, right? But the truth was, I couldn't do it, I felt disgusted being asked by strangers to make videos of adult content – this wasn't *me*. I had no desire to touch myself for a man.

I don't understand how so many people don't get traumatized by the endless comments about their appearance, about their breasts, their ass and demands to send videos masturbating for them.

It was actually disgusting.

This whole story about "It's women taking a stand and being in control" …

THIS IS NOT TRUE.

At the end of the day, the men ask for or pay you for 'special requests' and you do it.

Does that sound ... *right*?

I couldn't do it. It was a sick reminder of my past and I refused to live that and put myself through that kind of hell. In the end, the men reminded me of my painful past. I chose to prioritize my values over a quick monetary gain, reaffirming that compromising my integrity was not a path I was willing to tread. I knew it would take a long time to get my life where I wanted it to be, but I was certain that I was capable of doing that on my own.

In this new chapter of self-discovery, I found solace in the role of a freelance teacher and the success of my business English courses. The story of my life was shifting, and with each challenge, I learned to trust myself a little more, something that I thought I would never do again. The path ahead was uncertain, but I had learned to embrace the uncertainty, confident that everything happened for a reason, and my journey was far from over. Life had offered me a second chance, and this time, I was determined to seize it, and with it, an unwavering belief in my own potential.

Finding Love
May 2021

In the realm of post-prison life, the dating scene wasn't my top priority. Focused on goals and getting my life together, I didn't want anything to distract me. However, there were moments, casual dates with different women, and the enjoyment of exploring connections. None of them, though, seemed to fit into the mould of a long-term relationship. Crystal, my best friend, called me up one Saturday, and despite our recent drift due to busy lives, I dropped everything to be there for her. Often struggling mentally, she saw me as her strength and problem solver, affectionately calling me her 'prison mum.'

Crystal invited me to a nightclub to help her forget about a recent breakup. We ventured to a new club that offered both techno/electronic and Latin reggae music. I couldn't risk drinking due to fresh ink from a new tattoo, but I was determined to ensure Crystal had a good time. The gay bar area was our destination, as I preferred the atmosphere there. Recognized by the bar owner, I stood out as probably the only Aussie gay girl who had graced the establishment.

Crystal, having started her pre-drinks much earlier, was well on her way to a good time. We spent time in the VIP area before I suggested moving to the reggae section, my personal favourite. I danced alone, thoroughly enjoying the music, when I felt someone encroach on my dance space. Concerned it might be a guy, I asked Crystal to confirm. To my relief, it was a girl, a well-dressed tomboy named Tato. We spent the night dancing and chatting, and there was an instant connection. Tato's infectious smile, nervous laughter, and adorable personality made the night memorable. We clicked effortlessly, a feeling I hadn't experienced in a long time. Despite his occasional nervousness around me, Tato's presence made the night special, and our new-found friendship felt like a refreshing breeze in my post-prison life.

The serendipity of meeting Tato felt like the universe aligning stars. Crystal and I rarely ventured into nightclubs or saw each other, making that night out an unexpected rarity. Tato shared that it was his – Tato doesn't refer to himself as a 'she' and prefers 'he/him/his pronouns' – friend's influence that led him to the same club, creating an uncanny sense of destiny. As our friendship blossomed, we spent time together a few times a week, our connection palpable. Despite neither of us actively seeking a relationship, the growing tension between us was undeniable. In the initial days of our friendship, I decided to reveal my tumultuous past to Tato. Trusting him was instinctual, and I believed it was essential for him to know the scars that marked my history. I provided him with the option to walk away, but his response surprised me. Tato expressed understanding, emphasizing that everyone has a past, but what mattered most was how I moved forward. This revelation affirmed that he not only accepted me but also supported my healing journey.

The more time we spent together, the more I found myself missing his presence. Our daily conversations became a constant, and the unspoken tension lingered in the air. It reached a point where one of us had to make a move, but the uncertainty hung in the balance. On the eve of his birthday, I invited him to dinner to celebrate since I had to work on his actual birthday. Despite choosing a nice restaurant, Tato seemed unusually nervous. As we placed our orders, he surprised me with a heartfelt question – whether I would officially be his girlfriend. The mix of doubt and anticipation in his eyes was endearing. It was a relationship neither of us saw coming, yet it was consuming, making me feel vibrantly alive. In Tato, I found a person I wanted to have in my life.

Months went by. We had overcome many obstacles already and it had only ever seemed to make us stronger. I was completely convinced that Tato was *my* person. Tato's attempts at secrecy were futile. His nervousness betrayed any plans he tried to conceal. Despite his subtle attempts, I had become adept at reading people, leaving him with little chance of surprising me.

After several months together, the desire to explore Colombia, unsure if the opportunity would present itself again, led us to plan a trip to the picturesque coastal town of Cartagena. Our stay at the Hilton Hotel took an unexpected turn when we were personally greeted by the hotel manager upon arrival. Tato, visibly more nervous than ever, engaged in a conversation with the manager regarding a mysterious reservation. The hotel itself was stunning, sparking a fleeting vision of a potential wedding venue. Sensing there was more to this trip than a simple getaway, I couldn't shake the feeling that a surprise awaited.

At 7:00 pm Tato led me to a charming restaurant perched over the ocean. Despite the pesky mosquitoes, the ambiance was enchanting, with flowers and a bottle of wine adorning our table. My suspicions proved accurate when, after the entrée, Tato launched into a heartfelt speech about finding his soulmate, his other half. Expressing his desire to spend the rest of his life with me, he concluded his prepared words and, much to my delight, dropped to one knee. In that moment, he produced a ring and asked me to marry him.

Reflecting on past proposals, I acknowledged that those instances lacked commitment and were more about avoiding hurting others. However, with Tato, it felt as though I had been patiently waiting for this person to reciprocate my feelings. Without hesitation, my heart unequivocally responded with a resounding "Yes."

We married on the 19th of March 2022.

These were my wedding vows:

As I stand here before you, surrounded by the beauty of this moment, I find my heart overwhelmed with a love that words can hardly contain. Today, I vow to cherish you in every shade of life, to stand by you in the brightest days and hold you closer in the darkest nights.

I promise to be your confidant, sharing in your joys and shouldering your burdens. With each sunrise, I will greet you with love, and with each sunset, I will be grateful for the day we've shared. I promise to laugh with you in times of joy, and to provide comfort in times of sorrow. In building our life together, I pledge to be your partner in every adventure, your ally in every challenge, and your refuge in every storm. I promise to nurture the flame of our love, letting it grow into a beacon that will light our path through the years.

With an open heart and a deep sense of commitment, I take you, Tato, as my partner, my confidant, and my one true love. I look forward to creating a lifetime of beautiful memories with you, hand in hand, heart in heart.

Today, I choose you, tomorrow, and all the tomorrows that follow.

The Unveiling Freedom
7 June 2022

This was the day of the unofficial end of my sentence. The day held a paradoxical significance. I counted my time in Colombia, not because I wasn't enjoying my life with Tato, but because I yearned for a different kind of freedom. I craved the normalcy of a visa, the ability to secure a job without fearing inquiries about the specifics of my visa status. I longed to walk the streets without the constant anxiety of being stopped by the police, to break free from the looming threat of returning to prison. Though physically out of prison, I still felt like a mere number in the labyrinthine prison system. The excitement of impending freedom spurred me to call my judge's office, eager to know when I would receive my release documents. However, my enthusiasm met an unexpected obstacle.

The Judge was away, and crucial paperwork for the last six months of my sentence awaited her signature upon her return next month. In that moment, the freedom I thought I'd taste slipped through my fingers. Once again, disappointment enveloped me, and the weight of accountability rested solely on my shoulders. Despite the setback, I resolved to be patient, a virtue I had honed over many years.

This time, however, patience would be coupled with preparation. I meticulously organized a petition, a document outlining the two years, 11 months, and 21 days I spent in prison, the 11 months of sentence reduction through work, and the 28 months on parole in Colombia. My original sentence had been 72 months, yet I had completed 74 months and 21 days, and the count continued as I awaited the judge's return. A month later, the long-awaited reply arrived. My judge confirmed the finalization of my sentence – it was official, I had finished my term. The chains of incarceration were ostensibly broken, but one barrier remained:

immigration needed to release the block on my passport. Armed with the Judge's letter and my meticulously prepared petition, I headed to immigration, expecting a smooth transition. But, as if mirroring the tumultuous journey that led me here, immigration opted for one final obstacle. They claimed they wouldn't accept the Judge's letter unless it came directly from her – doubting its authenticity.

The bureaucratic hurdles seemed endless, reminiscent of a final test on this road to freedom. Frustration gnawed at me, but I reached out to my judge's assistant, who assured me that the issue would be resolved within the week. Amidst these bureaucratic battles, Tato and I began working on visas. He had decided to accompany me back to Australia, and the thought of not facing this journey alone brought with it a profound sense of relief. Together, we packed our suitcases, bid farewell to our apartment, and dispatched our belongings to Tato's family home. A tinge of sadness accompanied the process – the end of an era.

It wasn't always a nightmare; there had been moments of grace and growth amid the challenges. These six years had become my much-needed life experience lesson.

The Weight Lifted
August 2022

The first week of August cast long shadows, the anticipation thick in the air like an impending storm. I held my breath, waiting for any word from immigration about my passport. Days dragged by agonizingly slow, but deep down, a quiet certainty assured me that answers were near. And then, like a herald of change, the confirmation email arrived. It beckoned me to appear at immigration the next day. This was it. Finally, everything was falling into place. That night, a mix of excitement and nerves filled me as I booked our tickets home for August 17th.

The countdown had begun.

Immigration, once a faceless bureaucracy, now seemed to loom with a resentful, formidable presence. What should have taken an hour at most for anyone else stretched into a painstaking seven-hour ordeal for me. But nothing would deter me now. With the letter in hand at 4:00 pm, the key to my freedom, I felt the weight of uncertainty and legal battles lift.

Now armed with everything needed to return home, I couldn't shake the realization that it had been nearly six years since I'd left Australia. Part of me hesitated, reluctant to bid farewell to a place where I had been a nobody, where my past was hidden, and where I had found ways to cope with the shadows of hate and shame. Here, in anonymity, I had learned resilience.

As we prepared to face what lay ahead, I knew leaving Colombia wasn't an end; it was a new chapter. The echoes of my experiences would follow me, but this departure wasn't a severing of ties. Colombia had marked me deeply, and the journey ahead promised redemption and self-discovery.

The adventure hadn't ended; it had simply shifted course.

On that Thursday, a close friend came to the airport to bid us farewell. The airport stretched out before me – a maze of bustling travellers and distant echoes of announcements. Once a place I navigated with the innocence of a tourist, it now carried the weight of my darkest memories. The last time I passed through immigration here was when I was arrested. Just the thought of returning here sent my heart racing.

The terminal hummed with the rhythm of hurried footsteps, the mechanical whir of conveyor belts, and the subdued murmur of conversations. But beneath the surface normalcy, fear gripped me. I wasn't doing anything wrong this time, yet the spectre of past events clung to me, threatening to unravel my composure. As we checked in our suitcases, I avoided meeting the gaze of the lady behind the counter. I felt my unease radiate, setting off silent alarms for airport security. Paranoia took hold, whispering doubts and suspicions into my mind.

Immigration loomed ahead like a fortress, its officers the gatekeepers to my anxieties. Every step toward them felt laden with the weight of anticipated scrutiny. Tato, a pillar of strength beside me, provided some solace, but the fear lingered. I wasn't prepared for the visceral reaction as I faced the officers who once held the keys to my incarceration.

Interrogation lights flickered, reminiscent of distant storms in my memory. Their questions penetrated my defences, their gaze searching for any hint of deceit. They scrutinized every nuance of my demeanour, every twitch of my expression, seeking a guilt that no longer existed. Physically and emotionally stripped bare, I felt sick, the knots in my stomach tightening. The trauma of my past arrest seeped into the present, poisoning the air around me.

Tato's unwavering presence was my lifeline. Alone, I couldn't bear the weight of this harrowing revisitation. Police awaited us at the gate, their stern expressions heightening the tension. I was escorted back to customs, a familiar haunt that bore witness to my darkest hours. Minutes dragged on – an agonizing eternity of questions and searches. It felt like a cruel re-enactment of my arrest. When they finally released me after over 30 minutes, relief washed over me.

I just wanted it to be *over*.

Reflecting on my time in Colombia still brings forth a cascade of emotions – a tapestry woven from attacks, pain, and unexpected growth. The scars, both visible and concealed, bear witness to a journey that tested my endurance. Through moments of vulnerability and fear, amidst echoes of gunfire and shadows of unrest, I discovered reservoirs of strength I never knew existed. Each trial became a crucible for growth, forging resilience from despair. In the crucible of adversity, I transformed – not a victim, but a survivor shaped by challenges, refined into a better version of myself. The scars remain, but they no longer define me; they tell a story of tenacity, adaptability, and an unyielding spirit. I was ready to face whatever awaited me next.

Home
21 August 2022

Returning home after enduring the depths of one of Colombia's toughest prisons wasn't the triumphant homecoming one might imagine. Instead, it marked the beginning of an emotional labyrinth, a journey I wasn't prepared for. My reputation lay in ruins, torn apart by relentless media scrutiny, and the warmth of friends and family felt like a distant memory. Hope, that fragile thread in dark times, seemed to elude me completely.

Confusion and loss became my constant companions as I navigated the unknown, each step forward clouded in uncertainty. Rebuilding and moving forward were met with insurmountable obstacles. Banks, like gatekeepers of my past, denied me basic financial services. Medicare, crucial for many, remained out of reach, adding to my challenges.

Rejections from countless job applications stung, with insults like 'pathetic drug mule' echoing in my mind, leaving me overwhelmed with shame and self-hate.

Returning to the refuge of family became bittersweet. Living under their watchful eyes, their involvement in our lives became suffocating, casting a shadow over my marriage. Arguments over the sacrifices demanded for my sake became a persistent drumbeat, a reminder of the burdens I unintentionally brought upon them. The streets, once familiar, became a minefield of scrutiny where harassment replaced the anonymity I craved. Powerless to defend myself, I internalized the judgments, feeding my self-loathing.

Returning home to live with my mom and stepfather brought up unresolved issues. It felt like the sacrifices that my mother and her partner felt they had made were hanging over me.

I felt at times that my life was becoming toxic and my mother was attempting to dictate my life and relationships.

Eventually, I took a leap, found my own place, and cut ties.

Then there was the ordeal surrounding the charges from a tennis club.

Widely broadcast across Australia, the allegations suggested I had embezzled thousands of dollars from the club's funds. As the club's treasurer, I had used a personal account instead of the official account for payment as the club had a deposit only account and couldn't be used online. I promptly rectified the error once discovered. I had been accused of stealing thousands of dollars, yet I had meticulously documented each transaction.

After my lawyers had asked for proof, the accusation of theft was dropped.

My reputation was again tarnished.

Legal victories felt hollow against the backdrop of public judgment. The battle for redemption transcended courtrooms, seeping into my soul. The desire to vanish, to erase the pain and past, haunted me constantly. I questioned whether surviving prison was fate's twisted joke or a torturous sentence I couldn't undo. Yet, a flicker of hope remained. Deep down, I knew my past wouldn't define me forever.

Securing a job in recruitment felt like a small victory amidst my turbulent life. Gratitude mixed with trepidation as I navigated professional terrain, fearful of expressing opinions or standing up for myself. I felt vulnerable, believing I needed others more than they needed me. The strength I had found in prison seemed distant, and I felt vulnerable, akin to my 22-year-old self who could be easily manipulated out of fear of disappointing others.

Battlegrounds of Resilience – *SAS Australia* and Beyond
Late 2022 to 2023

Approached in September 2022 about participating in *SAS Australia* – a reality TV show that challenges people to 'survive' the *SAS* training program.

The prospect initially terrified me. It wasn't a show I had sought out; rather, my agent Max saw it as an opportunity to reshape the public perception of me. The offer came with the promise of redemption – a familiar narrative for anyone with a tarnished reputation for redemption. Of course, like all criminals. It's always redemption.

The truth was, I didn't prepare for *SAS*. Part of me always thought I'd have more time, but it wasn't even that. I didn't prioritise it like my other cast mates, my focal point was getting my life back on track, getting a job, having transport, all these small things that no one else had to worry about. The show wasn't even on that list, I knew it was coming but I just couldn't prioritise it.

What did I hope to achieve? I craved a chance for authenticity, to peel back the layers of 'Cocaine Cassie' and reveal the person obscured by sensationalised headlines. I knew I was strong, yet beneath that facade, I grappled with deep sadness and a sense of brokenness. Shedding the label and reclaiming my true self was paramount. I yearned to rediscover the buried strength within me, confront my fears head-on, and rebuild the self-trust needed to navigate life's decisions.

What did I want out of this? I wanted to be seen, for the real me, not what I had been painted out to be for six years, I wanted to be given a chance to give people the chance to see just a snippet of who I was, because I was strong.

But I was still very weak too.

I was sad and broken and because of the self-hatred I felt, I just wanted to shed 'Cocaine Cassie'. I wanted to find the strength that I had forgotten was within me.

I wanted to face my fears and know that I was going to be okay, no matter what was thrown at me, but most of all I needed to face my past to move forward – I needed to trust myself again to make the right decisions.

Many people thought *SAS Australia* was a 'fame' thing, or a 'get rich quick' thing, but that wasn't the case. It was something that didn't benefit my future. It DID NOT help me get ahead financially, but I had hoped that it would help me find the ability to be okay with myself again.

Eventually.

The unforgiving terrain of *SAS Australia* was more than a challenge; it was a battlefield echoing the haunting corridors of my past.

But during the recording of the program I was instantly transported back to my prison days, and I knew this process was going to break me. Somehow, returning to Australia had made me weak again, I didn't feel the strength I had within anymore, the pity, the self-hate, the shame, it followed me everywhere and it didn't allow me to live in peace with myself. For two days I endured, a mere blink in time, yet each moment etched with the weight of memories, reminiscent of the Colombian prison that held me captive for nearly three harrowing years.

Being buried alive – a chilling re-enactment of the isolation, the claustrophobia that had been my daily companion in that South American cell. As each shovelful of soil cascaded over me, it carried not just the weight of earth but the heavy burden of memories, a visceral connection to a past I had fought to escape. What you didn't see on screen, was the back-to-back anxiety attacks, a relentless onslaught that mirrored the psychological warfare of my Colombian incarceration. I tried to hold myself together until I couldn't anymore.

I knew in order to find my strength again. I thought I needed to let the trauma consume me, like it once had; however it was different this time, because I had been avoiding it for so long, the confrontation of feelings I refused to feel hit me harder than ever.

The mountains, stoic witnesses to my struggles, stood as silent sentinels against the backdrop of panic. The thin air, a scarce commodity, amplified the echoes of vulnerability, as if the very atmosphere conspired to recreate the breathless moments of despair. Asthma, an unyielding adversary, became the embodiment of the suffocation I once battled behind prison walls. Each attack, a cruel reminder of the fragility of breath, of life itself. The mountainside became a stage for this personal duel, where every gasp was a defiance, a declaration that I wouldn't succumb to the haunting spectre of confinement.

SAS Australia wasn't a mere reality show; it was a deliberate choice to confront the shadows of my past. It wasn't about showcasing physical prowess; it was a visceral journey into the heart of trauma.

The battlefield became a metaphorical canvas where I painted resilience with every step, refusing to be defined by the scars of my history. A part of me knew that I was capable of continuing the course, I might not have finished the tasks, but I knew I was capable.

However the moment came when I needed to decide.

The decision to leave wasn't an admission of weakness; it was a strategic retreat, preserving the strength that had carried me through the darkest corridors of my life. I had willingly walked into the crucible, facing demons that lurked in the recesses of memory. But as asthma tightened its grip, as anxiety threatened to consume, I made a conscious choice to protect the hard-fought strength that defined my journey.

SAS Australia was more than a physical challenge; it was a testament to the indomitable spirit that had propelled me forward. It became a mirror reflecting not just the traumas of my past but the resilience that defined my present. As I stepped away from the battlegrounds, I carried with me the unwavering belief that I had faced my demons, proved my strength, and emerged unbroken.

It wasn't until walking away from the *SAS* camp I felt the sudden release from the chains of my past, it was the first time that I felt like I was going to be OK. I had done what no one would understand, put myself into a position that would trigger traumas and break me, however those traumas were now an experience from my past, a lesson learned, and consequences faced.

Amidst the challenges, I painted resilience with every step, determined not to be defined by my scars. While I knew I had the capability to persevere, the decision to leave wasn't a retreat in defeat. It was a strategic choice to safeguard the hard-earned resilience that had defined my journey. Walking into that crucible meant confronting demons buried deep within my memory. As asthma tightened its grip and anxiety threatened to overwhelm, I made the conscious decision to protect the strength that had carried me through my darkest days.

Leaving the *SAS* camp wasn't just a relief; it marked a sudden release from the chains of my past. For the first time, I felt a glimmer of hope that I would be okay. Despite the hardships endured – a deliberate choice to confront triggers and potential breakdowns – the experience transformed traumas into lessons learned and consequences faced.

As the calendar turned to 2023, the world, it seemed, had not relinquished its grip on my vulnerabilities. Being spat on in public, an accusation of murder, forced me to change my hair colour, a futile attempt to escape the damning judgments.

The PTSD, dormant but never defeated, resurfaced through the crucible of *SAS Australia*, forcing me to confront traumas I had diligently avoided, including quite serious mental and physical health issues, cruel reminders of the consequences from my past, impacted my ability to cling to my employment as I couldn't commitment to the full-time hours, and I found myself swiftly discarded – a stark reminder of how disposable I was. To be honest, I hadn't expected it, although understanding, I had expected some sort of agreement in hours whilst recovering, however, one thing that life had taught me was that everything really did happen for a reason.

Something that I had promised myself upon leaving prison, was that I wouldn't stop helping people, that same sentence still echoed, no matter how bad you think you have it, someone else is going through something worse. Reaching out to my Instagram followers, I sought solace in helping struggling families with food vouchers and any support I could muster. In the midst of my own trials, extending a hand to others offered a lifeline, a tangible reminder that, even in the darkest depths, the capacity for compassion and support could endure.

As I navigated the maze of unemployment, each rejection letter felt like a weight, threatening to pull me back into the abyss of despair but I couldn't give up. I remember telling myself that I can do this. I worked briefly as an ESL teacher. It had its moments, part of it gave me my strength, as teaching English had helped me once before, but the toxic environment became untenable.

The elusive promise of financial stability continued to evade me. I was still unable to have a bank account, every time I would open one, they would be closed down a month later. Their justification, a haunting echo of the past, centred on the perceived risk to their reputation. Something so basic, it was so deflating, not being able to open something so basic, however it got worse. Medicare still remained an inaccessible mirage, an essential service denied, application after application denied, using excuses as to why it couldn't be given to me, while I continued to suffer serious health issues.

The job market persisted in slamming its doors, something that I knew I wasn't alone in however it was still disappointing.

Eighteen months of this relentless struggle became yet another crucible of transformation. Rather than succumb to the weight of my past and the systemic roadblocks, I chose to confront my demons. It was a period of intense introspection, a journey into the depths of my trauma. I emerged not as a victim, but as a survivor determined to rewrite her story. Refusing to be defined by the judgments of others, I shed the layers of the persona that had been thrust upon me. The metamorphosis was profound, and I unveiled the real me – a resilient, persistent woman who had weathered the storm. I no longer wished to hide, and my hair, once a shield, returned to its natural blonde hue – an external reflection of the internal transformation.

My fitness journey, the Hourglass Body Challenge, a project that I had worked on for months soon became an opportunity to assist other women who suffered with body image issues just like myself, was more than physical; it was mental healing. Months of dedication paid off, boosting confidence and marking my resilience and determination. It became a beacon of hope. It wasn't merely a physical transformation but a symbol of the strength that lay within. It had been part of my mental healing process, something that I spent months, almost years perfecting as it was what helped me.

Finally graduating from a criminology degree marked the academic culmination of my journey – a victory over adversity. I had wanted to be a lawyer in Colombia, I wanted to be there for those who had gone and will go through similar situations, and not be used and abused by the lawyers and most importantly, I wanted *justice*.

I wanted to get ahead of the corruption.

As I had studied in Colombia I had to sit the year 12 exam, in which I managed to get a score high enough to allow me to get into university. It hadn't been possible for me to study Law while on parole, however I was allowed to study criminology, which was perfect anyway, as it gave me the knowledge of crimes and the psychology of it all.

My law degree will be the next step.

But victories, as sweet as they are, were not the endpoint. The hunger for more fuelled my desire to create something more. Thus, I ventured into uncharted territory, of planning to open an English school in Colombia, because the truth was, I never forgot about all those nights sitting in my prison cell, dreaming about opening an English school that could help people grow and see their potential, I wanted to help those who were in prison find a way to turn their life around.

As I look back at my arduous journey, I know that the real triumph lies in inspiring others to find their strength. The struggles I faced were not isolated incidents but universal challenges that demanded a collective response. This realization fuelled my desire to help people, to be a source of support because I had once needed help and the only people who appeared were the ones who wanted to take advantage of my situation. Believing in myself when no one else did was my superpower. It was this unwavering self-assurance that propelled me forward, enabling me to pull myself out of the darkest recesses.

Now, armed with the wisdom gained from my journey, all I want is to extend a helping hand to those still navigating their own tumultuous seas. My story is not just mine; it's a beacon of hope for anyone who has ever felt lost, showing that transformation is possible, and the strength to overcome lies within. No matter what I did, the echoes of my past reverberated through every attempt to atone. Apologies and acts of restitution felt like drops in an endless ocean, swallowed by the magnitude of the judgment I faced. But within me, an unyielding determination blossomed – to illuminate the real me, to shatter the misconceptions that clung to my name.

As I had embarked on the journey of self-discovery, the world's scepticism acted as a formidable adversary. It didn't matter how sincere my apologies were or how much I gave back; the scepticism persisted. Yet, I refused to be defeated. The real me, obscured by the sensationalism of my past, was clawing its way to the surface.

The scars of my past were not erased, but they were no longer the defining narrative. I stood at the intersection of my journey, a beacon of inspiration, offering proof that one could rise from the ashes of their mistakes. The world's reluctance to accept my transformation only intensified my resolve. I knew the real me, and I was determined to share her with the world – flaws, mistakes, and all.

My story was not just a personal saga; it was an invitation for others to believe in their potential for change and growth, to rise above their own tumultuous pasts. The journey was far from over, but with each step, I walked closer to the person I aspired to be – one who embraced her past, forged her own path, and inspired others to do the same.

Mental health and image plays a huge part in vulnerable situations. Helping others feel confident and proud became my mission. Business success wasn't just triumph; it was defiance against those who doubted me. Despite public scrutiny and judgment. I persevered silently, helping troubled teens and making a tangible impact.

Looking back at my journey, I know true triumph lies in inspiring others. My struggles were universal, demanding a collective response. Believing in myself when no one else did was my strength, propelling me past dark times. I knew that if I could overcome all these obstacles that anyone else could too.

I know I haven't been the only one who had had to jump through these hoops, but not everyone has had to do it so publicly.

Just Call Me Cassie
Present Day – Mid 2024

In the quiet moments between reflection and redemption, I stand before the mirror of my past, not as the infamous 'Cocaine Cassie,' but as a woman reborn from the crucible of my own mistakes. The journey from despair to the cusp of redemption has been gruelling, paved with the shards of my missteps, but here I am – raw, transformed, and ready to share the harrowing chapters of my life.

My story isn't one of glorification; it's a stark admission of my imperfections. I stumbled, fell, and stained the canvas of my existence with choices that resonated far beyond my understanding. I don't sugar-coat the reality of my actions; I hurt others and tarnished my own soul. The weight of those transgressions is a burden I carry, not lightly, but with the gravity of remorse.

Yet, redemption isn't about dwelling on the mistakes of the past; it's about the resilience to rise from the ashes. I seek understanding, not sympathy, acknowledgment, not pity. My pain, my experience, isn't a plea for sympathy – it's a stark cautionary tale, a living testament to the perils of veering off course.

I hope my story serves as a beacon of caution for young adults and teenagers navigating the dangerous waters of the wrong crowd. Let it be a road sign that reads 'Proceed with Caution,' so others can steer clear of choices that could shatter their lives. For those who have served time and feel trapped in the belief that forward movement is an illusion, hear me: You can overcome the shadows of your past. I've felt the chains, heard the mocking echoes of confinement, and emerged stronger – not defined by my mistakes but refined by my resilience.

Strength, resilience, and accountability became my guiding lights. In the crucible of incarceration, I forged a determination not to let one moment define my life. I know the despair that whispers of a lost future, but I urge you to grasp onto the glimmer of hope. One mistake need not be the end of your story; it can be the catalyst for a triumphant comeback.

My life isn't a tale of despair; it's a symphony of second, third, fourth, and fifth chances. If my journey can inspire even a single soul to believe in the possibility of redemption, to find strength in adversity, and to shoulder the responsibility of their choices, then my story will resonate beyond the confines of my past. May my experiences serve as a lighthouse for those navigating stormy seas, guiding them away from treacherous rocks toward shores of redemption.

To those impacted by my actions, I offer a heartfelt apology. The echoes of remorse reverberate within me, a constant reminder of the hurt I've caused. If my story serves as a cautionary tale, a whispered warning to those teetering on the precipice of wrong decisions or tangled within the wrong crowds, then perhaps my experiences have not been in vain.

The crucible of my past transformed me, not into a victim of circumstance, but into a survivor sculpted by resilience. Lessons etched in adversity have taught me strength, compassion, and the profound ripple effect of our choices on others. Speaking out about my experiences isn't an appeal for sympathy but a plea for attention – a call for others to heed the silent warnings embedded in my journey. For those who've walked similar paths, I hope my words serve as a beacon, encouraging you to find your voice, break the chains of silence, and step into the light. The scars I carry aren't just reminders of pain but symbols of my metamorphosis. I refuse to let the shadows of my past dictate my future. The naive 22-year-old who stumbled into darkness is a relic of the past. The journey from despair to empowerment has been arduous, but today, I'm in control of my destiny.

I've chosen not to be defined by the mistakes that stained my history. Instead, I focus on the growth that blossomed from adversity. Gratitude fills my heart for the extraordinary individuals who became my pillars of support, standing by me as I navigated the turbulent terrain of redemption. These scars are a testament to my strength – a strength that defied the odds and transcended pain. As I stand on the brink of an unwritten future, I see the brightness that awaits. My future is a canvas awaiting strokes of resilience, determination, and triumph.

I'm unstoppable, not because I'm impervious to adversity, but because I've embraced the power within me to overcome. The scared, lost, and naive version of myself is a relic of the past. Today, I'm resolute, empowered, and capable of creating the life I deserve. This closing chapter isn't an end but a beginning – a prelude to the unwritten volumes ahead, my life. The echoes of my past may linger, but they no longer dictate my destiny. I'm the author of my story, and with every word, I affirm my resilience, my growth, and my unwavering belief in a brighter tomorrow.

I am not 'Cocaine Cassie'.

I am Cassie Sainsbury.

Acknowledgements

"I can be changed by what happens to me,
but I refuse to be reduced by it."
— Maya Angelou

Thank you to those who stood by my side and helped me through all these years, everything you did will never go unnoticed. Even if we don't talk anymore, I will forever be in your debt.

Special thank you goes to Fiona and the crew at New Holland Publishing – thank you for giving me a voice!

Thank you to my father, although we may be estranged, you taught me to be strong and resilient. I don't think I would have ever made it through all these years if you hadn't had brought me up the way you did. I love you.

A huge thank you to my darling partner, whom has been right by my side and has watched me fall to a million pieces while reliving these moments and always reassures me when I don't believe in myself. You are my motor, each and every day, you give the strength to keep on fighting.

And last but not least, thank you to all the people who have crossed paths with me over the last seven years, you have all taught me something, whether it be good or bad – it's all a part of learning and growing. Everything happens for a reason.